CHURCHILL AND IRELAND

CHURCHILL AND IRELAND

PAUL BEW

OXFORD
UNIVERSITY PRESS

OXFORD
UNIVERSITY PRESS

Great Clarendon Street, Oxford, OX2 6DP,
United Kingdom

Oxford University Press is a department of the University of Oxford.
It furthers the University's objective of excellence in research, scholarship,
and education by publishing worldwide. Oxford is a registered trade mark of
Oxford University Press in the UK and in certain other countries

Published in the United States of America by Oxford University Press
198 Madison Avenue, New York, NY 10016, United States of America

British Library Cataloguing in Publication Data
Data available

Library of Congress Control Number: 2015943022

ISBN 978-0-19-875521-0

Printed in Great Britain by
Clays Ltd, St Ives plc

To Patrick Maume
who has revolutionized the art of Irish biography.

ACKNOWLEDGEMENTS

I owe a very great debt to Patrick Maume. In his work for the *Dictionary of Irish Biography* he has displayed a scholarly sympathy for all shades of Irish life. This book owes a great deal both to his work and to his wise conversation. It also owes much to the generosity of Henry Patterson and David Shiels. Allen Packwood, Director of the Churchill Archives Centre, kindly showed me the de Valera material in the King-Hall papers also in his care.

In London, as I worked in the library at Westminster late at night, a number of colleagues displayed a kindly interest—Patrick Carter, Gordon Wasserman, Kenneth Morgan, and David Trimble. I am happy to thank them. In particular, Alastair Lexden gave most valuable advice on the early sections. The librarian, Elizabeth Hallam Smith, and her staff have been magnificent. I also owe a debt of gratitude to Brian Walker, Charles Lysaght, and Sarah McAfee. My friend Dean Godson maintained a constant support. Above all, I owe a massive debt to my family for their insight, support, and practical help.

On those Internet lists of the ten historical figures most hated by the Irish people, Churchill is always in the top ten—though always behind Sir Charles Trevelyan (who takes the blame for British policy during the famine) and Oliver Cromwell (who takes the blame for the massacres in Drogheda and Wexford). Even as this book goes to press, a sharp letter in *History Ireland* recalls his responsibility for Gallipoli in 1915 where so many Irish soldiers died. Writing a book on this topic was, therefore, something of a burden as well as a joy and I was lucky to have so many good friends to share it with.

PAUL BEW
Belfast
September 2015

CONTENTS

LIST OF ILLUSTRATIONS

It is a curious reflection to inquire why Ireland should bulk so largely in our lives. How is it that the great English parties are shaken to their foundations, and even shattered, almost every generation, by contact with Irish affairs? When did Ireland derive its power to drive Mr Pitt from office, to drag down Mr Gladstone in the summit of his career and to draw us who sit here almost to the verge of civil war, from which we were only rescued by the outbreak of the Great War?

Whence does this mysterious power of Ireland come? It is a small, poor, sparsely populated island, lapped about by British sea power, accessible on every side, without iron or coal. How is it that she sways our councils, shakes our parties, and infects us with great bitterness, convulses our passions, and deranges our action? How is it she has forced generation after generation to stop the whole traffic of the British Empire in order to debate her domestic Affairs?

Ireland is not a daughter State. She is a parent nation. The Irish are an ancient race. 'We are too,' said their plenipotentiaries, 'a far-flung nation'. They are intermingled with the whole life of the Empire, and have interest in every part of the Empire wherever the English language is spoken, especially in these new countries with whom we have to look forward to the greatest friendship and countenance, and where the Irish canker has been at work. How often have we suffered in all these generations from this continued hostility?

If we can free ourselves from it, if we can to some extent reconcile the spirit of the Irish nation to the British Empire in the same way as Scotland and Wales have been reconciled, then indeed we shall have secured advantages which may well repay the trouble and uncertainties of the present time.

(Winston Churchill, speech in Parliament in defence
of the Anglo-Irish Treaty of December 1921)

Introduction

On 3 December 1925 Winston Churchill told the parliament of the United Kingdom: 'The Irish question will only be settled when the human question is settled.' Winston Churchill took Ireland seriously: if anything, his engagement with Ireland was more serious than Ireland's engagement with him. Twice in his career, in Manchester in 1908 and Dundee in 1922, Churchill painfully lost his parliamentary seat. On both occasions, despite enjoying the support of the official Irish nationalist leadership, Churchill was deserted by the majority of the significant Irish vote in the constituency.[1] His embrace, first of home rule, then of the Irish Free State, did him little good.

Ulster Unionists loathed him during the home rule crisis of 1912–14, and some also loathed his role in the negotiation of the Anglo-Irish Treaty in 1921. Mainstream Irish nationalism has tended to regard him as an imperialist John Bull figure—unsympathetic to and ill-informed about Ireland. Even the most subtle and nuanced of Irish writers treat his interventions and attempted interventions in Irish affairs—especially in the context of his dislike for Irish neutrality during the Second World War—with some coolness. The one rather dramatic exception to this general rule was Garret FitzGerald, Irish prime minister, who declared on Irish television that Churchill was a personal hero. More typical was the contestant on the popular Irish radio quiz show *Question Time*, broadcast from Belfast in August 1942, who replied—to gales of approving laughter—when asked the name of the world's most famous teller of fairy stories, not Hans Christian Andersen, but Winston Churchill.[2]

In Hugh Leonard's play *DA*, the playwright's adoptive father tries to get his son a clerkship in the Land Commission. The incident, which Leonard took from real life, is also described in his memoir *Home before Dark*. The setting is early 1945 or possibly late 1944. Leonard's father is an Irish Republican Army (IRA) veteran and supporter of De Valera, though his military activities were pretty much limited to hiding guns in the grounds of the Jacob family big house in Dalkey, where he was head gardener. Leonard presents his father as generally decent if naive: in this conversation he is clearly trying to impress a possibly influential civil servant, Drumm, whom he believes might get his son a job:

> DA: Hitler's the man that's well able for them. He'll give them lackery, the same as we done. Sure isn't he the greatest man under the sun, himself and De Valera?
>
> MOTHER (not looking at him): Now that will do...
>
> DA: What the hell luck could the English have? Didn't they come into the town here and shoot decent people in their beds? But they won't see the day when they can crow over Heil Hitler. He druv them back into the sea in 1940, and he'll do it again. Sure what's Churchill anyway, bad scran to him, only a yahoo, with the cigar stuck in his fat gob and the face on him like a boiled shite.
>
> [pause. DRUMM just looks at him][3]

Churchill himself intensely disliked the idea that he was a 'Hibernophobe': in fact, he felt it was the very opposite of the truth. Speaking in the House of Commons in November 1948, Churchill faced a certain amount of heckling on the basis that he was in some sense crudely 'anti-Irish'. His reply is of some significance:

> I have my own mental contacts with that people, whose fortunes I have followed and been connected with in many ways, long before those who make these superficial scoffings were called upon to form, or were capable of forming, any intelligent opinion on this subject. I say that we on this side of the House harbour no ill towards the Irish people wherever they may dwell.

He wanted to see the two nations work closely together in the future.

Gough Statue and City Car, Phoenix Park, Dublin.

Fig. 1. The Gough Statue in Phoenix Park. The unveiling of the statue in 1878 by his grandfather was one of Churchill's earliest memories.

Winston Churchill made his first public appearance in Dublin in 1878, when a portrait of the young child was displayed before the slightly amused eyes of the Irish press. He had his first rather elementary lessons in politics from his nanny, who warned him against Fenian terrorism. Churchill's first major historical book, his biography of his father, devotes much space to the analysis of Randolph Churchill's role in Irish affairs. The sharpness and shrewdness of Churchill's discussion here are worthy of note: but so, also, are the rather notable *lacunae*. Randolph Churchill's Irish career was characterized by an initial unionist sympathy. This mutated into a friendly and intimate engagement with Irish nationalism, and then reverted back to a more unionist, or at any rate Ulster Unionist, position. Ironically, his son reproduced, with much greater historic resonance and over a longer period of time, the trajectory of his father.

In spring 1904, as a young MP, Churchill switched from the Unionist Conservative Party to the Liberal Party, the party of home rule for Ireland. This initiates a more complex phase in his relations with his eminent Irish Unionist cousins, the Londonderrys. On 15 October 1904, Churchill wrote to Lady Londonderry:

> It was nice of you to express regret at my severance with the Conservative party, and as I said to you and C, have a perfect right to express regret and even to formulate a reproach. Had everyone adopted a tolerant line the present situation would be vastly different. I appreciated your attitude all the more because I had gathered from tales told—as tales are told—that some times in the last few months you had commented upon my actions rather more severely than I had reason to expect from one who has known me all my life. But I was delighted to find at Blenheim that you still seemed to take a friendly interest in my fortunes.[4]

In fact, Churchill's relations with the Londonderry family were to become ever more tense and did not recover until after the First World War. In Lady Londonderry's papers Churchill is described first as a 'rat'[5] at the height of the home rule crisis in April 1914, and then as 'vindictive and unscrupulous'[6] in late May 1915, but in February

1918, when he offers her son a front-bench post (at the Air Ministry) in the Lords, he is 'at bottom…kind, when it suits him'.[7] For some years, Churchill–Londonderry relations were cordial, but they soured again over differing strategies towards Germany in the interwar period.[8] At first, as a Liberal, Churchill retained a unionist stance, but he rapidly began a complex process of public and personal reflection on the Irish question—which began with his Manchester speech in September 1904 on the devolution crisis and intensified during the completion of his father's biography at the end of October of 1905. This stage of Churchill's Irish journey concluded with his increasingly frank espousal of home rule by 1908—an espousal that was combined with a strong conviction that it would be desirable to make a special arrangement for north-east Ulster.

Fig. 2. Charles Vane-Tempest-Stewart, 6th Marquess of Londonderry. Churchill's Irish Unionist cousin.

Over time, Churchill's underlying guiding principles on the Irish question remained cast in this mould, though the mode of their application varied greatly as circumstances changed dramatically. There is, however, an unavoidable consistency. Churchill's preference was always for a grant of self-governance to nationalist Ireland. He favoured in the long term the political unity of Ireland—but this Ireland would be intimately linked to Great Britain, through either the mechanism of devolution or the connection of the Commonwealth. Nevertheless, Irish unity depended on the wooing of 'Ulster' not its rape. He was a strong and unwavering defender of what is called today the 'consent' principle as applied to Northern Ireland.

During the home rule crisis of 1912–14 Winston Churchill, as a senior Cabinet minister, was at the centre of everything. His visit to Belfast in February 1912 to make a speech in favour of home rule provoked a public order drama of the highest order—so intense, in fact, that it has distracted attention from the significant intellectual content of his speech as such. Churchill embodied in his own political personality the 'soft cop' and 'hard cop' approach to the unionist campaign against home rule. He was intimately involved in the Curragh mutiny crisis and in all the most sensitive negotiations up to the outbreak of the First World War. This was part of Churchill's early training in dealing with problems of nationalist extremism and domestic political violence. It is an important neglected clue to the understanding of his whole career.

In 1912 Churchill became the first Cabinet minister to kiss the Blarney stone in Cork. It was not his first trip to Cork; he had earlier stayed at Innishannon, his uncle Moreton Freweton's estate, to see his cousin Clare, later to be Clare Sheridan, a mistress of Trotsky and other Soviet leaders.[9] More importantly, this visit brought home to him the importance of Irish naval facilities at Haulbowline and Spike Island to the Admiralty. The preservation of these naval facilities was one of his key concerns after he had belatedly become convinced of the need to strike the bargain with Irish nationalism envisioned in the Treaty in 1921. He was three times seriously considered for the post of

Irish chief secretary in 1907, 1910, and 1916: when eventually appointed Secretary of State for the Colonies, in the critical year of 1921, Churchill achieved vastly more in Ireland than any chief secretary of Ireland since the act of union. One recent scholar, Kevin Matthews, has described his work here as producing a 'Churchillian dispensation' for Ireland. This is a decisive moment in Churchill's career. He had been an activist, humane Home Secretary in 1910–11[10]—but his record, in the eyes of many, was marred by an apparently overenthusiastic attitude towards the application of force. His reputation for love of action, even when he, in fact, acted with prudence, counted against him. He had been an active and, in many ways, effective First Lord of the Admiralty (1912–15), but for many his record was once again spoiled by a propensity for incautious strategy, particularly in the case of Gallipoli. In the Irish crisis of 1921–2, while often challenged at the time by the Prime Minister and others that he was repeating his characteristic error, he, in effect, got it right and delivered a settlement that worked from the mainstream British political perspective. Churchill's work, which had previously had an *alpha gamma* quality in this perception, now seemed to be pure *alpha*. Churchill held fast to a belief that James Craig in the north and Michael Collins should be supported: a complex and at times contradictory strategy. The two Irish states were born in circumstances of political violence. Churchill contributed directly to the violence both in the north and in the south. But he did so not on the basis of any imperialist sectarian policy of divide and rule. Rather, as his letters to his wife show clearly, in the hope that, once stability had been achieved, the way might be open to Irish unity by consent.[11] As Chancellor of the Exchequer in the mid-1920s he was intimately involved in the Anglo-Irish Agreement, which settled the complex issues of the Boundary Commission and the financial relationship between the two islands. In 1934 Churchill prepared a film script for Hollywood magnate Alexander Korda, in which a 'draft scenario' is a Belfast 'mixed'—that is a Catholic–Protestant—marriage.[12] In 1938, in his essay on Parnell, he lamented the fact that the 'youth of today' did not understand Ireland's historic importance within British politics. At the height of his power during the Second World War, Churchill was much troubled by Irish neutrality.[13] He watched nervously as Eamon de Valera, elected as premier in Dublin in 1932, began the process of destroying the Anglo-Irish Treaty settlement that Churchill had done so much to create with Michael Collins in 1921–2. He particularly denounced the British decision in 1938 to return the Irish port facilities, reserved for Britain under the Treaty, to Ireland: he predicted correctly that it was a strategic error of some importance. During the Second World War, he was a bitter critic of Irish neutrality; he genuinely believed that Ireland had turned away from the probability of unity on the island and was blind to the evil of the Nazi regime. His famous scathing comment on the Irish state's record in his victory speech at the end of the war has left behind scars that are still not entirely healed in the twenty-first century. In 1948, in his celebrated essay 'The Dream', in which Churchill engages with his father's memory and addresses the changes in world history since his father's death, Ireland plays a large and dramatic part.

More intimately, his most devoted friend and colleague Brendan Bracken was the son of a radical anti-clerical Fenian stonemason from Templemore in Tipperary.[14] His uncle Moreton Frewen stood for and won a Cork seat in the nationalist interest: his cousin Shane Leslie just failed to get elected in Derry for the home rule cause. He had, however, rather scratchy political relations with his unionist cousin, Charles, the sixth Marquess of Londonderry,[15] and also his son, the seventh Marquess.[16]

These are not his only personal connections with Ireland. Hazel Lavery, wife of the great Ulster painter Sir John Lavery, was the key person in encouraging his painting hobby.[17] He was able to buy his beloved house at Chartwell only because in 1921 he had inherited the Garron Tower estate in Antrim from his grandmother, Frances, Duchess of Marlborough, a Londonderry daughter.[18] As Dr Eamonn Phoenix has recently pointed out, he displayed a significant interest in his Antrim tenantry in the following years.[19] His cousin Ivor Guest, Lord

Fig. 3. Portrait of Shane Leslie (1932) by R. G. Eves.

Wimbourne, was—apparently as a result of Churchill's urging[20]—one of the last Lord Lieutenants in Dublin Castle from 1915 to 1918.

One of his favourite American politicians was the Irish–American (born in Carrowkeel, County Sligo) William Bourke Cockran, a six-term congressman and strong supporter of Irish causes. When Churchill praised Cockran's eloquence to Adlai Stevenson, Stevenson was amazed: he had regarded Cockran as just another Irish–American 'pol' produced by the machine of Tammany Hall. His first commanding officer when he joined the Hussars was Col. Brabazon, an impoverished Irish landlord. It was an Irish commander, Sir Bindon Blood, who gave him his first experience of battle, and an Irish admiral, Sackville Carden, who pointed him towards his first great career fiasco, Gallipoli.[21] The Kerryman, Lord Kitchener, as Minister for War, also supported Gallipoli.

From the moment of his youthful career as a war correspondent, Churchill was an admirer of Irish military prowess. Four of his most important generals in the Second World War were Northern Irish.[22] General Alanbrooke (from 1944 Field Marshall) was Chief of the General Staff from December 1941 until the end of the war and, as such, played a major role in Allied strategy. When he appointed Alanbrooke, Churchill recalled riding into Ladysmith in 1900 alongside two of the 'fighting Brookes', the family that, of course, produced Sir Basil Brooke, a later prime minister of Northern Ireland.[23] Alanbrooke's talents had been first revealed during the perilous retreat to Dunkirk. As a divisional commander, General Montgomery, the son of a Church of Ireland bishop, often 'accomplished almost the impossible', in Alanbrooke's words, during the retreat. General Harold Alexander was in charge of the final evacuation of the British Expeditionary Force—responsible for 340,000 servicemen. Alexander was a Tyrone man; beside Churchill in London was Armagh man General Sir John Dill, Chief of the General Staff and Churchill's then senior military adviser, soon to be translated to Washington in 1941. Dill was to die in Washington in 1944; his grave is in Arlington cemetery. Alanbrooke, Montgomery, and Alexander were to play critical roles throughout the war.

There were other less satisfactory encounters. He did, after all, sack General Gort. In 1942 an Irish officer in the British army lectured Churchill over lunch on his lack of grasp of military strategy.

The same man, Brigadier 'Chink' Dorman Smith, sued Churchill for libel arising out of a passage in Churchill's book *The Hinge of Fate*; the possibility loomed of a highly embarrassing conflict in the Four Courts in Dublin. Dorman Smith's legal team included John A. Costello, a former Taoiseach, while Churchill's included Arthur Cox, the leading Dublin solicitor, and the former Labour attorney general, Hartley Shawcross. In the end, a compromise settlement out of court was reached. 'Chink' completed his revenge by advising the IRA on the logistics of a raid for arms in Omagh in 1956.

On his personal wartime staff were three Unionist Northern Irishmen, Richard Pim, John Sayers, and Commander H. W. McMullan. Churchill had to give special permission to allow another No. 10 official and Ulsterman Tom Wilson (later Professor Tom Wilson) to serve on the D-Day landings, and only on the understanding that he would kill himself if captured, as he knew so many secrets.

Churchill shared with the Irish a temperamental affinity. His use of language was designed to stimulate rather than sedate. He wanted to quicken things up rather than slow them down. He wanted to resolve issues rather than simply manage them. The relative complexity of the position he took—in which he attempted to balance the just claims of Irish unionism and nationalism—did not forbid action but impelled it. The West Clare MP Arthur Lynch was an early enemy and later ally. Like Churchill, Lynch was a soldier, a man of letters, and politician. Lynch insisted that Churchill liked to quote Machiavelli in French: 'to govern is to discontent.'[24] (Harold Laski noted that Machiavelli was the only political philosopher Churchill had actually read.)

John Updike's fictional historian and presidential biographer, Professor Alf Clayton, believed there was a 'civilised heroism to indecision' (Clayton's subject was President Buchanan, whose strategies failed to avert the American Civil War). 'Real life is in essence anti-climactic,' adds Professor Clayton.[25] This was not Churchill's view: as Isaiah Berlin pointed out, Churchill's philosophy was the philosophy of action.[26] He admired intensity of purpose and action. This is the clue that linked him temperamentally to a leader like Michael Collins, despite their fundamental difference of outlook on so many political matters. It should, of course, be noted that both Churchill and Collins shared a similar manic depressive temperament.[27]

At first glance, there should be no need for a new book about Churchill and Ireland. So much, after all, has been written about Churchill in recent decades, some of it magisterial. Again, the literature on the politics of modern Ireland has expanded dramatically in sophistication and professionalism. There are three relevant books devoted to this topic: there are fine monographs by Mary Bromage and Anthony Jordan and a particularly important collection of essays devoted to the Churchill family as a whole and Ireland edited by Robert McNamara. Yet, despite this valuable work, some significant themes have not yet received a full and satisfactory treatment. These issues are important in themselves. Churchill determined—during the home rule crisis of 1912–14, the violent epoch of 1919–23, and the Second World War—the shape of the relationship between and within the two islands more than any other British politician. At a historiographical moment, when there is much renewed emphasis on the imperialist, racist,[28] and simply impractical elements[29] in Churchill's wider thought, such an argument is all the more important—in part, because this more broadly focused work has clearly been seen to have implications for the analysis of Churchill's role in Ireland.[30]

The defining feature of Churchill's career is a determination to confront rather than evade challenges. This can lead to some remarkable transformations of position in the course of an engagement; but these are always felt to be in pursuit of a preordained objective. This essential drama of Churchill's career is first played out fully in the case of Ireland. Churchill was well aware of Britain's long-term historical role in Ireland. He castigated the brutality of Cromwell in Ireland and criticized other aspects of the historical record. But he also notes that a British population dwarfed by that of France, for example, and not so very much larger than that of Ireland found itself challenged at its core by the spectre, and sometimes reality, of Irish and continental alliances. The union of 1801 had, of course, been in theory the answer to this problem. It is necessary, however, to place Churchill's intervention in its historic context: the collapse of the original 1801 concept of the union between Britain and Ireland. This had been a concept of creating an imagined identity of one people across two islands. By the 1880s it had been replaced by another more defensive concept that there were two peoples on one small island, Ireland, each with a right of self-determination. This diluted concept of unionism fought out an intensive battle with Irish nationalism: a nationalism that had the strong support of a Catholic community that interpreted the Union in terms of second-class citizenship and famine. Ironically, though, the Act of Union had one great success: the alienated Ulster Presbyterian community of the late eighteenth century fully identified with the British link by the late nineteenth century. But this success merely intensified Protestant hostility to Catholic claims. For Protestants, the union was seen as the necessary context for liberal advance, the rule of law, and economic progress. At the turn of the twentieth century, Irish Protestant and Catholic communities viewed each other with distrust and fear. This is the context of Winston Churchill's Irish career. Britain, as Churchill pointed out, was now so strong she no longer feared Ireland—but how did she manage her?

This was the Irish question as Churchill found it when he embarked on his political life. He described accurately the paradox of constitutional nationalism: exercising power and influence at the heart of the Westminster parliamentary establishment. Irish Nationalist Party MPs, he noted, often gained election by the exploitation of extremist, angry rhetoric. The Irish appeared to be supporters of every enemy of Britain abroad and every subversive movement at home. By such means they maintained their control of Irish domestic public opinion.

Yet this was not the whole picture. In practice, such is the influence of parliamentary institutions, the anti-British doctrines of the Irish Nationalist Party were sensibly modified.[31] If the Irish Party disrupted the House, its members also made many excellent speeches. If they were sworn foes of British institutions, they also helped pass valuable reforms.[32] Parnell even protested once in the mid-1880s when Randolph Churchill described him as obstructionist.[33] But Winston Churchill did not deceive himself; he knew that 'hatred plays the same part in government as acids in chemistry'. In Ireland there were, he said, hatreds that would 'eat the live steel' from a rifle butt, in Kipling's phrase.[34] He judged his own career by how much he had contributed to the management and dilution of these hatreds. His hopes for consensual unity on the island were consistently over-optimistic. His resolution of the mixed-marriage issue for Alexander Korda was typically sentimental: William Orange, Lucy's father, is so pleased by his Catholic son-in-law's decision to join the British army that all is resolved over a glass of Irish whiskey. There is a letter to his wife in 1922 in which Churchill does concede that, at some level, the Irish were beyond his comprehension, if not admiration: 'The session closed peacefully with a quiet Irish debate. I think things may yet turn out well there. Extraordinary people! They are all paying their taxes. Revenue is up to the mark. Cattle trade roaring. Record entries for the horse show. And civil war galore. All one could desire!'[35]

As a lieutenant commander, John E. Sayers, a young Ulsterman later to be the liberal unionist editor of the *Belfast Telegraph*, served on Churchill's permanent staff during the war. When Churchill died in January 1965, Sayers observed in an editorial that 'the time has not yet come to discuss fully Winston Churchill's attitudes towards Ireland, dictated as they tended to be by Britain's need for war and peace'.[36] Fifty years later, surely the time has come.

1

A Father's Legacy

'Ah', he said, 'how vexed the Tories were with me when I observed there was no English statesman who had not had his hour of Home Rule.'

(Churchill's father, speaking as a ghost in 1947 to his son)[1]

Winston Churchill's earliest memories were Dublin memories. From 1877 to 1880 his father, Lord Randolph Churchill, then 28 years old, was aide to Winston's grandfather, John Churchill, the seventh Duke of Marlborough, who was appointed Lord Lieutenant to Ireland by Disraeli. Randolph took up residence in Phoenix Park in Dublin with his American wife Jennie and his 2-year-old son Winston. It was a convenient move. Randolph had made himself unacceptable in court circles because of his intervention in a marital scandal involving his older brother George, the Prince of Wales, and Mrs Aylesford. The Dublin appointment removed him from the social consequences of this intervention: already the MP for Woodstock, Randolph now worked for his father's administration as an unpaid and unofficial secretary.

The vice-regal family socialized happily with various Catholic clergy and members of the hierarchy, such as Dr Delaney of Cork, Dr Molloy of the Catholic University, the future Archbishop Walsh, and the Reverend James Healy of Bray. The viceroy delivered a speech in Belfast in July 1877, in which he deplored the sectarianism and riot culture of the city. The duchess was an enthusiastic patron of native Irish textiles such as poplin, lace, and linen. Cardinal Cullen observed in early 1878: 'I see the Duchess is wearing shamrocks and green dresses and visiting convents.'[2] The Catholic hierarchy communicated to the duchess their preferred choices for the Intermediate Education Committee. These appointments were well received in the nationalist press.

The viceroy opposed the exaggerated language of the hard-line faction of Irish landlords. He insisted that they overstated the level of agrarian crime in order to make the case for repression. His son, Randolph, went further in a speech in his Woodstock constituency in 1877: he addressed the problem of 'obstructionism' in parliament, led by a new, less deferential breed of Irish MPs, chief among them C. S. Parnell, J. G. Biggar, O'Conor Power, and F. H. O'Donnell. These men infuriated English members by filibustering and achieving large-scale delays in all the business of the House. The gentlemanly leadership given by Isaac Butt to the advocacy of Irish demands in parliament was being pushed aside. Most Tory members regarded the obstructionists with contempt. But Randolph Churchill took a rather different view: he chose to be both accommodating and conciliatory:

> It was inattention to Irish legislation that had produced the obstruction to English legislation...We must remember that England had years of wrong, years of crime, years of oppression, years of general misgovernment to make amends for in Ireland...It was for these reasons that he should propose no extreme measures against Irish members, believing as he did that the cure for obstruction lay not in threats, not in hard words, but in conciliatory legislation.[3]

Randolph Churchill also began to focus on Irish educational issues. He criticized Protestant educational provision in Ireland and argued also for more funding for Catholic education. He voted against the government and with the Irish MPs on O'Conor Don's 1878 motion to establish a Catholic university. It is not surprising that the nationalist press began to suspect that one day Randolph Churchill might support a local Irish parliament in Dublin.

When the economic crisis of 1879 first hit Ireland, the anxiety of the British government was to prevent any hint of repeat of the great famine. The combination of falling prices and bad seasons in 1877–9 appeared to presage just that. The Duchess of Marlborough's relief fund was established, with great success—so much so that a *Punch* cartoon showed better-off farmers feeding themselves on the 'duchess', while giving their pigs the poorer-quality grain provided by lesser relief agencies.[4] Winston's father, Randolph, was at the heart of these efforts: in early 1880 he gave an expansive and well-informed interview on the topic to James Redpath, a radical representative of the Irish–American press. The tone of Redpath's article is interesting: Redpath was a militant democrat who was to involve himself in the Parnellite and Land League causes. Yet, he was clearly impressed by Randolph Churchill's grasp of local detail and determination to prevent any repeat of the Great Famine of 1846–50.[5]

> I called at Dublin Castle today and had an interview with Lord Randolph Churchill, who is the son of the Duchess of Marlborough, and next to his mother the most responsible manager of the Castle Relief Fund. He is a young man, slightly built, of fair complexion, very courteous and obliging, and a good conversationalist.[6]

Churchill's responses were essentially designed to stress the importance of local detail. He admitted that about a quarter of a million—'a moderate estimate' he said—were in distress. He did not believe in the likelihood of general starvation, despite the loss of two-thirds of the potato crops. 'And while in some districts the potato crop has fallen off one third, in others it has fallen off a half, and in others two thirds, there are districts where they have absolutely no potatoes at all.'[7] Churchill offered Redpath a detailed breakdown of conditions, poor law union by poor law union, in the west. He insisted that the objective of policy was to help small farmers, artisans, and skilled labourers: in other words, to prevent those just above the 'pauper' class from falling into it.

The Times of 19 April 1880 penned the Duchess of Marlborough a generous tribute: 'In the moment of doubt about what the dismal phenomena of peat sodden and unstacked, of potatoes unstored and rotting, might mean, a lady solved the problem which perplexed

Fig. 4. Winston Churchill, aged 5. 'Boy with Brogue'.

statesmen...that the glens of the west...have escaped the cruellest pangs of hunger is due to her.'[8] Yet, while such a verdict was uncontroversial in London, this was hardly the case in Dublin. It became essential for Irish nationalists preaching the virtues of 'manliness' and 'self-reliance' to denounce British charity. Young Ireland had done so in 1846–7, and it was far easier to do so in the less threatening circumstances of 1880. Parnell, the emergent leader of Irish nationalism, attacked the Duchess of Marlborough's fund: James Redpath now insisted that the 'Duchess of Marlborough deserved no thanks... rather reproaches' for her 'miserly' contributions to the relief of Irish distress.[9] Following the Liberal election victory in spring 1880, the Marlboroughs were pelted with eggs by Dubliners on their final departure from Dublin. James Redpath now insisted that the condition of the poor in the west of Ireland was worse than those who had lived on southern plantations before the abolition of slavery.

Randolph Churchill became increasingly concerned about the temper of mainstream Irish political life. He reversed his position on extending the Irish franchise. He became more sympathetic to landlords facing the full force of the Land League agitation. He opposed Gladstone's 1881 Land Act—designed to draw the teeth of the land agitation—as communistic.

There were some messages sent that were couched in a rather different tone: he regularly commented that Irish nationalist MPs were men of 'high intelligence'—much to the delight of these same MPs, who were used to frequent snubs in the Palace of Westminster. But the predominant tone of hostility to the new Irish nationalism is unmistakable.

But what did the young Winston Churchill retain from his early childhood in Dublin? He certainly learnt something about fenianism. The Fenian movement had launched an incompetent separatist insurrection in 1867, which had failed miserably. But it still had many Dublin adherents. Churchill recalled:

> My nurse, Mrs Everest, was very nervous about the Fenians. I gathered these were wicked people and there was no end to what they would do if they had their way. On one occasion, when I was out riding on my donkey, we thought we saw a long dark procession of Fenians approaching. I am sure now it must have been the Rifle Brigade out on a route march but we were all very much alarmed, particularly the donkey, who expressed his anxiety by kicking. I was thrown off and had concussion on the brain. This was my first introduction to Irish politics.[10]

Churchill, in his memoirs, also recalled Thomas Burke, a Catholic and the most senior civil servant in the Dublin Castle system during the 1870s. Burke was an invaluable source of advice to the English politicians sent over to lead the Irish administration: 'He gave me a drum. I can not remember what he looked like, but I remember the drum.'[11] Churchill recalled the gift because the man who gave it to him was to be one of the two victims of the most spectacular political assassination of the Victorian era.

What was the political context for this remarkable crime? Parnell and the Land League movement had convulsed much of Ireland from 1879 until 1882: a large part of the country was in the grip of a social revolutionary movement endeavouring to break down the Irish land-lord system. Britain reacted with a mixture of reform—the 1881 Land Act, which, in effect, reduced Irish rent levels by 20 per cent—and internment—the mass arrest of a 1,000 Land League activists, including, in the autumn of 1881, its leader, Charlie Stewart Parnell. The policy of mass internment caused considerable unease within the heart of Gladstone's Liberal government. As Winston Churchill was to explain in a 1938 essay on Parnell:

> Mr Gladstone, the champion of freedom and national movements in every foreign country, the friend of Cavour and Mazzini, the advocate of Greek and Bulgarian independence, now found himself forced by duress to employ against Ireland many of the processes of repression he had denounced so mercilessly (and we will add so cheaply) in King Bomba and the Sultan of Turkey.[12]

Conveniently, for a prime ministerial soul so troubled, Parnell began to exhibit—in particular through messages to Gladstone from his mistress, Katharine O'Shea—a growing political conservatism. The prime minister decided to gamble by releasing Parnell from prison on 2 May, even though it meant the resignation of his chief secretary for Ireland, W. E. Forster, a key figure in his Cabinet.

Forster was replaced by Lord Frederick Cavendish, an intimate member of Gladstone's circle. He arrived in Dublin on 6 May 1882. As Cavendish and his most senior official, Burke, walked towards his new office in the Phoenix Park, they were set upon by a gang of Dublin assassins, the 'Invincibles'. They were sliced to pieces by surgical knives: the bone of Cavendish's arm was cut clean through. Despite clear evidence that the Invincibles were not acting independently of the Land League—Mrs Frank Byrne, the wife of a senior Land League official, smuggled their knives into Ireland—the Kilmainham Treaty between Parnell and Gladstone remained intact and set the tone for

Anglo-Irish politics for the 1880s. The Liberals embraced the deal rather than return to 'illiberal' coercion; the Tories refused to accept Parnell's attempt to disassociate himself and his movement from the crime and denounced this not so tacit concession of governmental authority to crime.[13]

Following Mrs O'Shea's explanation of Parnell's essential moderation, Gladstone decided that he 'considered him a conservative force in Ireland'.[14] Gladstone was already, in principle, a home ruler, but his 'conversion' was made much easier by his perception of the essential moderation of Parnell. As Winston Churchill observed:

> Yet, he [Parnell] was himself a man of Conservative instincts, especially where property was concerned. Indeed, the paradoxes of his earnest and sincere life were astonishing: a protestant leading catholics; a landlord inspiring a 'no rent' campaign; a man of law and order exciting revolt; a humanitarian and anti-terrorist; controlling and yet arousing the hopes of Invincibles and terrorists.[15]

Churchill added:

> Without Parnell, Mr Gladstone would never have attempted home rule. The conviction was borne upon the Grand Old Man in his heyday that here was a leader who could govern Ireland, and that no one else could do it. Here was a man who could inaugurate the new system in a manner which would not be insupportable to the old.[16]

Randolph Churchill, one of the few people in British politics who would have known both Burke and Cavendish well, at first echoed the conventional conservative anti-Parnellite view. He observed of the Liberal government in March 1883 that 'so base was their policy that they forced the Crown to rely for their authority in Ireland on the assassins of the Phoenix Park'.[17] Even after leaving Ireland, Churchill remained close to some of his clever Dublin friends, especially those from the unionist and professional elites. The most important of these was the Irish government law adviser Gerald Fitzgibbon—whose legendary Christmas house party in Howth regularly drew

Randolph Churchill back to Dublin.[18] This group was 'modernizing' in outlook—its members passed on to Churchill a disdain for an already defeated Irish landlord class—but strongly unionist, and, in Fitzgibbon's case, prepared to call on the Orange Order to maintain the union. In December 1883 Randolph Churchill, speaking in Edinburgh, proclaimed: 'We must lose India, we must lose our colonies and still remain a great power, but if we lose Ireland, we are lost.'[19] In January 1884, before a Blackpool audience, he implied a link between the Parnellite Irish Party and the Phoenix Park murders and repeated his warning of a Gladstone–Parnell alliance as a 'monstrous and dangerous coalition' that would lead to repeal of the union and thereby strike at 'the vitals of Empire'.[20] In February 1884 he told the House of Commons that Orangemen 'merely adopted the attitude now generally assumed by the Tory Party in this country of offering vigorous resistance to Radical and subversive doctrines, and describing those doctrines in extremely plain terms of speech. If language of that kind produced riots in Ireland so much the worse.'[21]

Yet, over the next two years Randolph Churchill became increasingly close to the Irishman. As the likely leader of a party of over eighty members in the next parliament, Parnell was of obvious interest to Churchill. It was always a strong probability that he would hold the balance of power. Churchill, as the opportunist but active leader of 'Tory democracy', wished to impress his party with his power of political initiative. But why was Parnell so interested? It was obviously in his interests to make the two British parties engage in a bidding war, but the matter went deeper. As Winston Churchill explained of Parnell:

> His own Conservative instincts, his sense of realism, the anger excited against Liberal coercion, led him a long way towards the Tories. After all, they could deliver the goods. Perhaps they alone could do so, for the House of Lords in those days was a barrier which none but Tories could pass.[22]

By the middle of May 1885 Randolph Churchill had established a rapport with Parnell. He was certainly willing to drop repressive coercion as an instrument of British policy. In his biography of his father, Winston Churchill reported a conversation between Lord Randolph Churchill and Parnell at about this time at the former's London home: 'There was no compact or bargain of any kind,' Churchill said a year later, 'but I told Parnell when he sat on that sofa [in Connaught Place] that, if the Tories took office and I was a member of the government, I would not consent to renew the Coercion Act'. Parnell replied: 'In that case you will have the Irish vote at the elections.'[23] In itself this was hardly a remarkable deal. Lord George Hamilton later recalled:

> Churchill, whom I had got to know intimately, always assured me that the only understanding to which he had ever been a party was his statement that if the conservatives did take office in this parliament, they would not renew the existing Coercion Bill. It was a very safe proposition to lay down, because the mere fact of our taking office at the end of a session in a House where we were a comparatively small minority, made the re-imposition of such legislation an impossibility.[24]

Why did the two men get on so well? They were both still in their thirties, full of pride and ambition. Lord Rosebery liked to quip that they shared a common insanity. Both had tried to woo and win rich American women. Churchill had been successful; Parnell had failed; still he did not hold it against Churchill. Churchill seemed equally impressed. On 17 June 1885 Sir George Fottrell had lunch with Randolph Churchill at the Carlton Club: 'He has a great admiration for Parnell whom he considers a greater man than O'Connell. He says that Parnell's instincts are parliamentary and constitutional, he looks to him as a Conservative force among the Irish party after the election.'[25]

In July 1885 the *Spectator* coined the phrase 'Parnellite Toryism': 'The simple truth is that Parnell is now the true Lord Lieutenant of Ireland, and Lord Randolph Churchill the true prime minister of England.'[26] This strange alliance seemed to carry all before it: Belfast Tories stirred restively.[27] The leader of Ulster Unionism, Colonel Saunderson, was to claim that Churchill told him that he had 'decided' to give home rule to Ireland; Saunderson replied sharply that it was not in his gift.[28]

In August 1885, at an Arklow speech, Parnell revealed something of his private discussions with the Tories. He was challenged on the topic by a close ally, Andrew Kettle. Kettle asked him:

> You were at Arklow yesterday, I said, opening the granary and selling the stones to the Dublin Corporation, but what was the meaning of your strange speech on protection and Irish industries? Are you going to break with the free traders? 'Yes', he said, 'we have a rather big project on our hands'. He then explained the meeting with Lord Carnarvon and the project of aristocratic home rule, with the colonial right to protect our industries against English manufacture. I seemed to be knocked dumb, as I really was, by the unexpected news, and he went on to explain that it was not from a motive of justice or generosity that the Conservative party were making proposals. Inspired chiefly by Lord Randolph Churchill, the classes in Britain were afraid that if the Irish democratic propaganda were to continue, in conjunction with the English Radicals, class rule might be overturned altogether. So, to save themselves, they are going to set up a class conservative government in Ireland, with the aid and consent of Irish democracy, or in other words, with our assistance, having no connection with England but the link of the Crown and an imperial contribution to be regulated by circumstances.[29]

These remarks of Parnell reveal a great deal. As Winston Churchill was later to say, Randolph Churchill, at this moment, was 'in close and deep relationship with the Irish leaders'.[30]

In the end Parnell failed to deliver a Tory majority in the general election. Lord Randolph Churchill told Justin McCarthy, when the electoral results were known: 'I did my best for you and now I'll do my best against you.'[31] W. S. Blunt later wrote to Randolph's son:

> He [Randolph] was far more of a home ruler than you seem to know and I have always thought that if the election of 1885 had [worked out] rather more favourably and Gladstone had not taken up the Irish case when he did, your father would have persevered with it.[32]

This was Blunt's sincere, if obsessive view—but he was not alone in holding it. It seems clear that Winston Churchill gradually accepted the force of his criticism.

If, however, the Tory tactic had been to force Gladstone's hand, it worked remarkably well, opening the way to two decades of Tory electoral hegemony as the Liberal leadership split on the issue. Once Gladstone had committed to home rule in 1886, a new Churchill emerged. He spent the last days of the Tory government in early 1886 urging repression in Ireland.[33] These discussions were of little policy significance: the Tories were turned out of office a few days later. But his next move was of considerable significance.

Lord Randolph's closest Irish friend had been the distinguished judge Gerald Fitzgibbon; the originals of his correspondence have not survived. Winston Churchill, to his credit, chose to print many of these letters; one was to have a particular resonance. On 16 February 1886 Lord Randolph Churchill wrote bluntly to Fitzgibbon: 'I decided some time ago that if the GOM went for home rule, the Orange card would be the one to play. Please God it may turn out the ace of trumps not the two.' As Peter Clarke has noted: 'There is seldom a smoking gun in politics,' but this looks suspiciously like one: 'a devastatingly candid acknowledgement of its subjects' motives and methods'.[34]

On 22 February Randolph Churchill arrived at the port of Larne in County Antrim, fully intending to play the Orange card. He told a crowd in the town that the placing of the loyalists of the north of Ireland under the authority of a Dublin government would be a monstrosity of civilization. The loyalists must organize and fit themselves for the struggle for the maintenance of the union, which was beginning now, but which he predicted would assume grave proportions. Large bodies of Orangemen, wearing regalia, displaying banners, and headed by bands of music, met Lord Randolph Churchill at the depot in Belfast. The crowd unharnessed the horses of his carriage and made a point of dragging his vehicle from the station to the hotel. All along the enthusiasm—perhaps particularly of the women—was 'prodigious'. When Randolph Churchill actually arrived at the Ulster Hall, he was met by a wall of approving sound that lasted several minutes before he spoke. He then exploited fully his Ulster family connections—no one would have guessed that, a few months before, Ulster Tories had distrusted him.[35] His grandmother had ancestral connections with two leading northern Irish families, the Vanes and the Stewarts. She was the daughter of the Third Marquis of Londonderry, who was the half-brother of Viscount Castlereagh, the Irish chief secretary at the time of the 1798 rising and the Act of Union, who became Britain's greatest Foreign Secretary. Randolph Churchill's sister-in-law was married to the son of Sir John Leslie, a formidable Tory and Orange politician in Monaghan.

Churchill's speech in the Ulster Hall was hardly moderate in tone: he instructed his audience to wait and prepare in an orderly fashion, but he added: 'I am not of the opinion, and I have never been of the opinion, that this struggle is likely to remain within the lines of what we are accustomed to look upon as constitutional action.'[36] He finished his speech with a reference to the American civil war and a promise of physical support from England in the dark hours. He did not say 'Ulster will fight and Ulster will be right', but that phrase did appear in a public letter published shortly thereafter. The explicit, direct reference to Parnell was a brutal one. Parnell had nothing to be proud of. He had built his career on crime and pain. He did not represent the real Ireland.

> He denied that the Parnellites were the true representatives of the will of Ireland. As for Parnell himself, his only title to be considered in the party lay in an action of which no one could be justly proud. By playing upon the terrors of the peasantry and by means of brutal outrage upon human beings and animals, he had secured five sixths of his members of parliament.[37]

After this contemptuous reference, Churchill moved on to make an appeal to 'all, regardless of creed, to declare in favour of a freer and closer union'.[38] Amid all this bitter language, this formal appeal to non-sectarianism was even more empty than is usually the case in Irish politics.

This man whom Churchill so defamed was the same Parnell with whom he had had extensive sensitive political discussions. This was also the same Parnell whose fundamentally conservative outlook he had stressed in private conversation. It might be reasonably said that this was the paradox of Parnellism: the Irish leader led a movement with a significant criminal and intimidatory component. He was, on the other hand, anxious by the mid-1880s to quell Irish revolutionism. He believed that parliamentary politics was the way to advance Ireland's cause. For Churchill to emphasize only the subversive aspects of Parnellism was, therefore, to speak only a partial truth. In particular, he was rather more aware of the more complex truth—the contradictory aspects of Parnell's political personality—than his Belfast audience. Randolph Churchill might reasonably have expected Parnell to take personal offence; indeed, that was precisely the Tory politician's expectation.

Churchill fully expected Parnell would denounce him after his Belfast trip and further embarrass him by revealing his extensive contacts 'at my house' in 1885. But Parnell, who liked Churchill, did not do so.[39] Churchill now insisted that Gladstone was wrong. 'Salutary reform' was the answer to the Irish question: 'Were we to commit national suicide and involve millions of mankind in downfall and ruin at the bidding of Mr Parnell and his eighty autocrats?'[40]

Churchill contributed to what was for the British political class a winning argument. The Tory benches applauded him loudly on his return from Belfast.[41] The Gladstone government split and collapsed. The electorate moved away from the Grand Old Man. Churchill returned to power in triumph as Chancellor of Exchequer but lost a battle with the prime minister, Salisbury, and found himself out of office on the margins.

In the late 1880s and early 1890s Randolph Churchill struck an eccentric course on Irish matters. At first he welcomed the policies of Arthur Balfour, the new chief secretary in Ireland, then he described them as 'a blister' on Ireland. He remained consistently opposed to home rule: 'We can not, even for the sake of Ireland, assassinate the British Empire.' Yet he was not a reliable supporter of the government. He argued that evictions in Ireland should be avoided at all costs. Irish MPs who protested against them should not be sent to jail, even if they had broken the law.[42] Local government reform linked to land reform was necessary. On the subject of land reform in 1890 he was explicitly closer to Gladstone than the government.[43] He criticized the idea that Irish financial self-indulgence—the Dublin mayor was given a salary of £3,000 in 1890; the job in Belfast was carried out for nothing—was a case against conceding more local government in Ireland. There was plenty of financial indulgence, he pointed out, in England.

Sometimes Churchill's tone slipped. At Bolton he called the Irish members 'political brigands and nihilists'. The inevitable failure of home rule to bring prosperity would lead to a swamping of Lancashire by poor Irish willing to work for nothing. Worst of all, he challenged the basic concept of the union: a government was not legitimate if it relied on Irish votes.[44] But, on the whole, Randolph Churchill justified his son's view that he believed in 'equality of treatment' for the Irish.[45]

In one key respect Churchill remained attractively consistent. He opposed resolutely the government's attempt to 'criminalize' Parnell by means of the judicial special commission inquiry into Parnell and crime. Arthur Baumann, a Tory MP, has left us with a pathetic picture of a physically ailing Churchill, having completed a bitter attack on the commission, desperately asking for a glass of water from Tory colleagues, who ignored him.[46]

2

The Making of a Home Ruler

Winston inherited his father's late period unionism. As a young soldier he imbibed also the unionism of his fellow officers. As far as the 4th Hussars were concerned, we 'were all delighted' by the change of government in 1895, as the Liberals were very unpopular at this time in Aldershot, 'because they had been kept in office' by the Irish nationalists, 'who everyone knew would never be satisfied till they had broken up the British Empire'.[1] Churchill's 'brother officer' who joined the Hussars at the same time was Lieutenant Ian Hogg, a fact that was to be of some significance in later years.

At the age of 20, on his mother's recommendation, Churchill met the Irish–American politician William Bourke Cockran (1854–1923), one of his mother's lovers, in New York in 1895. Cockran, born in Sligo, had emigrated to America in 1871 and, by sheer hard work, became a lawyer and US congressman. Churchill was tremendously impressed by Cockran, a vigorous supporter of Irish home rule. It may have been his first serious discussion with someone of substance who did not share his instinctive unionism. He was to remain in regular contact with Cockran. In Cuba, a few days later, Churchill noted that the Spaniards talk of Cuba 'as we talk of Ireland'. Cockran certainly influenced Churchill in favour of classical liberalism, though, when he tried to persuade Churchill of the Irish nationalist reading of the Cuba case, Churchill rejected it.

On 29 February 1896 Churchill sent a copy of an article he had written on Cuba for the *Saturday Review* and requested Cockran's opinion. Cockran's return letter not only gave his views on Cuba but included his views on Ireland. Churchill thanked Cockran for his eloquent reply but pointedly did not accept his view on Ireland.[2] Churchill remained a unionist. 'I am a Liberal in all but name,' he wrote to his mother in 1897; 'my views excite the pious horror of the Mess. Were it not for home rule—to which I will never consent—I would enter Parliament as a Liberal.'[3]

In October 1899 the struggle for supremacy between the British and the Boers led to the outbreak of war in southern Africa. That November the adventurous young Churchill, now a highly paid war correspondent for the *Morning Post*, was captured by the Boers and interned in the State Model School in Pretoria. He was imprisoned alongside Cecil Grimshaw, the son of the celebrated Irish Registrar General T. W. Grimshaw, described by Churchill as a 'very energetic and clever young officer'.[4] Churchill escaped and became a war hero, but he displayed a consistent respect for the Boers. He also noted Irish bravery. He described them as the 'finest' infantry soldiers in the world. 'His description of these fellows, utterly immersed in the midst of bursting shells, is enough to cause a thrill of pride and pleasure in the hearts of Irishmen all over the world.'[5]

In the carnage of the Boer War, Churchill covered the struggle for the relief of Ladysmith. On 22 February 1900 the British army found itself in an exposed position in the valley of the Tugela River. General Fitzroy Hart's Irish brigade faced the brunt of the Boer fire:

It was four o'clock when the Irish brigade began to toil up the steps of what is now called Inniskilling Hill and sunset approached before the assault was delivered by the Inniskilling and Dublin Fusiliers. The spectacle was tragic. Though our glasses we could see the Boers' heads and slouch hats in miniature silhouettes, wreathed and obscured by shell-bursts against the evening sky. Up the bare grassy slopes slowly climbed the brown figures and glinting bayonets of the Irishmen, and the rattle of intense musketry drummed in our ears. The climbing figures dwindled; they ceased to move; they vanished into the darkening hillside. Out of twelve hundred men who assaulted both colonels, three majors, twenty officers and six hundred soldiers had fallen killed or wounded.[6]

In the end, the Boers were outflanked and Ladysmith retaken, but the price had been high. The Inniskillings had lost 72 per cent of their officers and 27 per cent of their men. For all this celebration of Irish pro-imperial patriotism, it remained the case that the Boers could draw on Irish brigades to support them: on one occasion after the battle at Dundee the Dublin Fusiliers surrendered to Irish brigade soldiers with whom they had been at school.[7]

On 30 October 1899 Hugh Carberry, an Armagh nationalist, fell fighting for the Boers at Modderspruit. Carberry became posthumously a national hero memorialized by a Celtic cross in his home town. Michael Davitt hailed him as a 'soldier of liberty' as against those 'hirelings' of the King. William Redmond MP proclaimed: 'We can not fight in Ireland as the Boers are fighting . . . I wish to God we could.' Patrick O'Brien MP declared: 'If we had Kruger's rifles, we would not be talking constitutionalism.'[8] The Irish Party quite simply was pro-Boer.

In 1901 Churchill, now MP for Oldham, decided to make his maiden speech in parliament on the Boer War. It provoked a certain amount of jeering from the Irish Party. But Churchill remarked on the 'courage, sacrifice and, above all, the military capacity' of the Irishmen in the British forces. Churchill was satisfied with the impact of his speech. 'I was up before I knew it . . . I got through it. The Irish—whom I had been taught to detest—were a wonderful audience. They gave just the opposition which would help and said nothing that would disturb.'[9] Interestingly, though, he claimed that the Irish Party did not really represent Irish views on the Boer War. It was an index of an early and pertinent failure to enter into the interior world of Irish nationalism.

There was, however, to be a significant footnote. Arthur Lynch, the commander of the Second Irish Brigade who had fought for the Boers, was elected for a Galway seat in 1901. When he returned from South Africa in 1902, he was arrested, charged with high treason, and imprisoned. Churchill fully supported this course of action; but, when the war was over, Lynch was released in 1904. Churchill wrote to him that 'I am glad to congratulate you upon gaining your liberty'.

Lynch's actions in South Africa, however 'reproachable', he added, involved 'no moral turpitude'.[10] Typically, the two men were to become friends and allies.[11]

Churchill's Toryism became more and more diluted. Nevertheless, at the moment of conversion to the Liberal Party in April 1904, Churchill signalled to the Liberals of north-west Manchester that he was not impressed by the great Gladstonian theme of home rule. 'I remain of the opinion that a separate parliament for Ireland would be dangerous and impractical.'[12]

On 29 April 1904 he told the Liberal Association adopting meeting:

> Now I have alluded in the letter which I wrote to you on the Irish question. No such proposal could be made except with an overwhelming majority for that purpose [hear, hear] and it would be to court destruction for a government elected—as the next government will be—mainly upon the free trade issue to embark upon such a policy. Let us rather consider the aspect of the Irish question in which we can all agree—the continued application to the Irish problem of Liberal principles, and the continued gradual extension of wider powers of self-government, and perhaps the creation of provincial councils, so that purely domestic questions, whether they be secular or whether they be religious, be settled in great measure in a greater degree in theory with Irish likes and Irish sympathies.[13]

He did, however, continue to address Irish issues. On 18 May 1904 he was sympathetic to the idea floated at the time of the Financial Relations Commission of 1896 that Ireland had been overtaxed in the nineteenth century:

> The money question was the root of all the existing bitterness. The discontent prevailing between England and Ireland arose not so much because of differences of religion and of race as from the belief that the English connection was not a profitable nor a paying one. If Ireland were more prosperous, she would be more loyal and if more loyal, more free.

On 16 June 1904 Churchill still insisted: 'It would put me, and others like me who wish to work for the Liberal party and help it win a great victory, in a position of hideous difficulty, in a most hateful and monstrous dilemma, if we are suddenly confronted with a definite proposal to create a separate parliament for Ireland.'

He accepted the view that Ireland would not simply blow over. But he reiterated his father's rejection of a parliament in Dublin, which would be 'a rival, perhaps an enemy of our own parliament'. Churchill was worried by the protectionist impulses of the Irish, but he wanted the Irish to feel more free and felt that administrative home rule might help in this respect. He then declared, in a passage that was to haunt him later:

> Our duty towards Ireland is undiminished. I would much rather deal with the Irish question on its merits, according to the conscience and conviction of the English people, than have to deal with it according to some bargain or pact which had been made in some lobby or some corner as the price by which a particular member received a particular number of votes, or a particular government assumed the reins of office.[14]

But a process of gradual softening on the home rule issue began soon enough. In September 1904 Lord Dunraven's Reform Association called for Ireland to be given more extensive powers of self-government. Dunraven had been Lord Randolph's political ally and the only Tory minister who resigned in support of Lord Randolph's resignation as chancellor. (He was also, allegedly, one of Lady Randolph's numerous lovers.) This was not simply the independent action of a reform-minded wing of Irish unionist and landlord opinion. Dublin Castle was sympathetic. Lord Dudley, the Tory Lord Lieutenant since 1902, had shown a consistent flexibility and openness towards popular opinion; he liked to talk about governing Ireland according to 'Irish ideas'. The Catholic under-secretary, the formidable Sir Antony MacDonnell, had helped to draft the Dunraven proposals—with the support of George Wyndham, the chief secretary. The leader of the Irish parliamentary party, John Redmond, had reacted with initial enthusiasm: he immediately stated that, 'with these men (meaning Lord Dunraven and his friends in the Irish Reform

Fig. 5. Moreton Frewen. Churchill's uncle, and an Irish Home Ruler.

Association) with us, home rule may come at any moment'.[15] The Ulster Unionists, however, were alarmed: in March 1904 they formed the Ulster Unionist council to express their hostility. Senior nationalists—in particular John Dillon—weighed in with a firm rejection. Redmond felt it necessary to abandon his friendly support, on the spurious grounds that it merely made life more difficult for Dunraven. At the end of September 1904 Winston Churchill supported Wyndham in a Manchester speech. The system of government in Ireland was 'rotten'.[16] The imperial parliament was overburdened. Irish affairs should somehow be returned to Dublin. Orange bigots should not have a veto on policy. His uncle Moreton Frewen—who was to be elected as a nationalist MP in 1910—wrote from his small estate in Cork praising the speech, saying that it would split the unionists.[17] Despite this foray, Churchill remained a unionist.

But there was to be some movement. In a speech in parliament on 20 February 1905 Churchill acknowledged the reality of nationality as 'a valuable principle'. He regarded it as absurd to suggest that 'Burns was as much an Englishman as Shakespeare, and Shakespeare as much an Irishman as Moore'. This assertion obviously implied—for his Irish readers at least—that certain political consequences followed.

Churchill then turned to a historically exceptionally well-informed dissertation on the subject of the English rule and rulers in Ireland. 'What was in the air of these Irish offices that so powerfully influenced distinguished public officials, chief secretaries and Tory viceroys, who were sent to watch the workings of the Irish governmental machine on the spot?' The recent example of Sir Antony MacDonnell was likely to have been on the minds of parliamentarians, but Churchill went much further, displaying a high knowledge of Irish officialdom going back to the 1830s. 'Sir Antony MacDonnell did not stand alone. Behind him there had been Sir West Ridgeway, Sir Robert Hamilton, Thomas Drummond and others. What was it disquieted those public officials?'[18]

Churchill then drew on his knowledge of the mid-1880s when Lord Carnarvon, in alliance with his father, had met privately with Parnell. 'What was it that drew Lord Carnarvon to the empty house in Grosvenor Square?' In his biography of his father he had re-created the moment. 'The two rulers of Ireland—coroneted impotence and uncrowned power—rambled discursively on such topics as self-government and national aspirations, colonial parliaments and a central legislative body, which might, it appeared, possess—a remarkable licence—the right of protecting Irish industries. Altogether a very instructive afternoon!'[19]

Indeed, a wide range of topics were discussed, according to Carnarvon: the protection of property, the possibility of a central board, the removal of Irish members from the House of Commons if an Irish parliament were established, the question of a land purchase bill and the improvement of industrial sources. Parnell later said: 'We were discussing a general outline for constituting a legislature for Ireland on the colonial model. When I took occasion to remark that protection for certain Irish industries against English and foreign competition would be absolutely necessary...Lord Carnarvon said: "I entirely agree with you but what a row there will be about it in England."'[20] Carnarvon denied that he had ever agreed to a statutory parliament with a right to protect Irish industries—but Churchill is right to seize the essential point: both men agreed that protection had been discussed. How had the topic come up except in the context of some sort of model of colonial home rule? He then moved on to the early twentieth century and discussed the Tory Lord Lieutenant Lord Dudley, who had openly said Ireland should be governed according to Irish ideas.

Churchill asked:

> What was it that induced Lord Dudley to cast away all his prospects of future promotion in the Tory party? Was it some dim understanding of a great truth which came to those who watched the working of the machine at close quarters or was it the clear apprehension of a great fraud? The Irish polity has its equal nowhere in the world...Ireland was governed by neither King nor people. The system of government was not democratic, autocratic or even oligarchical.

His tone towards Ulster Unionism was cold and contemptuous: 'They paraded their loyalty, using it to extort concessions and privilege from the British government; when any man attempted to do even-handed justice in the King's name, they complained they were being betrayed.'

The range and sweep of this speech are most impressive. Churchill's quite untypical use of historical references—often quite *recherché*—was not necessarily designed to appeal to Irish audiences, but it undoubtedly did. He had clearly been reading the work of R. Barry O'Brien, biographer of both Parnell and Drummond. It seemed, and indeed was, rather 'un-English'. This speech was delivered just as Winston Churchill neared the end of his biography of his father. In November 1905 he sent the book to press.

Churchill was now identified with a softer position on Irish nationalism. In May 1905 he spoke of the 'brighter days'[21] for Ireland that were in the offing. In October 1905 the nationalist leader, Tom Kettle, identified him as a clever, coming young man 'at present in the process of being converted'.[22] In February 1906 it was reported that Winston Churchill, 'until recently a unionist', now believed in a 'self-government for Ireland'.[23] Later in the year, he congratulated the Tories for the condition (peaceful) in which they had left Ireland but insisted that it did not vindicate Tory policy in the long term.[24]

In 1906 Churchill published the two-volume life of his father Randolph: designed, above all, to exorcise his father's long humiliating public death by embracing and explaining his career, it inevitably dealt with Irish matters. He laid considerable emphasis on his father's attempt to form an alliance with Parnell in 1885.[25] 'By 1906, after all, a newly minted Liberal, he was himself under pressure to support home rule. This is perhaps the single most embarrassing political dilemma that the biography has to confront.'[26] A key passage resolved the problem:

> A proposal to establish by statute, subject to guarantees of Imperial supremacy, a colonial parliament in Ireland for the transaction of Irish business may indeed be unwise, but is not, and ought not to be, outside the limits of calm and patient consideration. Such a proposal is not necessarily fraught with the immense and terrific consequences which were so generally associated with it. A generation may arise in England who will question the policy of creating subordinate legislatures as well as we question the propriety of catholic emancipation and who will study the records of the fierce disputes of 1886 with the superior manner of a modern professor examining the controversies of the early church. But that will not prove the men of 1886 wrong or foolish in speech and action.[27]

In 1906 Churchill took the post of Under-Secretary of State for the Colonies; he managed to convince his colleagues in government of his plan for early responsible self-government, elevating South Africa to the same status of autonomy within the empire as that of Australia, Canada, and New Zealand.[28] Jan Smuts, the former Boer general, immediately grasped this significant olive branch.

Irish nationalists were deeply impressed: if Churchill was capable of such empathy and insight, surely he would soon apply the same qualities to Ireland? If home rule was good for the Boers; surely it was good for the Irish? The *Ulster Herald*, the voice of Tyrone nationalism, was ecstatic:

> It is a transformation of momentous import, truly Mr Churchill was becoming the medium of 'making history' at an age when many young men are still troubled with making their choice of an occupation in life. He is, we believe, only 32. At this age he is the instrument chosen to confer a free constitution on a brave nation. William Pitt was 40 when he robbed a free nation of its constitution and doomed its people to misery, slavery and degradation for a hundred years and more. The time is fast approaching when the brilliant youth who announced this week the terms of the home rule settlement for South Africa will get his opportunity of saying whether he approves of a home rule settlement of the Irish question. There was not a single plea or argument in his speech on Tuesday night, which could not be ten times more justly applied to the case of Ireland—than to the case of the Transvaal.[29]

The same writer added:

> Had Mr Winston Churchill been through an 'Irish war for freedom', had he been captured on the Bog of Allen instead of on the Transvaal veldt, and held prisoner at Omagh instead of at Pretoria, he might have been supporting a home rule measure for Ireland this week...[30]

The *Daily News* saw Churchill as a serious candidate to replace James Bryce—who was moving on to become ambassador in Washington—as chief secretary in Ireland.[31] The *Globe* published a story that Augustine Birrell had turned the post down and that it would go to either Churchill or John Burns, 'though neither of them is keenly desirous of taking up the position'.[32]

On 8 May 1907 the Liberals attempted a cautious resolution of the Irish question. The new chief secretary, Augustine Birrell, offered in parliament a measure of devolution that fell short of home rule. The bill, Birrell explained, does not 'contain a touch or a trace, or a hint of or suggestion of any legislative power'. Birrell's bill proposed to set up an Irish council consisting of elected, but also nominated, members and the under-secretary of Ireland. To this council it proposed to transfer the control of eight out of the forty-five existing departments of government. It is clear that both John Redmond and John Dillon at the apex of the Irish Party were sympathetic to the bill, despite its limitations. But Birrell's tone, designed to reassure unionist opinion, provoked a grass-roots nationalist uprising against the bill. The *Freeman's Journal*, normally a supporter of the official Irish Nationalist Party line, declared sourly of Birrell's advocacy: 'He was full of reasons why no unionist should oppose the bill, but very bare of reason why any home ruler should support it.'[33] Public bodies began to denounce the measure—so rapid was the change in mainstream opinion that within ten days Redmond had decided to reverse his initial position and denounce the measure. An official party convention rejected the measure. On 3 June the bill was withdrawn, probably to Redmond's private dismay.[34]

Churchill once again indicated his disappointment. The rejection of Birrell's bill was another instance of a tragic, lost opportunity in Irish history. He praised the speeches of Tim Healy and William O'Brien, the two senior nationalists who had supported the Birrell project. Churchill insisted that the bill was not a low-grade political manœuvre designed to ease the Liberal Party's complex relationship with its Gladstonian inheritance. Rather it represented 'a great policy— because there was a policy behind the bill'. He spoke not of the details but rather of the Cabinet's desire to offer 'a large measure of self-government to Ireland'. He hoped, in vain as it happened, that Irish nationalists would not return to the 'tomfoolery' of agrarian militancy and cattle driving.[35] Privately, he was rather more scathing about Birrell's project: 'That stupid bill . . . has been one disaster. But it is a big one; for it leaves us without an Irish policy...Ireland at the moment is utterly pigged.'[36]

In 1908 Asquith succeeded Campbell-Bannerman as prime minister. Asquith introduced Churchill into the Cabinet as president of the Board of Trade. Following constitutional convention, Churchill was compelled to stand again for north-west Manchester. How would the Manchester Irish vote? The pro-Liberal mood of 1906 was evaporating, giving the Irish a particular significance. Even so, Redmond had to tread carefully before offering Churchill his support. The conventional wisdom among Irish MPs was that Asquith was playing with Redmond on home rule. Tim Healy forcefully expressed this in parliament. It all made Redmond look weak and too tolerant of liberal evasion. The pro-liberal mood in the countryside had subsided since 1906. The seat was obviously going to be hotly contested, with the Irish vote playing a central role. Churchill had been winning good opinions from the nationalist press in Dublin and some Irish MPs. He must have had every hope that the Irish electorate would carry him to victory, but was Redmond strong enough to help?

On the eve of the campaign, matters became even more uncertain. Redmond, anxious to extract himself from the devolution fiasco, put down a motion in favour of home rule in parliament. Asquith's response was perceived to be lukewarm. Asquith had defined his position on Home Rule as a conviction that the 'ultimate solution of the Irish problem can only be found in a system of self-government in regard to purely local affairs'.[37] Tim Healy, hardly an ally of Redmond's, gained enhanced credibility within the Irish Party by his waspish put-down of the prime minister. Churchill was well aware of the problem and tried to mollify the Irish.[38] But Redmond was still undecided. He was afraid of being perceived as a 'poodle' of the Liberals. On 16 April he praised the 'great strides' Churchill was making. A day later it was reported that he was still opposed to offering the Irish vote to Churchill.

Four days later the Dublin correspondent of The Times reported divisions in nationalist opinion in Dublin on the subject of Churchill.

Churchill had one great advantage. His conservative opponent, William Joynson-Hicks, was a particularly strong unionist. He was a supporter of coercion in Ireland. On 20 April Churchill made his appeal: 'He is the representative of bitter, aggressive repression in Ireland.'[39]

But it was not enough to stress Joynson-Hicks's reactionary unionism. The Catholic Church in Manchester liked the Tory candidate's stance on educational matters. The Bishop of Salford continued to urge his flock, mainly Irish, to support the Tories. Churchill had to insist that the Liberals had not gone cold on home rule. His solution was to say on 20 April that

> I am strongly of opinion and I say that with the full concurrence of the prime minister—that the Liberal party should have a full authority and a free hand to deal with the problem of Irish self-government without being restricted to measures of administrative devolution of the character of the Irish Council bill.[40]

Asquith was visibly annoyed; he made it clear that he had not authorized Churchill's comment, though he accepted it was consistent with government policy. Delighted to see Asquith's hand forced, the Irish Party executive in Dublin rapidly announced its support for Churchill.

> On behalf of the Standing Committee of the United Irish League of Great Britain, after having carefully considered Mr Winston Churchill's speech on home rule, we are of the opinion that the object we had in view has been substantially gained, as we have elicited a declaration on the authority of the Prime Minister, that home rule, in the sense of Mr Redmond's resolution, will be put by the government before the electors at the general election. Without such a constructive declaration it would have been impossible for us to ask support for Mr Churchill as a member of the cabinet, and as his personal pledges are, on the whole, satisfactory, we call upon Irish nationalists to vote for him.[41]

Those present at the Dublin meeting were John Dillon MP, Swift MacNeill MP, T. M. Kettle MP, J. J. Clancy MP, J. J. Mooney MP, David Sheehy MP. Redmond and Devlin in London had been in touch by telegram throughout the day. A day later Churchill, in Manchester, had a question-and-answer session with electors: he was asked if he had adopted home rule just to ingratiate himself with his new party and the electorate.

My questioner is wrong in supposing that I suddenly developed a faith in home rule when I separated from the Conservative party. At the last election, although I was prepared to advocate reforms in the government of Ireland, I was not then prepared to go so far as I have been prepared to go in the course of the present year. But I have been very much embold-ened by going for two years in the inner councils of liberalism. I have found myself working with men whose minds I knew and understood. I have found myself in full and complete sympathy with them, and I have got to know much more about the Irish cause. Then I have had South Africa to deal with. I have seen the advantages of freedom in that country; I have said what a far-reaching doctrine is the doctrine of 'trust the people'; I have seen what a boon is self-government when it is boldly and frankly conferred, and what a power it has to heal the wounds and sores of the past.—[Cheers.] That is why three weeks ago, when Mr John Redmond moved his motion in the House of Commons, I was able to give it conscientious and sincere support. [Cheers.][42]

This was Churchill's reply to the charge of opportunism. It is coherent and based on observable facts. It is a plausible narrative but also a convenient one. At any rate, all the fine talk was to no avail. The Catholic Church in Salford still preferred Joynson-Hicks and his posi-tions on denominational education. Most Irish voters seemed to have followed that line. Churchill lost, he said, thanks to those 'sulky Irish Catholics'[43] changing sides at the last minute under priestly pressure. Incidentally, Churchill's support within the Jewish community led by Nathan Laski held firm, but it was not enough to hold the seat.

There was one rather ironic footnote to the whole process. Andrew J. Kettle, the veteran nationalist lieutenant of Parnell, whose son had strongly supported Churchill, moved to criticize in public his son's action. For Andrew Kettle, British liberalism was a false friend to Ireland. Parnell had been right to explore an alliance with Randolph Churchill in 1885: 'Let it be always remembered that the practical contemplation of an Irish parliament originated with the advanced section of the British Tory party.'[44] Both Andrew Kettle's son and Randolph Churchill's son must have contemplated this message from a bygone era with some disdain. For both of them it must have seemed obvious that the way forward lay with an alliance between British democracy and Irish nationalism. Best to leave old men with their memories of what might have been. After all, even when Churchill moved to a Dundee seat, he needed, as John Valentine of the Irish party was not shy of pointing out, Irish votes.[45]

Churchill did not brood over the Irish 'betrayal' in Manchester. He moved on to the next task—election for Dundee—with aplomb. On 4 May 1908 Churchill told the Kinnaird Hall in Dundee:

> With these facts before us, upon the authority of men like Lord Dunraven, Sir Joseph West Ridgeway, Sir Anthony MacDonnell, Lord Dudley, and others who have served the Crown in Ireland—is it wonderful that we should refuse to turn our eyes away from the vision of that other Ireland, that Ireland free to control her own destiny in all that properly concerns herself; free to devote the native genius of her people to the purposes of her own self-culture, the vision of that other Ireland which Mr Gladstone had reserved as the culminating achievement of his long and glorious career?— [Cheers.] Is it wonderful that we should refuse to turn our eyes away from that? No, I say that the desire and the aim of making a national settlement with Ireland on lines which would enable the people of that country to manage their own purely local affairs is not an aim that can be separated from the general march of the Liberal army. [Cheers.][46]

Churchill was now firmly a signed-up contributor to the liberal consensus in Ireland: if anything, he was rather more enthusiastic than most about home rule. He had completed his 'conversion', just as Tom Kettle had expected.

3

Churchill in Belfast

To bridge the gulf that separates these two sectarian nations and combine them into one, to unite the strength and practical ability and effectiveness of the North to the sensibility and imagination and enthusiasm of the South, is a noble ideal for statesmanship; its fulfilment would heal a sore which has long poisoned British politics. It is, moreover, an ideal which is by no means unattainable from the nature of the case; for both nations, as has been said, are essentially Irish, and between Irishmen of every creed and class and province there is at bottom a common ground of sympathy and intelligence. In the very depths of their antagonism there is something essentially Irish. But to the realization of such ideals there is no royal road; time alone can do the work, and the problem for the statesman is how best to co-operate with time in its healing efficacy.[1]

All intelligent politicians guessed that home rule would stretch the unwritten rules of the UK Constitution to its limit and beyond. Randolph Churchill's aggressive and inflammatory language of 1886 was a clear warning. Talk of Protestant Ulster 'fighting' the democratically articulated demand of nationalist Ireland for home rule frightened and angered many. But talk of coercing a coherent community to the point where it had to surrender its pre-existing terms of membership of the British polity also caused great anguish and uncertainty. Churchill was among the relatively few senior politicians who felt both these arguments had merit. Like the *Times* writer W. F. Monypenny, he saw the clash of the two Irish nations as a clash of 'two rights' and classically tragic in that sense.

In the summer of 1910 all party leaderships—Nationalist, Tory, and Liberal—flirted with the concept of federalism. All intuited they were on the eve of an intensive, brutal conflict. The senior figures of the unionist press were also attracted by the notion.[2] If, somehow, the constitution of the United Kingdom could be remodelled in a way that permitted the benign resolution of the Irish question without justifying in any way Ulster Unionist cries of betrayal, was this not a prize worth obtaining? 'Home Rule All Round' was, in the end, an illusion but an attractive one—it certainly attracted Churchill, who was involved in these discussions.

Moreton Frewen (1853–1924), an English adventurer from a landed family, had later become the MP for North-East Cork, standing for the moderate O'Brienite nationalist faction, the All for Ireland League. As brother-in-law of Randolph Churchill, he reinforced Churchill's interest in these schemes. But Frewen, who had some personal links to Edward Carson—and, indeed, was to be related to him also in later years by marriage—could not win Carson to support the federalist concept; nor, in truth, could Redmond have taken the bulk of the Nationalist Party. So Churchill drifted back towards a more conventional home rule position.[3] 'You say we are going to pass home rule in this parliament—so we are,' he proclaimed in 1911.[4] But this was now a parliament after the 1910 election in which Redmond held the perceived balance of power—exactly the circumstances that Churchill had said earlier were the wrong ones for dealing with the home rule issue.

In early 1912 it became known that Churchill was prepared to speak for home rule at the Ulster Hall—a venue where his father had declared his support for the Ulster Unionist cause in 1886. This seemed to the Belfast Unionists to be a gross act of impiety and provocation. Churchill was himself more than a little concerned. The Master of Elibank, the Liberal chief whip—'a genial Scotsman with a profound ignorance of Ireland in general and Ulster in particular'[5]—had urged the move upon him. At this point, Churchill's concern related to the political wisdom of such a meeting, not his own personal safety. In particular, he wished to make a personal appeal and not to be surrounded by nationalist politicians.

On 13 January 1912 Churchill wrote to John Redmond: 'I have been reflecting a good deal upon the meeting which has been arranged for us both to address in Belfast in February.' Churchill made it clear that he would be delighted to share a platform with Redmond and Devlin at the Eighty Club in Manchester. 'But,' he added, 'I am extremely doubtful whether our joint appearance in Belfast will really conclude to the public advantage'.[6] Churchill added ominously: 'The arrangements have been made without my being consulted, otherwise I would have expressed my view at an earlier date. What we want in Belfast is not demonstrations but discussions.' Churchill felt that the event gave a possible advantage to the 'violent Orange faction'. The only viable tactic was to display extreme flexibility in the face of unreasonableness—in order that English public opinion, the key factor in the whole crisis, was not misled. Churchill indicated that he wanted to use the speech for a serious discussion of the anxieties of Ulster Protestants. There was no point in appealing to nationalists—they were already strongly in support of home rule. He believed that he could best appeal to unionist concerns if he spoke alone and sought, unsuccessfully, Redmond's acquiescence on this score.

Disagreement on this point should not occlude the fact that Churchill and Redmond actually shared rather similar world views. Both had recently penned introductions to pro-home rule booklets; they were remarkably aligned in tone. T. M. Kettle's *Open Secret of Ireland* was published with an introduction by John Redmond, dated 12 December 1911, which hailed the 'advent of that brighter day when the grant of full self-government to Ireland will reveal to England the open secret of making Ireland her friend and helpmate, the brightest friend in her Crown of Empire'.[7] Churchill's language, in a pamphlet published a few months later, was rather more wide-ranging in scope, but after a survey of the world it reached the same conclusions.[8]

In his introduction to Jeremiah MacVeigh's *Home Rule in a Nutshell*, Churchill wrote: 'We see the four consolidations of the human family, which, measured in terms of energy and force, realised or latent, are in the ascendant—the Russian power, the Yellow races, the Teutonic alliance and the English-speaking peoples.'[9] From this he deduced: 'The road to the unity of the English-speaking races, with all that carries with it ... we can not see the end of it. But it is a road, and an Irish parliament, loyal to the Crown ... is assuredly a milestone upon it.'[10]

However, Belfast unionist opinion was infuriated by the suggestion that Churchill and Redmond would speak in the Ulster Hall. It seemed to them to be a vulgar assault on the memory of his father's celebrated speech. Churchill, it was said, wanted to dance on his father's grave. It was widely believed that the gesture was intended to be particularly needling and offensive. The air was filled with threats, while English unionists nervously urged on their Belfast allies respect for free speech. On 18 January 1912 the *Irish Independent* reported: 'The declaration of the Standing Committee of the Ulster Unionist Council to prevent the holding of the Churchill meeting in the Ulster Hall, Belfast, on the 8th of next month, has created quite a sensation in political circles, and is discussed by the Press and public men of both sides.' On the same day Moreton Frewen, speaking for the moderate O'Brienite faction in home rule politics, which had often suffered physical bullying and denial of free press, published a letter in the *Pall Mall Gazette* saying that the Redmondites had no right to protest at Unionist tactics.[11] 'The decision will certainly be carried out,' said a distinguished Ulster Unionist, who had just returned to London from Belfast, to a representative of the *Pall Mall Gazette*.

> 'Then the meeting,' he was asked, 'will not be held, if it is in your power to stop it?'
>
> 'It will not. The feeling in Belfast, and in fact throughout the whole of the North of Ireland, has been slowly gathering force ever since the announcement was made that Mr Churchill was to speak in the Ulster Hall. Loyal Ireland is determined that he shall not. Ulster has this great opportunity of proving that it is capable of doing what it says it will.
>
> As to the method to be employed, it will be,' he said, 'the most effective. There may be bloodshed—I think there will. The only way it can be avoided is by Mr Churchill staying away. His presence on that platform is an insult to loyal Ireland.'

But no one believed that it was easy to discourage Churchill. 'Will he stay away, do you think?' asked the *Pall Mall Gazette*. 'No. He is probably as determined to speak as we are to stop him, so I suppose we shall share the responsibility for what takes place.' The local Liberals sought to move the meeting from the Ulster Hall to the Opera House. Fred W. Warden, the Belfast theatrical manager, insisted that he had been in receipt of a serious offer of a knighthood if he allowed the Liberals to book the Grand Opera House.[12] Matters were becoming at one and the same time squalid and threatening.

When the wise decision was made to switch the meeting from the Ulster Hall to Celtic Park in Catholic nationalist West Belfast, there was widespread relief. The Ulster Unionist Council (UUC) responded to the nationalist decision and called on 'all unionists to abstain from any interference with the said meeting, and to do everything in their power to avoid any action that might lead to disturbances'.[13] The Grand Master of the Orange Lodge, Colonel Wallace, also issued a statement: 'We call upon our brethren to abstain from interfering in any way whatever with the nationalist meeting advertised to be held in Celtic Park Football Club.'[14] It was now widely expected that the meeting would pass off peacefully. For that reason the chief whip announced that he would not accompany Churchill to Belfast.[15] For the same reason, Churchill thought it was safe to take his wife, Clementine, who was pregnant.

The spirit of relief found vent in an outbreak of jokes. The Celtic Ground was known locally as 'Paradise': this led to an evening paper placard in Belfast bearing the legend 'Mr Churchill for Paradise'.[16] The proximity of the city cemetery provoked further quips. The boxing ring at Celtic Park led others to suggest a joust between Churchill and Lord Londonderry, his kinsman and a prominent Ulster Unionist.

Meanwhile, behind the scenes, the discussion of policy was ever more complex. At the Cabinet meeting on 6 February Churchill and Lloyd George moved a formal proposal for Ulster's exclusion from the bill. The majority, however, opted for applying the bill to the whole of Ireland, while leaving the government free 'to make such changes as fresh evidence of facts, or the pressure of British opinion, may render expedient'.[17] Asquith thus opened the way for two and a half years of rising tension in Ireland, but, nonetheless, two and a half years in which he retained the Irish Party's support in parliament. Having failed to persuade his colleagues, Churchill set off for Belfast with inevitably mixed emotions. Getting on the train in London for Belfast, Churchill was genially mobbed by a group of young women who implored him: 'Give our love to Ireland and the Irish radicals in Ulster.'[18] He was hailed by the home rule press: 'Mr Churchill is the politician of the living moment. He is young, prominent and, as Belfast will readily admit, audacious.'[19]

Churchill and his wife reached the Grand Central Hotel in Belfast safely enough—but the mood was hardly pleasant. The hotel was full of furious local businessmen who shook their fists at Winston in the corridors. Freddy Guest, Winston's cousin, who had accompanied the Churchills, insisted on carrying a loaded revolver: even this was not particularly reassuring. Clementine felt that it might go off at any moment and wound one of them in the leg.[20] When Churchill and his wife attempted to leave the hotel for their political meeting, he found a large crowd of angry shipyard workers in threatening mood. (They included William Grant, who was to be Minister of Public Safety in Northern Ireland during the Second World War.)[21]

According to the *Irish Times*:

> Indeed, from the very moment that they emerged on the footpath until they got clear away, they appeared to be in danger, and had it not been for the prompt and vigorous action of the police, serious consequences might have followed. An ugly rush was made for Mr Churchill as he walked across the footpath. Some men aimed blows at him, but fortunately a police constable frustrated the effort. From the opposites of the street, a half loaf of bread was thrown, but it fell short.[22]

The London *Times* commented: 'The vehicle was, for a second, poised on the nearside wheel. I am convinced that the crowd had no intention of overturning the car, but this is what might have happened if the

Fig. 6. Mob Violence in Belfast. Illustration from *Illustrated London News*, February 17, 1912: 'Anti Home-Rulers in Action: The "First Lord" Mobbed'.

police had not driven off the people immediately.'[23] *The Times* added: 'It seemed to me that Mr Churchill was running a far graver risk than ever he had expected. But he never flinched. He took the hostility, visualised as well as vocalised, calmly and no harm befell him.'[24] Then the car made the short journey to the Falls Road and everything changed: here there were crowded streets and cheering thousands. Mrs Churchill (in a long fur coat) looked pleased with the warmth of the greeting.[25]

Churchill opened the speech with a windy phrase. 'Contact with Ireland is contact with history'—a piece of rhetoric that was to have an unconscious echo in 1998 when Tony Blair arrived in Belfast for the talks leading to the Good Friday Agreement. Churchill in 1912 identified himself with the Liberal tradition in Ireland. For more than twenty-five years, the Liberal Party had been taught by Gladstone that home rule was the right answer to the Irish question. There were three key arguments in its favour. The first of these was the argument that home rule would strengthen the empire. In particular, the Irish were now the 'most serious obstacle to Anglo-American friendship'. But the Irish in Ireland were 'monarchical' by 'character' and 'tradition'. The King had travelled extensively throughout the world but nowhere had he received a better reception than in Catholic and nationalist Dublin. 'Here, as elsewhere, throughout the British Empire the crown may become the supreme and central link of unity and acceptance.'

The royal visit to Dublin of 8–12 July 1911 had indeed been a success. King George, known to be personally supportive of home rule, was confronted by small-scale republican and radical socialist opposition, and, in a rather more mainstream gesture, the decision of the Dublin Corporation not to offer an official welcome. On the whole, however, the visit was a triumph: the royal party thought that the enthusiasm of Dublin crowds outdid even the warmth of the reception for King Edward VII in 1903.[26]

He addressed the unionists at this point: 'Are British governments to be condemned to maintain a perpetual quarrel with the Irish nation? For it is a nation [cheers]'. At this point, he was interrupted by a suffragette demanding votes for women. Churchill sidestepped the argument by saying—to cheers—that this issue must await an Irish parliament. As that 'belligerent' Irish 'liberal' Michael J. F. McCarthy noted:

> The speed and ruthlessness with which a number of suffragettes were consecutively hurled out of the meeting showed the strong hand of Mr Devlin and Mr Redmond. No English meeting ever handled the sisterhood so roughly. One would have imagined that a body of New York policemen constituted the stewards.
>
> 'Will you give self-government to the women of Ireland?' cried a suffragette, just before she was hurled out of the tent into the rain and marsh. A pertinent question, for under a Romanist Parliament the women of Ireland would become as the women of Spain and Portugal—prisoners and slaves to be kept in subjection and espionage.[27]

Churchill, however, had little choice but to keep to his prepared script. He had to reassure his audience that talk of federalism did not constitute any denial of the specifically national nature of the Irish case, but the problem was, of course, that there would have been no talk of federalism without the weight of the Irish problem on the British political system. Churchill declared:

> How often have we been reminded of the handful of Irishmen who voted against us in the Boer War? Have we forgotten the brave Irishmen that never failed in their duty to the Queen and to the army? Why, in these days, when Irish catholics are assailed with so much ill-nature, are they never to be remembered too? I can not help thinking of the scenes of which I was a witness when the heights of the Tugela were stormed, and when Ladysmith was at last relieved [cheers]. On the west of the hill firing the fire of sixty guns, in a veritable whirlwind of exploding shells, stood the valiant Boers. Up the slopes marched unflinchingly the Dublins and the Inniskilling Fusiliers [cheers]. That was a struggle of heroes, ranged by fate and duty on opposite sides. What a tragedy, what a cruel pity, that such noble breeds of men should be locked together in hateful carnage! [hear, hear] And now we have got them both [cheers]. We have made friends of our enemies. Can we not make friends with our comrades too?

It was possible to keep the Boers and the Irish within the 'shell' of the great 'mother empire'. Surely the Ulster Unionists took these imperial considerations at least as seriously as discussions about *Ne Temere* or *Proprio Moto*. *Ne Temere*, the papal decree on mixed marriage, in particular, infuriated Irish Protestants. This last observation was greeted by laughter and cheers. It was interpreted by his audience as a cut at the Ulster Presbyterian convention held a week before, which was much taken up with these fears of Catholicism. He continued: 'Meet the grievance, hear the quarrel, bury the hatred, but the interests, conciliate, consolidate, and unify—by this and this alone shall we be able to surmount the toils and the perils which the future may have in store [cheers].' Churchill then advanced his argument that the House of Commons was anyway overburdened with business and some way had to be found of lightening the load.

> There is only one thing we can do. We must divide our business up into imperial business, affecting the Empire and the United Kingdom as a whole, and internal and local business, affecting particularly each of its component parts. Then there will be plenty of time for both [another suffragette interruption and ejection], and every subject can be dealt with fully and in the proper place. But members of Parliament who are on this platform know perfectly well how this argument can be extended and illustrated by almost every day in parliamentary life at Westminster. If the House of Commons is to last—if it is to hold its position as the great representative Assembly of British Empire—it must be freed from the mass of business by which it is at present congested. This division of business is vital. It is the only way in which vast composite communities of civilised men can in modern times inform themselves. Look at our two most important rivals—Germany and the United States of America. Both these powers have developed their giant energies, effective as they are for all purposes of peace or war, the one through 26 separate parliaments, the other through more than 50.

He recognized that Ireland could not be governed simply in the light of this conception; but it still helped to give the Irish case a wider imperial logic. As Churchill warmed to his theme, yet another suffragette interloper tried to intervene, crying out 'and the women', before being speedily ejected. This continued a pattern that might have dismayed those young women in London who had urged Churchill to pass their love on to the Irish radicals. But Churchill laboured on:

> We recognise that the case of Ireland stands in a different position from that of other parts of the United Kingdom [hear hear]. On historical grounds, if on no other, it is clear that the same measure and the same form which would be applicable to Scotland or to Wales would not be applicable to the needs of Ireland [cheers]. This great and urgent public necessity of clearing parliament from the congestion of business is sufficient in itself, from a British point of view, were other arguments lacking, to justify the measure which we shall shortly place before the House of Commons [cheers].

Churchill turned to the fears of Ulster Protestants. There had been alarms and excursions before about perceived pro-Catholic reform—going back to Catholic emancipation. These had always proved groundless—had the prosperity of Protestant Ulster not continued to advance remorselessly? He did, however, warn the Ulster Protestants not to become the 'catspaw' of the Tories in England: after all, many Ulster Protestants broadly supported the policies of the Liberal government.

What is missing here is the force local sectarian and, indeed, widespread religious conviction gave to a political cause in this era. Presbyterian leaders asserted that they knew the will of the Lord. They asserted that God opposed home rule—Catholic priests were just as sure He supported it. The authority of the religious leaders derived from the fact that their audiences also believed in God. The religious leaders were often relatively moderate—Presbyterian leaders like the Reverend J. C. McDermott asserted that the 'any means' of opposition referred to in the Ulster Covenant meant only the withholding of taxes. But this moderation on elements of strategy is not the point. The religious leaders had the authority—which they used—to unify their community for political purposes.

Churchill then turned—in a passage that in its conclusion was to alarm nationalists more than it reassured unionists—to the question of safeguards. He argued that an Irish parliament would reject religious intolerance, but, if it did not, the Westminster parliament retained the power 'in law' and 'in fact' to intervene.

Churchill then turned to the difficult issue of finance. He insisted that Great Britain was 'at the moment paying on the balance...a subsidy to Ireland...which equals the sum of £2,000,000 a year'. This sum was certain to rise substantially as existing legislative commitments, such as to old age pensioners, were rolled out. Some wanted to cut this subsidy with the advent of home rule. Churchill dismissed the idea: 'A prosperous and loyal Ireland lying a great breakwater across our Atlantic flank' was so vital that on 'military grounds' alone the comparatively small sum was easy to justify; anyway, it was desirable that home rule should get off to a good start on generous, workable terms.

The Cabinet had been puzzling over various schemes of home rule finance. The problem lay in the recent growth of Irish dependence on the British Exchequer to pay for reforms like the old age pension. It was not just the Cabinet, but Ireland itself. One critic sourly commented: 'Ireland is rather puzzled between other peoples' money and a cabinet of its own.'[28] In the end—and despite the advice of the specially commissioned experts of the Primrose Committee— the Cabinet adopted Herbert Samuel's scheme, which retained substantive British control over finances. This flew in the face of a substantial body of Irish public opinion, expressed, above all, in this case by Tom Kettle MP, which sought to wean Ireland away from dependence on British 'doles' by giving greater fiscal independence. Nevertheless, the Irish Party leadership of Redmond and Dillon calculated that they had to tolerate Samuel's scheme rather than risk wrecking the wider prospects for home rule. This is important background for Churchill's Belfast speech. In this economic context, Churchill regarded separation as an impossible notion. The trend was for ever greater integration:

Churchill then turned back to the need for compromise. Only eighteen months earlier, the unionist press had shown great interest in a federal solution. Surely a compromise of 'reconciling' statecraft was possible. The unionists, by their extreme language of recent times, had disqualified themselves from ever being able to govern Ireland again. 'The flame of Irish nationality was inextinguishable,' he declared. Churchill then appealed to the selfish interest of the Tories. With a lower Irish membership at Westminster, was not a Tory majority more likely?

The word of the Imperial Parliament has been passed and so long as we have the strength to maintain our civilisation against external dangers, so long as the navy guards our shores, so long as the Union Jack flies over the parliament and the people of the United Kingdom, every old age pensioner, man or woman, will draw his pension which the House of Commons had provided as their last refuge on the side of the grave [cheers].

The Home Rule Bill will give the Irish Parliament a real responsibility in finance [hear, hear]. That parliament will be able to grip and control large areas of taxation, and it will have the power within reasonable and wise limits to supplement its income by new taxation...

Why should the empire, why should the world at large be deprived of a new contribution to the sum of human effort? History and poetry, justice and good sense alike demand that this race, gifted, virtuous, and brave, which has lived so long and has endured so much, should not, in view of her passionate desire, be left out of the family of nations, and should not be lost for ever among the indiscriminated multitudes of men [cheers]. What harm could Irish ideas and Irish sentiments and Irish dreams, if given their free play in the Irish parliament, do to the strong structure of the British power? Would not the arrival of an Irish parliament upon the brilliantly lighted stage of the modern world be an enrichment and an added glory to the treasures of the British Empire [cheers]?

He concluded:

There is the task which history has assigned to them, and it is in a different sense that I accept and repeat Lord Randolph Churchill's words, 'Ulster will fight and Ulster will be right'. Let Ulster fight for the dignity and honour of Ireland. Let her fight for the reconciliation of races and for the forgiveness of ancient wrongs. Let her fight for the unity and consolidation of the British Empire. Let her fight for the spread of clarity, tolerance, and enlightenment among men. Then, indeed, 'Ulster will fight and Ulster will be right' [loud cheers].

This was a brilliant and dramatic trope: rhetorically effective but quite without substance. Churchill refused to run from his father's legacy, seemed to embrace it formally, and even then practically subverted it. Randolph Churchill's words had been deliberately bitter and divisive. Turning them on their head was wonderful political theatre, but hardly a serious response to the issue of the day. What to do about Ulster Unionist opposition to home rule? Redmond's response was warm. 'After some 20 years of labour in the home rule cause, I can say with absolute sincerity that I would not have been absent from this meeting for any earthly consideration...I will accept all that he has said, and with reference to the safeguards that he has announced will be inserted in the Home Rule Bill, I accept every one of them.'[29]

Meanwhile, a threatening loyalist crowd gathered again outside the Grand Central Hotel in Belfast. But Churchill's car did not return: instead, it drove through a series of back streets to the York Street Railway Terminus, where a special train, which was in readiness, conveyed him to Larne. He boarded the *Princess Maud* some two and a half hours early. A loyalist crowd had already gathered on the quayside: Churchill walked on board slowly, carefully smoking his cigar.[30] Once on board, Churchill and his wife looked down 'smiling ironically but good-humouredly' at the 'singing mass'. They shouted 'Traitor', 'Turncoat', 'You are worse than John Redmond' and other slogans, but made no effort to get on the boat. Churchill did tell the *Irish Times* reporter on board that it had been a 'splendid meeting. The wicked dug the pit into which they tumbled themselves.'[31] But other newspapers noted that, during the few hours Churchill had spent in Belfast, 'he had to move about like a hunted man'.

For unionists the speech had been a notably lacklustre affair: Churchill 'probably never delivered a "duller speech". It lasted an hour and ten minutes. He appeared to be reading it and he indulged in little rhetorical gesture.'[32] The only drama had been the brutal ejection of the feminist protestors. The London letter of the *Belfast Newsletter* pointed out: 'Mr Churchill said a good deal about what the home rule parliament can not do but omitted to describe its power and duties. It was strange that he did not tell us hearers of the kind of legislation it might be expected to pass.'[33] The *Belfast Telegraph* noted: 'When Mr Churchill spoke of the empire and imperialism there was a chilling silence save from the Liberals.'[34] This was a reference to the relatively small body of Ulster liberals who had remained loyal to Gladstone after his conversion to home rule, and who had attended his Celtic Park meeting. Carson stressed the 'real' nationalist position on the Boer War: 'The Right Hon. gentleman was really eloquent when he spoke of the storming of Tugela, but he must have forgotten he was speaking in the presence of men who had prayed for the success of the Boer army.'[35]

Similarly, Churchill's emphasis on Ireland's economic dependence did not reassure Unionists. Churchill, after all, mentioned an Irish executive with 'real responsibility in finance' and 'able to grip and to control large areas of taxation'. As Michael J. F. McCarthy noted: 'When the Ulster merchants and mechanics read this the next day, they must have felt the grip of Mr Redmond already on their savings and earnings.'[36] W. F. Monypenny offered his own analysis of the words of Churchill:

> The separation of Ireland from Great Britain is absolutely impossible. The interests and affairs of the two islands are eternally interwoven ... the whole tendency of things, the whole inevitable drift of things is towards a more intimate connection. The economic dependence of Ireland on England is so absolute and quite apart from moral, military and constitutional arguments ... the two nations are bound together till the end of time by the national force of circumstances.

For Monypenny, such a statement had a more obviously unionist than nationalist implication: 'it is a curious kind of fatalism or political antinomianism that tells you an interest is so great that you can afford to neglect it, and common sense will prefer to see in the words quoted an argument for jealously guarding the connexion.'[37] Monypenny also felt that Churchill had been forced to face the reality that there were two nations on the island of Ireland:

> Mr Churchill was compelled almost against his will to give it recognition. He devoted the greater part of his speech to what he called the 'Irish argument', and the time so spent was divided between an elucidation of the fetters that are to be placed on one of the Irish nations to save the other from oppression, varying in tones of entreaty to expostulation to sink its own identity.[38]

It is hard not to accept, a century later, that Monypenny's analysis had raised questions that Churchill had not fully answered. The experience of 'actually existing' devolution in Scotland in a far more benign historic context has encouraged greater scepticism about the reconciling potential inherent in devolution as such.

Churchill's attempt to address religious fears was less than successful. The Vatican had recently published the *Ne Temere* decree, requiring that the non-Catholic partners in a mixed marriage pledge to allow all the children to be raised as Catholics. Churchill had played down these issues, but the significant Presbyterian convention, a week before Churchill's Belfast speech, reiterated strong religious feeling.

> Our Scottish forefathers, in their struggles for religious freedom and civil rights, cast their burden on the Lord Omnipotent, who gave their signal victory. Facing, as we now do, dangers similar to theirs, we shall follow in their footsteps and emulate their faith. In the profound belief that God requires, we commit our cause in all confidence to him.[39]

Even the most liberal Irish Presbyterians felt that Irish Catholics pushed the *Ne Temere* decree to the limit.

But it is perhaps more important to note the lack of enthusiasm in the nationalist response. The Central Board of Sinn Fein in Dublin seized the opportunity to carp. The board's chairman Sean MacGiobuin declared that 'a home rule measure which left England's hands in our pockets would be as worthless as the Irish Councils Bill, and more dangerous'.[40] However, even the mainstream Irish Parliamentary Party was unenthusiastic. The *Roscommon Herald*, owned and edited by the local MP, Jasper Tully, proclaimed: 'A calm perusal of Mr Churchill's speech brings a grand disillusionment.'[41] Patrick O'Growney insisted that Churchill had been well received by the 'Liberals' in Belfast but not by the nationalists. Redmond had to welcome him, but he led a party that was less than enthusiastic about the themes of Churchill's speech.[42] On 10 February 1912 Patrick White, MP at Rathkenny, a small village 10 miles from Navan, declared:

> Mr Churchill said that Ireland was a nation. Irishmen had always maintained that Ireland was a nation. How did this speech treat it as an independent nation? He thought that Mr Churchill was somewhat inconsistent, for subsequently [Churchill] said that the Imperial Parliament could repeal or enact any law. Was there any free parliament in the world that would allow an outside parliament to repeal its laws?[43]

The South Louth executive of the Irish Parliamentary Party was held in the Drogheda Mayoralty House. The secretary of the town Tenant Branch referred to Churchill's speech in critical terms:

> unless Ireland got hold of the excise and customs the financial arrangements of the home rule measure would not be satisfactory. Mr N. T. Murphy said the only home rule measure that would satisfy Irishmen would be to give free power to deal with everything concerning Ireland [applause]. He told the local MP, Joseph Nolan, that, if he voted for any other kind of a home rule measure, [he], Mr Murphy, would be one of the men who would be against him.[44]

In the normally conformist world of home rule politics, this was rebellious talk.

4

The 'Plot against Ulster'

Churchill's long and unusually careful speech had done little to lighten the mood. When Asquith introduced the home rule bill on 11 April 1912, the House was less than engaged. No one was 'at all excited nor interested in home rule', noted John Burns, one of sixty-seven survivors of the 1893 debates in the Commons: 'a jaded House, overworked ministry, stale subjects, indifferent public'. In Dublin the reaction was quiet. *The Times* editorial asked—save for John Redmond's fine effort—what had happened to the rhetorical skill of British and Irish politicians?[1]

Within a few months Churchill returned to Ireland on admiralty business, as First Lord. Churchill kissed the Blarney Stone on the fourth of July 1912. It was actually only a small incident on a visit of inspection at Queenstown Harbour. 'Local political feeling was kept discreetly in the background for all parties were anxious to secure a larger share of admiralty patronage for the naval works at Haulbowline.'[2] Churchill does, however, seem to have retained a strong sense of the strategic importance of Irish naval facilities.

In August Churchill continued his attack on the double standards of the unionist opposition. In an open letter to Sir George Ritchie, his local Liberal Party chairman, on 12 August 1912, Churchill denounced Bonar Law for inciting Ulster to revolt. Clearly still smarting from the effects of the Belfast visit, Churchill accused Bonar Law of giving encouragement to 'every street bully'. He pointed out: 'There are very many millions of very poor people in England who have little to lose except their lives, to whom these doctrines of violence and mutiny might not be unattractive.'[3] The *Standard* said the speech was one of the most bitter given by any English politician about another; the *Telegraph* saw it as Churchill's attempt to reassure fellow Liberals of his loyalty to the home rule cause, while the pro-government *Chronicle* found it a 'piece of measured eloquence'. What had happened to the Tory party, so often the party of law and order?

Carson replied that the Gladstonian Liberal Party had supported agrarian law-breakers in the late 1880s: 'I was myself present on many occasions when Liberal members of parliament thronged the court-house of Ireland with a view to encouraging those who were being presented and intimidating the magistrates!' The *Irish Times* added: 'Mr Churchill fails to point to any precedent in any civilised country for the betrayal of such a people—to this [is] added the fact that they are being asked to acquiesce in a constitution which has never been submitted to the people.'[4]

Once again Churchill's relations with his cousin, Londonderry, became strained. Londonderry felt that Churchill had in his Tory days been happy to denounce Liberal sympathy for home rule. At a Tory gathering at Wynard Park, Lord Londonderry concluded his reply to Churchill:

> What should they say of the office-holder who left the Unionist party when troubled days came near and joined a party for the purpose of accepting office from it, which he had but a short time ago likened to a 'toad in a block of coal hiding from public view a filthy object to be hewn limb from limb by the Tories when it stood forth in its hideousness'.[5]

Then, in the autumn, Churchill turned back to one of his old themes—federalism—in a speech at Dundee.[6] 'If it is desired to set up a workable federal system we shall have to face the task of dividing England into several great self-governing areas'—the so-called 'heptarchy'. Arthur Balfour noted sarcastically that Churchill had learnt in Belfast that home rule was impossible—his federalism proposal was designed to make it redundant.[7] Relations with the Ulsterman did not, however, improve. In November 1912 Churchill taunted the Unionists in parliament by waving his handkerchief at them, provoking Antrim Unionist Ronald McNeill MP (a fellow Harrovian) to hurl a small bound copy of the Standing Orders at Churchill's neck. He did not miss.[8]

Despite this unpleasant incident, Churchill did not become more anti-unionist. Indeed, as 1913 progressed, Churchill became more and more identified with the idea of concession to the Ulster Unionists. All the time, though, he was sure that the state would continue to operate effectively: 'Still less have I any doubt about the power of the state, as a state, apart from Liberal and Conservative politics, to maintain the law and put down disorder by whomever it is threatened.'[9] Churchill had received accurate warnings in 1913 of the army mood on the Ulster question—but he appears not to have taken it too seriously.[10] He did not anticipate any refusal by the army to carry out government policy; this, in part, explains his willingness to 'placate' Ulster. He did not doubt that, once the government had taken reasonable steps, the army would give its full support to any necessary action. In other words, Churchill proceeded on the basis of a lack of grasp of the underlying realities. He proclaimed: 'I do not agree with those who would not parley with men who threaten violence and illegality...the claim of north-east Ulster for special consideration for herself is very different from the claim to bar and defy home rule, and block the path of the whole of the rest of Ireland.'[11]

Following a Dundee speech to his constituents, the Unionist *Irish Times* declared on 9 October 1913: 'Mr Churchill's offer is plain enough. He proposes the exclusion of north-east Ulster from the Irish Parliament in the hope that she would grow weary of her isolation.' The Unionists in outer Ulster fretted: they detected a Churchillian scheme to split them from the four north-eastern counties,[12] but the nationalists fretted more. A few days later the journalist Lovat Fraser observed Redmond on the eve of a Limerick speech: 'I watched Redmond very closely at dinner and at breakfast this morning, as well as at the meeting, and if he is not damned anxious about the situation, I am no judge of men. His speech read like a poem of triumph, but there was no triumphant note in his voice and demeanour, only intense anxiety.'[13] Redmond at Limerick dismissed Churchill's suggestion as totally impracticable and unworkable. Redmond's reply to Churchill's speech at Dundee took a classic form:

> Irish nationalists can never be assenting parties to the mutilation of the Irish nation...united Ireland is and united Ireland must remain. [Loud cheers]...We would be degenerate Irishmen if we became assenting parties which would say that in the future there should be two nations among Irishmen and a dividing line between catholics and protestants. [Cries of 'Never' and cheers]...The two-nation theory is to us an abomination and a blasphemy. Ulster is as much a part of Ireland as Munster. [Great cheers][14]

Churchill's speech a week later in Manchester, however, seemed to dilute slightly the message of the Dundee speech.[15] At Manchester Churchill had simply said: 'We shall, I think, progress much better towards a settlement if we Liberals cultivate a habit of thinking about the genuine needs and legitimate apprehension of Ulster protestants, and if Conservatives all over the country turn their minds increasingly to the problem of satisfying the rights and claims of the overwhelming mass of nationalist Ireland.'

Nationalists were understandably alarmed. Tim Healy wrote to his brother, Maurice, that 'the line taken by Churchill...is that there must be a general election before the Home Rule Bill can come into operation, and that the Tories can repeal it'.[16] 'Churchill goes about saying he will leave the cabinet if there is any attempt to coerce Ulster. The Tories know this. So Carson has only to "keep it up".'[17] The unionists, meantime, seemed to grow in confidence.

> James Campbell says Ulster would form a 'provisional government' the day the Home Rule Bill became law, and that the Belfast protestants would never allow themselves to be ruled from Dublin. I asked if he thought that the British would allow them to seize the Custom House in Belfast, and he said their men would take it and get shot down and

the moment protestant blood was shed, Asquith's life would not be worth much.[18]

Both sides seemed to be rushing towards conflict. They were both convinced that the first deadly blow that they received would end the argument in their favour. But how best to arrange that moment?

On all sides this was the great obsession. As the unionists marched and mobilized in the Ulster Volunteer Force, what would the government do? When would the clash come? Both sides believed that the first to strike a heavy blow would lose the political battle. On 22 February 1914 Sir Arthur Paget, Commander-in-Chief of the Armed Forces in Ireland, addressed the Corinthian Club in the Gresham Hotel in Dublin. It is a speech full of foreboding. He told his elite audience in Dublin that he was aware that his grandfather had been recalled as Lord Lieutenant from Dublin because his pro-Catholic emancipation views were too liberal. As for himself, over many years, 'I have got rather fond of the Irish'. He said that they were in 'rather troubling times'. 'I have been assured over and over again that there is no intention on the part of the government to make use of the troops in this country, except for one purpose—a very proper purpose—to maintain law and order (hear, hear).'[19] His subsequent words were perfectly clear in their meaning. Speaking of the soldiers under his command, he declared:

> What they are going to do or what part they play I do not know, but certainly it is not thinkable, it is not possible for me to contemplate even being asked to concentrate my men to move against the forces that are, I believe, being formed in the north of Ireland [applause]. But at the same time you must remember that in our lives we soldiers have to do things that we do not like...
>
> When you have to deal with large bodies of men who understand the meaning of the word discipline, it means that, however distasteful it may be to them, they will carry out any orders given to them, they will carry out any orders given to them by their King [hear, hear]—and it may be— God forbid it should be—my lot to be ordered to move to the north. I should regret it. I have no doubt that many of the officers present here

tonight, many officers, friends of you all, would hate the idea of moving one mile north of Dublin, but if that order comes, that order must be obeyed.[20]

The least that might be said is that Paget was giving a public signal of the potential difficulty involved in using the army against Unionists. Within a month this idea would be put to the test.[21]

In March 1914 Asquith was drawn to make the proposal that he hoped would avert the danger of civil war and, of course, keep him in office. He made a significant concession to the Unionists. Unfortunately, it did not quite succeed. Asquith proposed an amendment to the home rule bill that would allow the electorate of each Ulster county, together with Belfast and Derry City, to vote on whether it wished to opt out of home rule for a period of six years and to be treated practically as an English county. At the end of six years, an excluded county was to come in automatically, unless the imperial parliament voted for its continued exclusion. The provision for inclusion after six years was intended to please nationalist opinion, whereas the unionists were supposed to focus on the possibility of a reprieve provided by a likely Tory victory in the intervening elections. In Belfast, the Presbyterian weekly, the *Witness* summed up unionist dissatisfaction: 'We are sure unionists would make any sacrifice for peace but to sacrifice the peace and safety of the future for a period of suspense, which would not be peace, is what no Ulster unionist would do.'[22]

In particular, the unionists disliked the idea that Derry City could be inside the Irish parliament but the county of Londonderry outside it. Above all, they disliked the idea of living under a 'sentence of death', as Carson was to put it. Senior Redmondite figures felt also that an opportunity had been lost. The party had dropped opposition to any talk of partition—and thus created much anger in nationalist Ireland—without gaining a new position of strength in dealing with the Unionists in parliament and thus bringing about a historic compromise.[23] On 16 March Carson dismissed the offer:

In offering exclusion and at the same time retaining a condition which he now knows renders the offer impossible of acceptance, Mr Asquith is, in the opinion of Ulster protestants, making no genuine effort to achieve a settlement, but is only trifling with a serious and dangerous situation, in the hope of gaining useful platform material to be used by Mr Churchill and others for party advantage.[24]

Winston Churchill was furious. He had pushed Asquith to the point of a decent offer to the Ulstermen—now it was being thrown back in his face. Churchill felt he owed Asquith some loyalty. According to the C. P. Scott diaries:

Ireland. Asquith decided to make statement on terms offered to Ulster immediately upon meeting of parliament. These go so far that impossible for opposition to abet rebellion in face of them. Cabinet united in determination to meet force by force. Churchill had now finally agreed to stand with the rest of the cabinet on this...[25]

More than anyone else in the Cabinet, Churchill had publically identified himself with the idea that a significant concession should be made to the Ulster Unionists; now, the concession having been delivered, it was expected of him that he would call the Ulster Unionists to order.

In a speech at Bradford on 14 March, urged on by Lloyd George, Churchill appeared to explode: the opposition to home rule had broken all the rules of civilised politics.

I am sure and certain that the first British soldier or coastguard, blue jacket or Royal Irish Constabulary man who is attacked and killed by an Orangeman will raise an uproar on this country...of a kind they [the Conservatives] little appreciate, or understand, and will shake to the very foundations the basis and structure of society.

He added: 'Let us go forward together and put these grave matters to the test.'[26] Clementine Churchill foolishly boasted at dinner to unionist supporters that 'Winston is going to land 25,000 troops in Ulster'.[27]

Lloyd George explained:

I got him to do it. I said to him this is your opportunity. Providence has arranged it for you. You can make a speech which will ring down the corridors of history. I could not do it. The PM could not do it: you are the only member of the cabinet who can make such a speech. You are known to have been in favour of conciliation for Ulster. Now you can say that having found a compromise the Ulstermen will either have to accept it or to take the consequences.[28]

The reaction in the press was harsh—one powerful press magnate refused even to discuss Ulster with Churchill.[29] One distinguished editor, J. L. Garvin, at this point an admirer of Carson, noted in the *Observer*: 'Every wise man realised instantly that an evil event had happened. Mr Churchill had reduced himself in a moment from one of the highest positions among statesmen who have a national and not merely a partisan influence—a position recently and laboriously gained—to an inferior level among demagogues.'[30] On the same day, General Sir Arthur Paget was instructed by the War Office to take the necessary steps for securing four vital points and arm depots in Ulster—Carrickfergus, Armagh, Omagh, and Enniskillen. But what evidence was there for thinking that the Ulster Volunteer Force intended to seize arms from the British army? The Unionist leadership, in fact, had put in place a plan to import them. Still less, given the tactical awareness on all sides about *not* striking the first blow, why would the UVF attack soldiers? The soldiers who reached Omagh and Enniskillen, in that part of the operation that went ahead, were greeted by cheering crowds of loyalists.

In Belfast, the *Witness* responded:

Mr Churchill's bellicose language in Bradford on Saturday afternoon indicated a serious and sudden drop in the political barometer of peace . . . It is not long since the meteoric genius was a flamboyant unionist; now he is a rampant home ruler with the noisy zeal of a turncoat.

But yesterday he was the advocate in Dublin of local parliaments, including one for Ulster; today he is all for mobilising the force of the

Crown to shoot Ulster unionists if they do not at once proclaim his latest plan for the parcelling out of Ireland.[31]

On 17 March Churchill informed a Cabinet committee that he would dispatch the Royal Navy's Third Battle Squadron to Lamlash, within striking distance of Belfast, to overawe the Ulstermen and secure arms depots. Field guns were taken on board the ships of Battle Squadron I.[32] On 19 March the Ulster Volunteer Force moved its weaponry to a place of safety, and, it was reported, the Dorset Regiment refused to move against the residence of one of the Unionist leaders.[33] According to H. A. Gwynne, on 20 March Churchill told the Chief of the Imperial General Staff, Sir John French: 'If Belfast should fight he would leave the town in ruins in twenty-four hours.'[34] On that day, a squadron of destroyers was dispatched to Lamlash. It was later reported that warrants for the arrest of some of the Belfast leaders were actually drafted by Churchill, with the knowledge of Asquith.[35]

On the same day, senior British officers at the Curragh camp in Kildare engaged in a remarkable act of insubordination. Technically, no orders were disobeyed, but the effect was the same. 'Are you ready to lead your men against Ulster? If you are not, send in your resignation within two hours,' said General Paget. No orders were actually disobeyed, because Paget gave offers of resignation as an alternative to moving north. The great majority took up the offer, but, within days, the War Office capitulated and the resignations were dropped. It was said that a large number of high officials in the War Office threatened to resign if anything was done to the officers, and there would have been a number of resignations in the command at Aldershot.[36] Churchill, when he realised the unreliability of the army, still hoped, for a moment, to use the navy. There is no doubt that Churchill was full of militancy at this moment. He seems to have convinced himself that the loyalist grass roots were in a more explosive condition than they actually were: perhaps also he underestimated the top-down discipline of the UVF.

When he first heard of the so-called 'Curragh mutiny', Churchill was defiant and 'talked very big about bringing the officers over in a battleship to be tried by court martial'.[37] To his frustration Churchill was told on the night of 20 March that no ship could be found.[38] But at the Curragh camp Colonel Ian Hogg, 4th Hussars, exclaimed: 'I can not resign, I am a poor man.'[39] Hogg may have been overstating the case—he was the Etonian son of the Hon. Quintin Hogg—but it is a fact that resignation meant, after all, loss not just of salary but of pension rights. Hogg decided to act. After dinner on Saturday, as an old friend and 'brother officer' at the Curragh, Colonel Hogg sent Churchill a telegram. Paul O'Brien, in the most recent book on the Curragh incident, has written: 'Churchill did not reply. He may not have received the wire as he was busy planning for the deployment of his naval force.'[40] In fact, Churchill definitely received Hogg's telegram and entered immediately into a dialogue with him. It was a dialogue that was to be of the utmost importance for his subsequent presentation of the 'Curragh mutiny'.

The Hogg telegram combined with other developments. On Saturday, 21 March, *The Times* broke the Curragh story in its later editions. The King, who had been kept in the dark, gave Colonel Seely in the War Office what is known in the army as an interview 'without coffee'. Asquith told Churchill to delay the movement 'of ships'.[41] Like Churchill, Sir John Seeley was first elected as a Tory MP in 1900 but switched to the Liberals in 1904. Ronan Fanning has shrewdly observed: 'Seely's and Churchill's swashbuckling temperaments, compounded by an engrained militarism, and, perhaps, an insecurity about their common past as Tory renegades, encouraged them to behave more belligerently towards the Ulster Unionists than cabinet colleagues with less suspect liberal credentials.'[42]

At this point, a word of explanation as to the significance of Colonel Hogg for Winston Churchill is required. What does the phrase 'brother officer' mean exactly? The lieutenant in the 4th Queen's Own Hussars in 1896 next junior to Churchill was Ian G. Hogg. Hogg received his commission on 15 January 1896 and joined the regiment in February. Hogg enjoyed an active and successful career. He was seconded for service in the Niger Coast Protectorate in late 1899 and served with the West African force until May 1905. During this time, Hogg received the Distinguished Service Order. He was promoted to captain in 1900 and major in 1904. Hogg was promoted to lieutenant colonel on 15 May 1913. In the summer of 1914 Hogg was in command of the 4th Hussars, 'having risen to the top after 17 years of duty'.[43] In fact, he was believed by right-wingers to have been promoted over others because he was more acceptable to the Liberal government.[44] Hogg was an old friend and an exemplary professional soldier—inevitably he commanded Churchill's respect and attention.

Churchill received Colonel Hogg's telegram on Sunday morning.[45]

> Today all officers Cavalry Brigade required to decide whether prepared to accept liability of active operations in Ulster on pain of dismissal. Enormous majority prepared to accept dismissal, but later adopted proposal that authority should be asked defining employment. Brigadier and great majority ready to undertake duties preserving order and property, provided no initiative or offensive action against Ulster contemplated. Convinced, if tactfully handled, Brigade can be saved. If unconditional service demanded Brigadier and practically all officers will accept dismissal. Appeal to you to ensure sensible handling.[46]

By now Churchill realized that the revolt in the army had 'important ramifications'.[47] Major General Henry Wilson observed that 'Winston tumbled to the situation, i.e. the army refusing to act, quicker than Seely, who up to 8 pm, was telling me he would court martial officers etc.'[48] On Monday, 23rd, Churchill had lunch with Hogg at the Admiralty in London.[49] Hogg wrote his account of this lunch on 25 March:

> He [Churchill] told me that my telegram was the first intimation that the government had received of any alternatives being put before us, that from the telegraphic report of the incident from Sir A Paget it had appeared to the government to be a concerted refusal to obey any orders which might be given to us to proceed to Ulster engineered by our brigadier. He admitted that my statement put an entirely new complexion on the incident and that his assistance would be at our disposal. He also

gave me his personal assurance that no coercive measures had been contemplated unless Ulster assumed the initiative.[50]

Hogg had played a decisive role. Everything was now to be smoothed over—as much as it could be.

The leading 'mutineer', Brigadier General Hubert Gough was well aware of Hogg's role:

> Hogg is in close correspondence with Winston. Hogg sent secretly to the correspondent of the *Irish Times* from Dublin the other day, and was closeted with him for an hour. The gist of it all was to get it published that the whole affair was a stupid misunderstanding. I suppose Winston was the instigator here. This was discovered by the accident of the correspondent (or editor) concerned travelling back to Dublin in the same carriage as C. R. MacEwen [Commander of the 10th Lancers], and as they were great friends, the *Irish Times* then asked M what sort of fellow Hogg was and told him what had occurred.[51]

He added: 'Of course, you know that Hogg is not trustworthy, but he is not dangerous as he has neither courage nor nerve.'[52]

Churchill's understanding with Hogg was, however, decisive. It allowed him to escape the consequences of his miscalculated obeisance to party unity. This 'misunderstanding' thesis served his interests supremely. With one bound, he was free. Of course the Asquith circle was less than impressed. Fourteen months later, Margot Asquith recalled: 'When he talked loud over the Curragh affair, pre-Curragh, and talked too loud about what he—Winston—would do in the event of such and such, that it almost amounted to a plot.'[53] This is the point. Churchill had himself ratcheted up the tension in ways that contributed to Sir Arthur Paget's nervousness. He had ignored the likely difficulties within the army. Colonel Hogg's telegram and later conversation alerted him to the danger. The 'misunderstanding' thesis was born and fed not just to the Cabinet and parliament but also to the press.

Churchill was able to settle himself in with a new narrative. Paget had been given modest orders but overinterpreted them.[54] Some Cabinet members accepted this version.[55] Not everyone followed this line—Liberal MPs as well as the *Spectator* blamed Churchill.[56] Yet, Churchill's explanations became ever more confident:

> We had received police reports from many parts of the disturbed districts, and we had also received military opinions and military advice as to the insecurity of those depots. What was the position? Carrickfergus Castle, with 88 tons of ammunition, held by 15 or 20 men only; a weak battalion in the Victorian barracks of Belfast of 500 or 600 men, with about 30 tons of ammunition in the possession...at Omagh, a small garrison of 80 or 100 men...and then again we had about 30 tons of ammunition. At Armagh the position was practically the same.[57]

The Irish nationalist press looked on with great interest. The *Irish Independent* paraphrased Churchill's argument. The *Independent* London editor was anxious to make sure that his readers were well informed on this most sensitive matter. Mr Churchill reviewed at great length the precautionary military movement that the government claimed it advisable to take. It felt it necessary, he said, to send troops to Ulster to protect the military stores, and in justification he quoted the letter, written by Sir Edward Carson after his rejection of the premier's proposal, saying the Volunteers intended 'to make good in action as they had been saying'. Mr Churchill regarded that letter as a cruel and barbarous blow 'at the prospect of a peaceful settlement—Sir Arthur Paget appears to have shared his sentiment. Paget was told only that indulgence might be given to officers domiciled in Ulster, but he was not told to give the alternative of resignation.'[58] The key point here is Paget's belief in serious unionist violence against the army. Churchill argued that it was understandable that Paget believed this might well happen. But, nonetheless, no one in the government believed him or had promoted the idea.

As Churchill was to put it:

> Paget had to have in mind the possibility of an 'organised warlike movement' by the Ulster Volunteers...
>
> I am bound to say that this was not a consideration which had entered my mind or into the minds of my colleagues in the government. But it

was present to Sir Arthur Paget's mind, and the Right Hon. gentleman has shown that it was a real contingency against which provision had to be made by the military commander.[59]

On 1 April 1914 Leo Amery challenged him in the House: 'Will the Right Hon. gentleman state whether he expected and hoped that purely precautionary measures to protect stores in Ulster would lead to fighting and bloodshed [opposition cheers]?' Churchill replied: 'As the question has been asked, perhaps, with the permission of the House, I may repudiate that "hellish insinuation".'[60] Perhaps so—but Churchill conveniently forgot the tone of his own Bradford rhetoric. Modest 'precautionary' measures do not put 'grave matters to the test', to use the Bradford language; nor did it require an initial decision to send north the highest calibre of siege artillery possessed by the army in Ireland.[61] The unfortunate Paget can hardly have been blamed for his interpretation of the context. Poor Paget was blamed both for exaggerating the case—telling his men that they would probably be at war in Ulster—and then for offering them a way out. Churchill, however, in his defence of the 'misunderstanding' thesis, contributed a narrative that, while technically credible, ignores the mood of the moment: a mood he had himself created.

Revealingly, on 20 April, Churchill—unusually for him—displayed visible signs of perturbation in the House. Sir Clemens Kinloch Cooke, a West Country unionist, asked a question about a letter to Churchill from a colonel of the Hussars. On hearing this, Churchill 'started violently, turned white to the lips, and hastily interposed with the protest that this document was private. It took him something like a quarter of an hour to recover his equanimity.'[62] The next day, a rather more composed Churchill returned to this issue, as the *Manchester Guardian* reported:

Mr Churchill said he desired to make a brief personal statement. The previous day at Question Time, the Honourable Member for Devonport asked him a question as to what communication had passed between himself and Colonel Hogg of the 4th Hussars. (Sir C Kinloch Cooke:

If any.) It was very unusual in that House for questions to be asked about the private correspondence of ministers or members, and he was sure that any member would say that such a procedure would be greatly to be deprecated from every point of view. However, he had obtained permission to reply, though the Honourable Member must not assume that he did not resent the gross personal intrusion in his private affairs [ministerial cheers] and he was now in a position to read the communication. Before he could do so he had to communicate with Colonel Hogg, and Colonel Hogg had sent a personal telegram. He telegraphed that morning in answer to his (the Right Honourable gentleman's) inquiry whether he might publish the telegram or not, and he replied that he had no objection to the telegram being published, provided that it was stated that it was sent with the knowledge of his general, General Gough, and that his general agreed to its being sent.

[An opposition member: It is not private. It is official.]

Mr Churchill said he wished to show that Colonel Hogg had acted fair and square by his commanding officer. It was a private and personal telegram, which reached him on Sunday morning. Of course Colonel Hogg was an old brother officer of his. Mr Churchill then read the telegram:

Personal. Today all officers in the Cavalry Brigade required to decide whether prepared to accept liability active operations in Ulster on pain of dismissal. Enormous majority ready to accept dismissal, but later adopted proposal that authorities should be asked to define employment. Brigadier and great majority ready to undertake duties to preserve order and property, provided no initiative of offensive action against Ulster contemplated. Convinced if tactfully handled brigade can be saved, but if unconditional service demanded from outset Brigadier and practically all officers will accept dismissal. Appeal to you to ensure sensible handling—Hogg.

To that telegram Mr Churchill said, he, of course, sent no reply. Now he had stated the entire correspondence that had passed, and it rested with the Honourable Member how and from what source he obtained information of this purely personal and private telegram. [Ministerial cheers]

This begs an obvious question—if Churchill had sent no message to Hogg, how come Hogg turned up for lunch with Churchill in London the following day? There were other issues. Everyone knew that Churchill had in a sense 'forced' the Curragh crisis. Everyone knew that it was a disaster. Yet, while Colonel Seely at his War Office had

had to resign and Paget's reputation as a commander had been damaged, Churchill had escaped scot free. 'Churchill was the dominating spirit in raising the Napoleonic scheme for ending the resistance of Ulster to the Home Rule Bill.'[63] Perhaps so, but he lived to tell the (carefully rewritten) tale. The simple truth was that Churchill was more important to Asquith. Churchill had to play the key role in dousing the fire he had himself sparked.

After the Ulster Unionist venture into illegality, the Larne gun-running *coup* of late April, became known, Churchill had more room for manœuvre. At the end of April he made a new approach to Ulster, which dismayed the Irish Party. Churchill had responded to the unionist vote of censure on 28 April 1914 with an elegant sarcasm: 'uncannily like a vote of censure by the criminal classes on the police'. But, as so often, he could not resist the urge to make—on his own initiative—a new offer to Carson. At first he appeared to castigate Carson. Carson, he said, had been running great risks for conflict, as was demonstrated by the Larne affair. 'Why will he not run some risk for peace? The key is in his hands now—why can not [Carson] say boldly, "Give me the amendments to this Home Rule Bill which I ask for, to safeguard the dignity and interests of protestant Ulster, and I in return will use all my influence and goodwill to make Ireland an integral unit in a federal system".'[64]

Carson responded the next day with a carefully calculated generosity of tone of his own. He offered, in the event of the home rule passing—'much as I detest it'—his earnest hope and prayer that the government of the South and West might prove such a success in future that 'it might even be for the interest of Ulster itself to move towards that government, and come in under it and form one unit in relation to Ireland'.[65]

The *Westminster Gazette* noted: 'We are heartily glad that Mr Churchill concluded his vigorous speech on a note of peace.'[66] The lobby correspondent of the *Daily Express* insisted 'that the whole position has been transformed by Mr Churchill's speech'. The correspondent added:

> Opening with defiance and bluster, it ended with an appeal for a federal settlement. The surprising character of his provocation had clearly been considered by the cabinet. It certainly means that the immediate coercion of Ulster, which Mr Asquith suggested yesterday as inevitable, is abandoned but it means much more. It means that the offer of temporary exclusion of Ulster is to be amended and enlarged.[67]

The *Pall Mall Gazette* agreed:

> If there is any real meaning in Mr Churchill's final hint that the government will apply the principle of exclusion pending federalism to protestant Ulster on condition that Sir Edward Carson will use his influence to make Ireland one country again when devolution is extended on fairly equal terms to the whole United Kingdom; this seems, at last, a recognition of the dominant fact that without the voluntary co-operation of protestant Ulster and its leader, the Irish problem can not be solved, and home rule can only lead to disastrous calamities.[68]

The problem for Irish nationalism lay in the fact that the Ulster Unionist leadership was given an effective veto on Irish unity, in exchange only for a promise—vague indeed—to keep its mind open on the topic.

Redmond did not confine his dismay to the briefing in the lobby. He wrote that night to Asquith that he and his colleagues could not go one step beyond the concession already offered, and could not agree to any demand to enlarge the exclusion beyond the four counties, or that the exclusion should last until a federal scheme was completed, 'in other words, for a period that may be anything from five to 50 years from now'.[69] On 28 July, the nationalists replied to Larne with their own gun-running at Howth, which led to loss of life as British soldiers arrived on the scene in a way they had not done at Larne.

Even up to the last week of July 1914, Ulster and the Irish crisis still appeared in the headlines in competition with the impending world war. Churchill, however, who grasped the seriousness of the international scene, was getting bored by Ireland. In fact, on 24 July the Irish party leadership privately dropped its insistence on temporary exclusion of four counties.[70] In Churchill's assessment the Irish issue had narrowed down to 'parishes' and 'groups of parishes' in Fermanagh and Tyrone. 'Failing an Irish agreement, there ought to be a British decision,' Churchill wrote to Sir Edward Grey.

> Carson and Redmond, whatever their wishes, may be unable to agree about Tyrone, they may think it worth a war, and from their point of view it may be worth a war. But that is hardly the position of the forty million who dwell in Great Britain and their interests must, when all is said and done, be our chief and final care ... I want peace by splitting the outstanding differences with Irish acquiescence, but if necessary over the heads of both Irish parties.[71]

By the end of July, Churchill was at the militant heart of the government's preparation for war.[72] Carson may have been rather slower to see the transformation in the political situation. Carson later told Lionel Curtis that he was about to give the signal for the setting-up of a provisional government in Belfast when he received a note from Asquith saying that war with Germany was only 'a matter of hours'. He may have been dramatizing a little when he told this story in 1917, but there is no doubt that the onset of war transformed Irish political life.[73]

For all the tension in Ireland, the Irish elites were not so far from a compromise, with little now separating the mainstream leaderships. Churchill was, in essence, right about this. Anyway, the mainstream political leaderships both wished to support Britain in the conflict with Germany. Reconciliations were certainly quick following the outbreak of war. On 5 August, the day after war had been declared, Carson wrote to Churchill:

> I know too well what a strain you are going through and at such a moment a friendly line from an opponent may be a little help. Whatever bitterness has existed in the past, believe me, I desire to show to you my appreciation of the patriotic and courageous way you have acted in the present crisis.[74]

The sudden rapprochement of Carson and Churchill reveals much about the realities underlying the bitter rhetoric of the Ulster debate. Churchill wrote later: 'Was it astonishing that German agents reported, and German statesmen believed, that England was paralysed by faction and drifting into civil war, and need not be taken into account as a factor on the European situation? How could they discern or measure the deep unspoken understandings which lay far beneath the froth and foam and fury of the storm?'[75]

From the start of the home rule crisis, Churchill's position had been complex and, in a sense, conflicted. He had argued unsuccessfully in Cabinet for an Ulster exclusion from the bill. Asquith, anxious to hold on to office and reliant on nationalist votes, rejected the argument. Churchill then headed to Belfast to argue the classic Gladstonian case for a united home rule Ireland, even though, as Ronan Fanning has pointed out, he shared the anti-Catholic assumptions of the Ulster Protestants.[76] He sustained this Gladstonianism throughout the summer of 1912, and then in the autumn in a Dundee speech turned again to the need to placate and make special provision for Protestant Ulster. For a year and more, this 'partitionism' was believed to be his real position by home ruler and unionist alike. Then, in March 1914, Asquith had, in effect, responded to Churchill's advocacy of a major concession to 'Carsonism'. When Carson seemed to reject the offer with contempt, Churchill exploded with anger. He was, as Margot Asquith noted, at least close to attempting a coup against 'Ulster': certainly his language gave every suggestion that this was his position. When he found the army—to his surprise—unwilling to help, he then, with the help of his 'brother officer', put out the idea that the 'Curragh mutiny' was simply a misunderstanding. Many people, rather than face the truth and rather unpleasant facts, wanted to believe this, but Churchill (with Colonel Hogg's help) gave them every encouragement. Churchill returned to the more conciliatory line on Ulster with which, in effect, he triumphed on the eve of the war. Within weeks Colonel Hogg would be dead and the Curragh a mere embarrassing footnote in the history of the British army.

The sharp controversy of the 'Curragh mutiny' faded quickly. It became impossible to argue, as Armageddon descended in Europe, that fatal damage had been done to the discipline of the army. John Ward, later Captain Ward, the Stoke Labour MP who made the most brilliant speech in parliament denouncing the arrogance of the Curragh 'mutineers', later declared that, of course, Ulster could never be coerced. On 9 September 1914 the prime minister, Asquith, noted sadly the death at the front of Colonel Hogg, 'who behaved so well at the Curragh'.[77]

5

Ireland at the Front

Ireland will fight and Ireland will be right.

(Winston Churchill to his cousin Clare Sheridan in 1914)

On 3 August 1914, Sir Edward Grey's speech to the Commons persuaded the House to accept that Britain was compelled to participate in war with Germany. He declared, somewhat oddly, that the country would suffer 'terribly in this war whether we are in it or stand aside'. Nonetheless, Liberal and Labour MPs, who had refused to accept the argument that Germany was irredeemably militaristic, now accepted the case that an invasion of Belgium would signal a challenge to British prestige that could not be shirked. On the afternoon of 3 August, Carson and John Redmond had met Grey. Following that meeting, Grey felt able to reassure the House of Commons:

> One thing I would say, the one bright spot in the very dreadful situation is Ireland. The position in Ireland—and this I should like to be clearly understood abroad—is not a consideration among the things that we have to take into account now.

Carson saw tears trickling down the cheek of Winston Churchill as Grey spoke. Carson went up to him as they passed behind the Speaker's chair and silently shook hands.[1] The bitterness of the Bradford speech and the 'plot against Ulster' was buried in that decisive moment.

Ireland suddenly ceased to dominate the headlines as soon as the First World War broke. Indeed, Ireland was now referred to as the only bright spot in an international tragedy. A civil war had been averted, and both Irish leaderships—Redmond and Carson—committed their supporters to the aid and assistance of the British war effort. 'Ireland will fight and Ireland will be right,' Churchill told his cousin Clare Sheridan.[2] But the consequences of the home rule crisis—mounting escalation of tension in Ireland from early 1912 to the late summer of 1914—were not so easily swept aside. There were continued tensions between nationalist and unionist soldiers at the front, though the officers on the whole had better relations.

Nationalists were on the alert for British failures to recognize their sacrifices. The Unionists, on the other hand, were on the alert for a perceived British tendency to exaggerate nationalist sacrifices at the expense of their own. Politicians professedly loyal to Redmond were to win all five of the contested by-elections in Ireland between the outbreak of the war and the Easter Rising, but there was now clearly a more militant nationalism in play—a more militant nationalism that drew strength from the delay of the home rule project but also, at bottom, rejected the vision of home rule—economically dependent and strengthening the British Empire—that Churchill had outlined in his Belfast speech, with, it should be noted, Redmond's complete approval. Redmond refused any concession to the separatist, republican militants. Also now with Redmond's approval, tens of thousands of young Irishmen were joining the British army. The first Victoria Cross of the war went to Lieutenant Maurice Dease of Westmeath.

Of particular importance here was the 10th (Irish) Division, the first of Ireland's 'New Army' divisions to be employed in battle. It was less closely identified with nationalism or unionism than the two other 'New Army' divisions—the 16th (Irish) and the 36th (Ulster) respectively. Redmond 'proudly saw the Tenth Irish as Ireland's "first" national army in the field'.[3] For Sir Edward Carson it was 'full of old friends and well known to him, and in command, his cousin, friend of his youth, old school fellow at Portarlington, Lieutenant General Sir Brian Mahon'.[4] One of Carson's close political colleagues, Arthur Bruce O'Neill, the Antrim Unionist MP, was to be the first British MP to die at the front—casually executed as he lay wounded at the Battle of the Marne in October 1914.

As First Lord of the Admiralty, Winston Churchill was to play a decisive role in British war strategy and therefore in the fate of many of these recruits. Influenced by the Irish admiral Sackville Carden, though strongly opposed by the Irish general Henry Wilson, he became convinced that the only answer to end stalemate on the Western Front was a flanking assault in the Dardanelles. Gallipoli was a catastrophe from the beginning. There was to be no dramatic breakthrough, no transformation of the balance of forces. Rather there was to be a dramatic loss of life, much of it Irish.

The stress of the Gallipoli campaign induced a nervous and physical collapse in Admiral Carden. He was replaced as commander by another Irishman, Admiral Jack de Robeck, born in 1862 near Punchestown in County Kildare. Within days, de Robeck had decided that there would be no further naval attacks on the Dardanelles until ground troops had taken the high ground at Gallipoli and neutralized the Turkish guns. Infuriated by this change of strategy, Churchill demanded that the Admiralty War Group telegram de Robeck to renew the attack. The War Group refused, arguing that de Robeck, as the man *in situ*, was better placed than Churchill to understand the situation. 'One of the big "what ifs" of the Great War is what if de Robeck had renewed the attack as Churchill wanted, broken through the Turkish defences and advanced on Constantinople?'[5] The outcome in the end was a celebrated British military disaster—but also, significantly, an Irish disaster. Within a month of landing at Suvla Bay in August, nearly half of the 17,000-strong Irish Division were dead, wounded, sick, or missing. It had suffered terribly in the landing and subsequent fighting, and a fraction of its personnel escaped death or wounds by enemy fire or illness by diseases caused by the climate and the conditions.

The Irish Division at Gallipoli—the 10th—was composed of young volunteers, many Protestant and unionist but also a large number of Catholics and nationalists.[6] They were 'clerks from offices and counting houses, assistants from drapery and grocery shops, and servants, public school boys, artisans, labourers and farm hands—a heterogeneous collection of youths from all walks of life—and officered chiefly by barristers, solicitors, engineers and university students who had only been a few months in training'.[7] Dublin gossip insisted that their only training consisted in saluting one another in the Wicklow mountains. They were in a certain sense a 'citizens' army', very different from the professional soldiers Ireland had always provided to the British army. Lieutenant Michael J. Fitzgibbon, son of legendary agrarian radical MP John Fitzgibbon,[8] became the first of the eleven sons of Irish nationalist MPs to die in the war. The elite who led Ireland into war in 1914 may have been mistaken in their politics, but they were prepared to pay the price of their convictions.

Churchill was well aware of the role of the 10th Irish Division at Gallipoli. He recalled their resolve and their losses in his later writing—he must have been reminded of his account of the slaughter of the Inniskillings at Tugela.[9] He personally knew men who died— Major Cecil Grimshaw, for example, who had been imprisoned alongside him in the Boer War.[10] Nonetheless, his later account of Gallipoli is designed, above all, to protect his own reputation. Gallipoli may have cost him his position at the Admiralty, but Churchill was determined to present the expedition in the best possible light.[11] As a result, he did not face up to the significance of the event in Irish history: it was a key moment in popular disillusionment with the British war effort. It is not, therefore, surprising that Kevin Myers in his book *Ireland's Great War* describes Churchill as a 'ruthless narcissist'.[12] The scale of the sacrifice, combined with an apparently ungenerous War Office response to Irish sacrifice, annoyed both Redmondite nationalists and southern unionists alike. The idea later to be formalized in the republican song 'The Foggy Dew' that it might be better to 'die 'neath an Irish sky than at Suvla' began to form in the minds of young men. The loss of life at Gallipoli undoubtedly helped create the atmosphere in which Ireland's separatist and republican leaders felt morally justified in launching their insurrection in Dublin in 1916.

After the Gallipoli failure, Churchill left the Cabinet and attempted to redeem himself by serving at the front in France. He was well aware of the doubts about his lack of judgement that had surfaced again. On 15 November he made his dignified resignation statement in the House: Arthur Lynch, the West Clare MP, immediately told him he had 'scattered his enemies', but Churchill knew this was not quite so. Lynch was an ardent Francophile and supporter of the war; the little matter of his Boer War 'treason' earlier in the century was now quite forgotten by both.[13] Churchill arrived on 18 November 1915 at Boulogne and dined there with John Redmond, a very friendly occasion. Fortunately, in strictly Irish terms, for Churchill, his timing meant that he was not in office when Dublin erupted in April 1916. He received neither the blame for lack of preparation nor the criticism for the harsh treatment of the rebel leaders. In later years he took a wry pleasure in pointing out to Asquith and his followers that Asquith, that humane liberal, had been prime minister when the wounded James Connolly, the socialist nationalist leader, was tied to a chair and executed by the British state. Connolly, Churchill recalled in 1920, was taken from his hospital bed, even though his leg had been shattered by a bullet. As he could not walk, he was carried to execution. Churchill famously opined in this context that grass did not grow over a scaffold—but can we be sure he would have behaved differently if actually in power faced with a rebellion that proclaimed the 'gallant' Germans allies?

Churchill had tentatively returned to parliament in March 1916 to make a defence of his Gallipoli policy, which was at best only partially successful. He was on the lookout for allies seeking a more active prosecution of the war. He could not afford to be choosy. Interestingly, he asked his wife to ascertain Carson's view of his performance. Carson had resigned over the Cabinet failure to support Serbia and, therefore, was a possible friend. Churchill was seeking an important ally in the struggle against the 'procrastinator', Asquith. Carson gave an honest, unflattering report but also 'spoke with great admiration of your qualities'.[14] The truth is that Carson was well aware from his Dublin friends how appalling the Gallipoli experience had been for the Irish soldiers. He also knew that there had been five Ulster battalions—the 5th and 6th Royal Inniskilling Fusiliers, the 5th and 6th Royal Irish Fusiliers, and the 6th Royal Irish Rifles—in the 10th Irish division. But, despite this, and despite their conflicts in the pre-war era, Churchill and Carson became closer. On 24 April 1916 Ruby and Edward Carson dined with the Churchills in London. On the same day in Dublin, the Easter Rising took place. Irish insurrectionaries, led by James Connolly and Patrick Pearse, had seized buildings in central Dublin. They proclaimed an Irish Republic allied to imperial Germany. British forces crushed the revolt, but for the first time in over a century Irish revolutionaries were perceived to have put up a decent fight. Several of the leaders were soon executed, and the chief secretary, Augustine Birrell, announced his resignation. This resignation led to press speculation that Churchill was in line for the job.[15]

In mid-May Churchill formally returned as a regular member to parliament. On 15 May the *Manchester Guardian* noted: 'Winston Churchill, now distinctly redeemed for political service, settled down by Sir Edward Carson's side and began to take notes for an early intervention in the debate.' Carson was one of a group of senior politicians considered capable of displacing Asquith's perceived weak wartime leadership. The debate dealt with the exclusion of Ireland from the conscription bill. The Ulster Unionists—led by Sir John Lonsdale—made their case in a relatively moderate fashion. The Unionists genuinely believed that Ireland could produce ten more divisions of first-class troops, and this could be the difference between winning and losing the war.

Carson, just returned from a trip to see Dublin's post-Rising condition, however, was in a restrained mood. There is a reason. He knew that his own Irish conduct was under scrutiny. Liberal MPs, like R. L. Outhwaite, challenged him in this debate: was he not responsible for the Rising because he, after all, had first imported arms from Germany into Ireland? At the height of the home rule crisis, Carson had found it easy to dismiss liberal charges of lawlessness. Why? Because he well remembered liberal encouragement of Irish agrarian crime in the late 1880s, when he had begun his legal career as a prosecutor. But after Easter 1916 he found it less easy to defend the Larne gun-running—a move he had always been uneasy about and that he had certainly wished to postpone at the last. The idea that the unionists had given nationalist Ireland a bad example was dismissed by his Ulster Unionist colleague Ronald McNeill—were the men of 1916 not simply acting in response to their long-term separatist tradition? But Carson, a southern Irishman after all, who contemplated the fate of the southern Protestant minority, was uneasily aware of the limitations of this argument. Instead, in the aftermath of the Rising, Carson encouraged the idea that there could be a new understanding with Redmond that would move Ireland forward. Formally, in this debate, Carson supported conscription in Ireland, as did Churchill, but Redmond described the idea as 'insane', and Carson openly accepted that Redmond had a veto. In support of this new Irish accommodation, Churchill was judicious and statesmanlike: 'With the two Irish leaders working together, there was hardly any difficulty they could not overcome.'[16] Redmond was decidedly impressed by the 'speech'. It was a well-received piety, but Churchill's speech the next day on defence against naval attack and making the case for an air ministry had rather more political force.[17] In the aftermath of the Easter Rising, both Redmond and Carson were prepared to compromise.[18] The reality is, however, that, as far as Ireland was concerned, Churchill did not grasp how weak the Redmondites had become; perhaps Redmond himself did not. Churchill was later to blame Asquith for the failure to strike a Redmond–Carson deal in 1916, but it was an unfair criticism. The type of accommodation once possible between those two men was now impossible, as Irish grass-roots opinion polarized rapidly. But Churchill was right to take notice of Carson's willingness to break with the old allies in order to reach a deal with Redmondism: he was also right to note the seriousness of intent within constitutional nationalism.

Lady Londonderry was among those who noticed that Carson and Churchill were sitting side by side. Carson had the respect of perhaps 100 MPs. At this point, this gave him rather more influence than Churchill. For some years, his Londonderry relations, after all, felt Churchill's 'betrayal' on home rule matters more strongly than did Carson. 'And W Churchill sitting on the same bench? *Certainly not!*' Carson's wife, Ruby, replied: 'The bench doesn't belong to Sir Edward! *He* can't help Winston sitting on it!'[19] This answer, Ruby Carson well knew, while truthful was not the whole truth, as it did not acknowledge the full extent of the private rapprochement between Churchill and Carson. By the end of 1916, as Churchill had hoped all along, Lloyd George—with vital assistance from Carson—had forced Asquith's resignation. Not that every engagement at the Carsons was an absolute joy. It was not possible to suppress all talk of pre-war controversies. Clementine, thinking of her lost child (she has suffered a miscarriage the month after the Belfast visit), cannot have taken much joy from a November 1917 luncheon. The talk was less than relaxed.

> Ruby was very funny about W C[hurchill] who lunched with them the other day. His wife was there, too, and Lloyd [George] and W C had the tactlessness to start talking about his disastrous visit to Belfast and said that he had no idea there was any danger in his going there, never dreamt his life would be endangered, or, of course, he would never have taken his wife. Offended by this slightly implausible story, Ruby Carson argued that the 'Ulster people' had been very forbearing in not killing Churchill. Lloyd George agreed and said he had told the cabinet as much. Clementine Churchill was 'purple in the face'—rather understandably—while Churchill buried his face in the food.[20]

It says much about Churchill's need for allies after the Dardanelles fiasco that he put up with this kind of thing. No wonder Clementine's face went 'purple'; no wonder he buried his head in his food. But there was a reward. Some months after displacing Asquith, Lloyd George, as premier, brought Churchill back to the government as Minister of Munitions. However, again Churchill's impact on Ireland was less than positive.

In March 1918 Churchill supported the Chief of the Imperial General Staff, Sir Henry Wilson, in his desire to extend conscription to Ireland.[21] It was an ill-fated idea, which merely assisted the revolutionaries in Ireland. Churchill in the end accepted the point; but it is clear at the time he was still slow to see the growing power of Sinn Fein, the political movement now led by the surviving leaders of the Rising. The Irish Party appealed to its record of solid achievement on land and educational matters, but eaten bread is soon forgotten in popular politics. The Irish people had a focus on the immediate future. The threat of conscription assisted Sinn Fein in a way no other issue could have done; the way was clear for a Sinn Fein landslide in nationalist Ireland in the 1918 election. Churchill later said:

> The question of Irish conscription was handled in such a fashion in 1918 that we had the worst of both worlds, all the resentment against compulsion, and in the end no law and no men. The English demand for compulsory service in Ireland spread disaffection through the whole Irish people. 60,000 Irish soldiers were serving at the front, but 60,000 British troops were simultaneously guarding Ireland, and on balance our resources were not increased.[22]

These were wise words but they came very late in the day. In 1918 Churchill simply did not see how quickly the political culture of Ireland was changing. Nor did he understand his own role in that phenomenon. After the Easter Rising there was a brief moment of uncertainty in nationalist Ireland, before the revolutionaries established their authentic Catholic nationalist credentials. To make matters even more difficult for the British government, as the nationalist position hardened, so did that of the Ulster Unionists. The young nationalists of the parliamentary tradition who might have fought the new men were in the trenches in Europe or, in many cases, dead at Gallipoli.

In his speech at Dundee in December 1918 Churchill emphasized the impossibility of coercing Ulster in the matter of home rule for Ireland. He added:

Before the war we had reached a definite agreement with the leaders of the Nationalist party that Ulster was not to be coerced. It never was the policy of the late Liberal government to take coercive steps in Ireland. Why do not the Irish leaders come forward now and take up the burden of responsibility of government within the British empire? Why do they not by a spontaneous feeling of comradeship with Ulster?

The government is most anxious that the Irish question be pressed forward vigorously to a solution. Great Britain goes to the peace conference ready to bestow self-government upon Ireland. It is only the quarrels and disputes of the Irishmen themselves that prevent a solution to this great question.[23]

By this stage these words had an entirely wistful quality. The moderate nationalists felt their sacrifice had been spurned by Britain. The Ulster Unionists felt that in the 1916 Rising Catholic Ireland had shown its true colours. The executions of the 1916 leaders, combined with the threat of conscription, had created a new, more aggressive nationalist sentiment in Ireland. Support had moved from the Redmondite tradition towards the separatists in Sinn Fein. It was impossible for the constitutional nationalists and Ulster Unionists to strike a viable accommodation allowing for tangible progress on home rule. Meanwhile, Ireland was full of young men who, having passed up on their adventure of war abroad, were determined to have it at home.[24]

6

War in Ireland

Personally, I wished to see the Irish confronted on the one hand with the realisation of all they had asked for and of all that Gladstone had striven for, and upon the other with the most unlimited exercise of rough-handed force.[1]

On 21 January 1919 Dan Breen and IRA colleagues fired the opening shots of what is still called in Ireland the 'war of independence', killing two Catholic policemen in Soloheadbeg, County Tipperary. The IRA avoided conventional military clashes with the forces of the state. But their campaigning and violence did enough to break down the normal operation of the legal system in Ireland. Churchill's disdain for the IRA's mode of warfare was genuine. He saw it as claiming a right to kill local policemen at one's convenience. It ignored the fact that for the weaker side in such a conflict there was no alternative. It ignored also that a polarizing momentum fuelled the IRA, as it forced the ordinary Irish citizen to make a choice—always likely to be made for the 'lads' of one's own community. Devolution as a concept simply collapsed in most of Ireland. The level of British concession to Irish nationalism envisaged in the Government of Ireland Bill introduced in the House of Commons on 23 February soon appeared to be inadequate. The IRA's method of war, however, gave it one of the greatest advantages in warfare, the advantage of surprise. How was that to be countered? The forces of the British state—army and police alike—were soon involved in a 'dirty war' in which the methods employed were shocking to domestic UK public opinion. Churchill felt it necessary to support the men in the field: 'Nothing is more unpleasant to our soldiers than the repeated conflicts . . . it would be quite impossible to expect them to do their duty . . . if the authorities, when anything occurred . . . which was the subject of comment in the newspapers, were ready to go and look for some victim on whom to pounce and of whom to make an example.'[2] This is a brutal and honest statement. In 1922 Churchill looked back on this period:

> When officers of the Crown, military and police, were ambushed and murdered under circumstances of the grossest treachery, it was quite impossible to prevent the police and military taking reprisal on their account. It would exceed the limits of human nature. Everyone knows that armed men will not stand by and see one after another of their number shot down by treachery, without to some extent taking the law into their own hands. Although the government did their best to restrain them, it is perfectly true that we did not punish with the full severity persons who had been mixed up in this sort of affair. We have never concealed that nor could we punish them while there was no other redress open to them, while no court would convict, while no criminals were arrested. These were the satisfactions of self-preservation when they saw comrades weltering in blood from a foul blow.[3]

Churchill, at least, did not shirk an exact description of what was actually involved. He avoided stale abstractions, easy moralism, and hand-wringing. The language does not obscure a grim reality, but was it a grim reality British public opinion was willing to accept? These are the words of the man who, after the successful election of 1918, had been rewarded by Lloyd George with the War Office and the Air Ministry—a politician who had a wide range of distractions— especially in the Middle East—but who retained a significant interest in Ireland, even chairing a Cabinet committee after the summer of 1920. There is clearly an element of personal subjective engagement with Ireland here. Lloyd George watched cautiously Churchill's con- sistently aggressive tone in the face of the 'war of independence'. Was Churchill trying to displace him, as the premier's friends believed, by exploiting 'anarchy' in Ireland? The prime minister was determined not to be outflanked.

Both Lloyd George and Churchill remained in apparently uncompromising mood throughout May 1920. Churchill argued for the establishment of a special tribunal to try murders. 'It is monstrous that we have had some 200 murders and no one hanged.' Churchill was keen to see IRA men hanged. At one point he turned to Lloyd George and said: 'You agreed six or seven months ago that there should be hanging.' The answer from Lloyd George was: 'I feel certain you must hang.' Throughout the autumn, Lloyd George and Churchill regularly boasted in public that the Irish 'murder gangs' would be crushed.[4]

At a conference of ministers on 11 May 1920, Churchill undertook to submit to the cabinet a scheme for raising a special Emergency Gendarmerie, which would become a branch of the Royal Irish Constabulary. Maurice Walsh has sarcastically described Churchill as operating like a modern manager 'engaging in blue sky thinking at a company away day'.[5] At a Cabinet meeting on 31 May, Churchill seemed to have lost some of his enthusiasm for this idea, principally because he was not sure if he would get recruits. Lloyd George shared his scepticism on this point. Yet, remarkably, two months later, the government adopted Churchill's original proposal and began the recruitment of a 'special corps of gendarmerie, the auxiliary division'.[6] The 'Auxies' were to prove formidable adversaries to the IRA, by the simple expedient of borrowing the method of assassination with rather better weapons. Churchill insisted that they had been selected from 'a great press of applicants on account of their intelligence, their characters and their records in the war';[7] Irish public opinion has always insisted that they were men of bad character. The Black and Tans also, in Churchill's words, 'with increasing information were striking down in the darkness those who struck from the darkness'.[8]

Churchill also had ideas for the north. According to Sir Henry Wilson, former Chief of the Imperial General Staff:

Winston suggested arming 20,000 Orangemen to relieve the troops from the North. I told him this would mean 'taking sides', would mean civil war and savage reprisals, would mean, at the very least, great tension with America and open rupture with the Pope. Winston does not realise these things in the least and is a perfect idiot as a statesman.[9]

But the basis of the A, B, and C Special constabularies was being laid. Churchill was also an enthusiastic believer of the potential use of air power in the Irish conflict—but a truly effective utilization was, in this case, never applied.[10]

It is, however, very important to set these warlike 'repressive' utterances in context. As Sir John Anderson later explained in a 1928 letter to Churchill,[11] Lloyd George was even at this moment operating a peace policy. It was initiated by the clear-out in April–May 1920 of the old Dublin Castle administrative elite in Ireland under Sir John Taylor and its replacement by a new one led by Anderson, Mark Sturgis, and Andy Cope. They were accompanied by General Henry Tudor, an old friend of Churchill, who brought with him Ormonde Winter, a ferocious but effective partisan. Their job was to intensify the physical struggle against the IRA, while at the same time Cope, in particular, encouraged peace negotiations leading to a new settlement for the south and devolution within the United Kingdom for the north. As C. J. Phillips, a Foreign Office official, told the American journalist Carl Ackerman at this point: 'Within three years Ireland would be a republic in everything but name and in less time than that all the British troops would be out of Ireland.'[12] Anderson insisted that he and other officials were always clear as to the prime minister's intentions—in this sense, the key change in policy, the 'vital reorientation' in Anderson's phrase, came not in May 1921 but in April 1920. Anderson acknowledged in his letter to Churchill that, in some respects, it was a little odd that he, a senior official, should claim to know the prime minister's mind better than a fellow Cabinet member. But with all due deference—and all the caveats involved in the analysis of a complex process—he stuck to his interpretation. 'God's Butler', as Brendan Bracken called the greatest Whitehall mandarin of the era, did not really doubt himself.

In the midst of all this militaristic rhetoric, there is a decided logic to Churchill's actions. It is the clue to Lloyd George's support and the clue also to Sir Henry Wilson's unease. When, in April, the Irish viceroy, Lord French, asked for more troops to be sent to Ireland, Churchill sent one-third less than was sought.[13] For a classical old-school unionist like Sir Henry Wilson, the former Chief of the General Staff, Churchill's methods could never secure Ireland for the union. For Wilson or French, it was essential simply to commit regular army forces. But Lloyd George was not really attempting to do this, and nor was Churchill, who emphatically stated it would take 100,000 troops. Their object was to meet terror with counter-terror and thus enable a compromise with Sinn Fein to be negotiated while not radically reducing the British army presence elsewhere in the empire. Ireland might have been costing the British taxpayer £20 million annually, but Mesopotamia cost £56.5 million in 1920–1 alone: 7,000 empire soldiers (800 of them British) were killed in Mesopotamia, contemporaneously with the 'Irish Troubles', as Churchill was well aware. Ironically, Churchill was much more responsible for the heavy-handedness of the 'Black and Tans' in the south or the 'B Specials' in the north than Henry Wilson, who was a critic of both forces. It was, however, Henry Wilson who was blamed most and who was, indeed, to lose his life on this account.

As IRA violence continued, it appeared to many in London that Britain was countenancing a dirty war of 'reprisals' in Ireland as the only viable response. It appeared to be so, because it was so. On 20–1 September, Balbriggan was the first Irish town to suffer a major reprisal following the opportunist IRA killing of Head Constable Peter Burke, a popular officer. Two prisoners were executed and the town sacked by visibly drunk men. Henry Wilson wrote in his diary: 'Winston Churchill saw very little harm in this, but it horrifies me.'[14] Reflecting on the idea that the British were now behaving as badly in Ireland as the Germans in wartime Belgium, the *Manchester Guardian* talked of 'an Irish Louvain'[15]—and spoke of a rampage by drunken men firing rifles and burning houses at will. For some in England, a terrible war on the Continent had been fought with decent national honour, but now that honour was being destroyed in the villages and hamlets of Ireland.

Churchill, needless to say, did not run away from this debate. On 16 October 1920 Churchill spoke on the subject of 'Russia and Ireland' at the King's Theatre, Dundee: 'Ireland is a country which like Russia is deliberately tearing itself to pieces,' he proclaimed. He described the IRA campaign as this 'brutal business of popping up and down behind hedges and shooting poor policemen in the back'. Churchill said it was 'amazing' that Irishmen themselves 'can not react against them and mow them off'. He noted sadly: 'It is amazing that a nation so gifted should allow itself to be robbed of its birth right and of its dignity by these shameful and paltry methods.' He did not add that many of the Irishmen who might have been expected to do just that had died at Gallipoli. But it was the duty of the 'stronger island and nation' to help. The best chance of solving the Irish question had come. The former prime minister, H. H. Asquith, was now calling for the release of Terence MacSwiney, the IRA Commander and Mayor of Cork, who was on hunger strike. Churchill replied:

> If we do, the whole system of justice will have broken down. Already 115 policemen and 22 soldiers have been killed and not a single person brought to justice. I am told by those who have gone through it that the strain on a man's nerves far exceeds the bombardment of the trenches. Assassination will not be allowed to change the history of the British Empire.[16]

Churchill's figures were not exaggerated: indeed, by the end of 1920, 199 police officers had been killed by the IRA.[17] 'We can not give up— the alternative is civil war in Ireland and what is the American response likely to be?' Churchill was alarmed that the United States would become involved in ways detrimental to British prestige.

> Nor can we allow terrorists to bargain. One hundred policemen are murdered, so give dominion home rule. Another 50, concede control of

the army and navy, with conditions; shoot another 50 and we will give up these conditions; go on shooting and we will throw in the control of foreign relations [laughter and cheers].

Churchill's black humour became more and more uncontrolled as he played up to his audience.

Kill a thousand British policemen and soldiers, kill if you will a few more Cameron Highlanders, shoot more of the Black Watch for a change— cries of dissent, of booing—and then for the sake of a quiet life [laughter] we will give them sovereign independence. Indeed, we shall be very lucky if we get off without paying an indemnity.

This was a brilliant and accurate description of the effect of negotiating under duress during a terrorist campaign. In effect, it is at least a partial description of what actually happened.

Churchill was asked a question from the floor: 'Are we to understand that the women and children of Balbriggan were notorious Sinn Feiners?' This was a reference to the twenty-five houses in Balbriggan that had been burnt to the ground. He replied: 'So far as I know only about a dozen lives had been taken in the reprisals, but, of course, there had been destruction of property which has caused suffering to other people. It is very regrettable.' But he insisted, above all, on the need to stand firm:

Surrender, based on impotence, would mean an independent Irish republic. An effective measure of home rule could be given to Ireland before the end of this year, but there we must come to a full stop.

If, in a moment of weakness or feebleness, a republic was granted to Ireland, its arms would stretch across the water and grip the vitals of America.

A few years of an independent republic would mean open war and the British people would never rest until they had rid themselves of so fearful a danger. Could a republic be given to a miserable gang of cowardly assassins like the human leopards of West Africa, the speaker asked? Surrender of that kind would be followed by passionate repentance and fearful atonement.

What was the meaning of Churchill's reference to the human leopards of Africa? His source appears to have been *Human Leopards: An Account of the Trials of Human Leopards before the Special Commission Court: with a note on Sierra Leone, Past and Present by K. J. Beatty of the Middle Temple, Barrister-at-Law for some years resident in Sierra Leone* (London, 1915). The Leopard Society was a West African secret society active in the early twentieth century that practised cannibalism. It was centred in Sierra Leonne, Liberia, and Côte d'Ivoire. Members dressed in leopard skins, waylaying their human prey with sharp clawlike weapons in the form of leopard claws and teeth. The victims' flesh would be cut from their bodies and distributed to members of the secret society. The principal activists appear to have been men who were well past their prime: when they consumed the most coveted portions of their victims, they were, it was believed, hoping to increase their virility. It has been argued that they were largely an imperialist–colonialist fantasy nightmare. They did not, however, bear any resemblance to the IRA. It is a clear example of Churchill losing control of his rhetoric. But he continued to speak in an unrestrained fashion:

> In the south the Sinn Feiners would naturally lose no time in organising their own army. Indeed, it is practically in existence. They would buy arms from abroad, and from the United States men would come over in large numbers to join them. They would avail themselves, as they were ever ready to do during the late war, of any German assistance that might be forthcoming. In particular, they would no doubt get the services of many German officers who are now out of employment.
>
> Thousands of volunteers would go over from England and Scotland to help the North, and when they were organised and armies were marshalled on both sides, when you had allowed the furnaces of hell to be stoked up to full blast, a fierce and furious struggle would begin with the double bitterness of civil war and the triple bitterness of religious war.
>
> The arrival of reinforcement and supplies from the United States would arouse in acute form the partisanship of that great people and might not this process and tension and antagonism bring us to the verge of the greatest danger to all the civilisations of the world, namely, a deep quarrel between the United Kingdom and our kith and kin across the Atlantic?

I say quite frankly that I would far rather face two or three years of the sort of difficulties we are now going through in Ireland than open the floodgates to organised war on a great scale in the country and run the risk of such a war embroiling us with powerful elements in the United States.

Once one starts on the road of flight and panic, no one knows where he will stop. There is no limit to the shame and disaster which must be drained from the dregs. Are we now, fresh from victory in the great war, fresh from the sacrifices of the greatest of all wars that men ever fought, having struck down the most terrible antagonists that ever marched forth in strife in the whole history of mankind—are we now to collapse miserably and impotently before the meanest, basest, cruellest yet, and if they are only stood up to, the feeblest of all foes?[18]

It is the classic answer to those who question the costs of a military campaign. Churchill argued that not to fight would be worse. The door would be opened not to peace but to even more intense and complex conflict. As an aside, Churchill mocked the strategy of hunger-striking. The well-connected American journalist John Steele reported: 'Mr Churchill employed his cleverest verbiage in ridiculing the fast of the Lord Mayor of Cork, which brought loud laughter from his audience.' Churchill believed it took more courage to endure trench warfare than to hunger strike. His words were, indeed, contemptuous: 'It was during the silly season that Mr MacSwiney assumed his determination to starve himself to death. If the government had given in to him, the whole administration of criminal justice would have broken down. MacSwiney did not want to die. The government didn't want him to die but he had many friends in Ireland who wished he would die. Now, after nine weeks of fasting, he still is alive.'[19] The tone of these comments did not impress significant elements of British public opinion. In the Commons, Commander J. M. Kenworthy pointed out that Churchill himself could not get through a day without a drink. Churchill knew of secret negotiations designed to end the hunger strike. He may have felt that the negotiations were likely to succeed. Carl Ackerman, the American journalist and back channel, who revealed their existence, also believed they had a chance of success. Even so, Churchill's language was unwise. The strategy of the whole speech—'Could a Republic be given to a miserable gang of cowardly assassins like the human leopards of East Africa'—was to mock and to frighten; to invoke the demons. Precisely because some of these demons—such as the danger of a sectarian religious civil war or increased Anglo-American tension—were real, it was all the more necessary to be precise in the use of language.

The Dundee speech provoked an interesting response in the American press. John Steele of the *Chicago Tribune*, alongside Carl Ackerman, the leading US journalist covering 'The Troubles', headlined his article: 'Mayor of Cork ridiculed by war minister | Winston Churchill says that Britain will fight Sinn Fein'.[20] The particular interest in this report lies in the fact that the author, John Steele, like Carl Ackerman, had already inserted himself as a secret back channel between the Sinn Fein leadership and the British government. On 12 October Steele had taken an Irish envoy, a leading businessman, Patrick Moylette, to meet a Cabinet minister. At this meeting, the envoy was asked if Ireland would insist on the full republican demand. 'I am a fisherman. I fish for salmon but never reject a trout.' The minister, H. A. L. Fisher, replied: 'Suppose we gave you salmon trout.'[21] Given his knowledge of these contacts, it is not surprising that Steele considered Churchill's Dundee speech to be 'sensational'. Churchill had said: 'We are going to break this murderous gang in Ireland as sure as the sun rises in the morning.' But Steele was aware that a negotiation had begun based on an entirely different presumption.

Four days after Churchill's Dundee speech, Terence MacSwiney, IRA Commander and Mayor of Cork, died. As J. M. Kenworthy MP pointed out, the effect was dramatic: the corpse of the Mayor—a 'wizened little monkey' formerly a 'robust man'—had an impact on British and Irish opinion that decisively helped Sinn Fein.[22] Kenworthy, who filed past MacSwiney's corpse in Westminster Cathedral, recalled: 'I have seen many corpses but nothing like this.' Churchill did not deceive himself on this point: he knew a critical battle for British, as well as Irish, public opinions had been lost.[23]

When Churchill visited Sir John Lavery's studio, the painter, without comment, put a portrait of MacSwiney on his easel.

> Churchill studied it and then said to Lavery, 'Well, what could we do?' Lavery remained silent and Churchill after a while continued looking at the picture, 'He was a brave man! They are a fine people, we can not afford to lose them. We shall be shaking hands together in three months.'[24]

In November Churchill was still in defiant mood in public:

> What of India, Egypt and Ireland? Do you not think it is possible there is some connection between all the revolutionary and subversive elements by which we are now being assaulted? Why does [Lenin] . . . send money to Sinn Fein? The rascals and rapscallions of mankind are now on the move against us, whether it is the Irish murder gang or the Egyptian vengeance society, seditious extremists in India, or the arch-traitors we have at home, they will feel the weight of the British arm. It was strong enough to break the Hindenburg line.[25]

Deciphered Soviet signals revealed plans to place cells in Sinn Fein.[26] In fact, Basil Clark, the ex-*Daily Mail* man who was head of propaganda in Dublin Castle, felt there was no proof of an actual Sinn Fein–Bolshevik connection of this sort.[27] But there was a plan to kill more British officers. On 21 November the IRA leader Michael Collins ordered the killing of fourteen suspected British secret service agents in Dublin; eight of them were actually British agents, the others were regular officers. Rather oddly, Churchill described the British victims as 'careless, mindless fellows'[28] who ought to have taken precautions. It was a remark that revealed much about the difficulties of the government position. It is as if he wanted to hear news from Ireland only of IRA dead and not of the death of British operatives—because it showed the strategy was faulty. In fact, the strategy—though lacking in moral dignity—was not faulty. For many British soldiers in Dublin, the cold-blooded murder of popular officers in their pyjamas on 21 November legitimized later acts of brutal revenge. The methods of assassination now being employed moved much of the advantage of surprise and random terror to the British forces. In Dublin Castle a few weeks later, a leading official, Mark Sturgis, hoped for a compromise, precisely because, as he noted, the British were now 'profiting' by methods 'which they could not admit'.[29]

Sinn Fein's representative in London picked up on this mood of uncertainty. London was full of such gossip. No one could agree on the correct policy. Art O'Brien wrote to Michael Collins on 12 December 1920:

> Many of the military people are getting afraid of what I may call the Black and Tan theory. They see visions of disintegrating their own army. I am told on what I would say at all events is fairly reliable authority that even Sir Henry Wilson, who, of course, with Churchill is chiefly responsible for the whole reign of terror, is getting nervous of these results. I am also told from another source that Churchill himself is peevish and doubtful.[30]

Then, just as strong men were beginning to lose their nerve, the unexpected happened: the application of superior force and repression had its due impact. The policy of waging a brutal 'dirty war' against Sinn Fein, combined with the offer of negotiation on a decent compromise basis, became ever more successful, even as Churchill's wife complained to him of 'reprisals which fall from Heaven upon the just and the unjust'. In actual fact, British policy was brutal but hardly random. There are, for example, no stories of the murder of constitutional nationalists: this group was more at risk from the IRA. The advantage of surprise now lay with British intelligence in Dublin, as successful raids and attacks mounted. Munster was placed under martial law, and the west was relatively quiet. The attraction of negotiation for the Sinn Fein leadership increased markedly. The only difference in the policy-making elite was a question of timing. Anderson, as he later confessed in his 1928 letter, was unaware until later of precisely how weak the IRA was in the early summer of 1921. Churchill, in fact, wanted to negotiate more quickly than most. In this respect, Churchill probably had the timing just about right.[31]

He was helped by Sir James Craig, the leader of the Ulster Unionists. As Sir John Anderson explained later in his 1928 letter to Churchill, Craig had a broader, more statesmanlike vision than that 'shared by many of his followers'. It was Craig who initiated the idea that he would take part in a conference with the Irish leader, Eamon de Valera. Anderson supported it because it would de-mystify de Valera and bring him into closer contact with reality. Helped by Andy Cope—with whom Craig had worked alongside Churchill in Whitehall during the war—a meeting was arranged on 5 May 1921. Cope, at this time, had excellent contacts with de Valera, through Darrell Figgis and John Cahill, the Dublin printer.[32] But Anderson decided to employ the Bishop of Killaloe, a strong supporter of Sinn Fein, as the intermediary to persuade de Valera of the need for the meeting. Little was said of substance at the encounter, but this was hardly the point. If 'Orange' Craig could meet with de Valera, why not the British premier? Churchill paid close attention to the meeting and later published a graphic account, which included the near arrest of Craig and his Sinn Fein 'handlers' by a Black and Tan convoy. As Craig put it after the meeting, he 'would rather be tolerant than have before us an ideal that we fight these people'. Craig fought off critics in Belfast by saying that he had a responsibility to southern Protestants to seek peace. This was the true meaning of Orangeism, he said—he had to think of isolated southern Protestants always vulnerable to attack.

When the Cabinet committee discussed the issue of a truce on 12 May 1921, Churchill was one of a minority in favour. He voted alongside Fisher, Addison, Montagu, and Monro. The opposing majority consisted of Greenwood, Winton, Macready, Anderson, Balfour, Chamberlain, Horne, Lloyd George, Shortt, Curzon, Worthington-Evans, and the great Ulster Catholic lawyer Denis Henry. For Churchill a truce was no longer a sign of weakness: the forces of the state had the initiative against the terrorists. He had a point, but it is worth noting that the British quietly dropped their 1920 demand for an IRA hand-over of weapons. Meanwhile, the ongoing conflict was bad for the international image of the country, especially in the United States. 'We should do everything to get away to a settlement,' said Churchill.[33] Urged on, as Roy Jenkins has shown, by his wife,[34] at the Cabinet on 12 May 1921 he called for negotiation and compromise.

> I don't agree that it would be a sign of weakness. It would have been six or eight months ago. Then we were not in a position to make any concessions and we had to stand firm and we did so . . . Now our forces are stronger and better trained; auxiliaries are now stronger . . . our position is vastly better in a material sense . . . If you are strong enough you should make the effort.[35]

Churchill later argued that the very fact that Britain had defeated the might of imperial Germany made concession to Ireland easier—no one could say that the recently triumphant British nation was decadent. Kevin Matthews insists that Churchill's account of the government's volte-face is evasive—in particular, that it omits Churchill's own efforts to destabilize Lloyd George's leadership by appealing to discontent over the 'anarchy' in Ireland.[36] In fact, Lloyd George had, perhaps to protect his own back, kept publicly close to Churchill on this issue; but now that Churchill had made his break for 'peace', Lloyd George was certainly freed up to act. The following day was the nomination day for the Irish parliaments established by the Government of Ireland Act of 1920. All candidates for the Dublin parliament were returned unopposed, 124 Sinn Feiners and 4 independents; in the north, Unionists won 40 seats in a 52-seat parliament.

In effect, a negotiation had begun. The government began to refine its terms. The Cabinet decided that the PM should impress on Sir James Craig before he saw de Valera again.[37] These terms are of some interest: (i) No separate navy, army or air force. (ii) A financial contribution by Ireland towards imperial expenditure. (iii) No imposition by Irish parliaments of customs duties on goods of UK origin.[38] Montagu, Churchill, and Fisher placed on record their dissent from point (iii).[39] Churchill, of course, knew that the Tories had discussed the concession of the power of protection as far back as 1885.[40] He clearly felt it would be wrong to try to hold the line on this point in 1921. They did not agree that it was impossible in all circumstances to permit Irish parliaments to do so.

On 15 June 1921 Churchill wrote to the former Conservative MP Sir Francis Newdegate: 'The situation in Ireland shows little improvement but it is something gained to have an Ulster parliament firmly established in Belfast with an overwhelming loyalist majority under the resolute and patriotic leadership of Sir James Craig.'[41] Anderson's account of Craig's role in May 1921 helps to explain this warm praise. Speaking some days later to a delegation from the state of Virginia in London, Churchill praised the greater closeness of Anglo-American relations since the First World War. He wanted to see an ever closer emotional tie between Britain and America.

> But there was only one great obstacle to its attainment—the tragic state of Ireland. But here there was hope. Once again we were at one of those points in history at which a settlement might be reached. Unreason might well again dash away the cup. But at any rate, the question was no longer one which concerned England and Ireland alone, but was inextricably bound up with worldwide problems.[42]

Churchill was now a dove in the Anglo-Irish war. He entertained Collins at his own house on 30 October and joked with the Irish leader about their mutual experience (Churchill in the Boer War) of having a price on their heads. Lloyd George talked to Collins that night of a Belfast parliament being subordinate to a Dublin one. On 5 November Duff Cooper noted: 'The only reason Winston is taking such an intransigent line with regard to Egypt is that he hopes by doing so to make the Irish settlement more palatable to the Tories.'[43] Yet on 7 November Lloyd George, who was trying without success to put pressure on Sir James Craig, kept Churchill at a distance from this operation. Perhaps feeling the exclusion, Churchill wrote to the prime minister:

I wish to put on record that I consider that it is our duty to carry forward the policy about Ireland in which we believe, until we are defeated in the House and thus honourably relieved from our duty to the Crown. Such a policy might well include the creation and recognition of an all-Ireland parliament, subject only to the condition that no physical force must be used against Ulster from any quarter.[44]

Lloyd George and his closest ally on this point, Tom Jones, agreed; but they were prepared to use economic pressure. 'We are pledged not to coerce Ulster,' wrote Tom Jones, assistant secretary[45] to the Cabinet. On 10 November 1921 he added significantly: 'some would confine that to physical force.' By 14 November Lloyd George thought he had persuaded Bonar Law to support his broad Irish policy—though Lloyd George had not told Bonar Law of his desire to include taxation penalties on the new Belfast government.[46] Throughout November Sir James Craig in Belfast resisted this pressure, but Churchill and Lloyd George continued to apply it. On 29 November Churchill, with Lloyd George alongside him, tempted Tim Healy, a link to Collins, with talk of a Boundary Commission so constituted that it would reduce Northern Ireland to three counties in size.[47]

There was still room for bombast, especially if it might be reported back to the Irish. In early December Harold Laski, the LSE don, reported a

conversation with Churchill, in which Churchill was full of threats of John Bull laying about with a big stick. We had utterly broken rebellion in the sixteenth century. Why not now with vastly greater power? Yes, replied Laski, but the condition of Ireland today is the result of our policy then.[48]

Within days Laski and Churchill were working together on the details and language of the Treaty compromise.[49] The Churchill–Laski connection had its roots in Manchester politics from 1904 to 1908: Laski's father, Nathan Laski, had been a senior figure in the Jewish community, which had remained loyal to Churchill in 1908 (Joynson-Hicks was then a perceived anti-Semite) when the Irish voters did not. Before long, Churchill—obviously impressed by Laski's argument or never really believing in his own—personally chastised Sir Henry Wilson for believing in a renewed English conquest, somewhat to Wilson's amazement.[50] As soon as Collins assured him that Britain could retain facilities in Ireland for the Royal Navy[51] and dropped the formal demand for a republic, Churchill was fully committed—possibly the more so as it became clear that he would not have to betray Sir James Craig in the north.

At the end of the Treaty negotiations, on 5 December, there were, Griffith indicated, still some Irish reservations. Lloyd George said that, if the Irish delegation did not accept the terms, no document would be presented to the Ulster PM—fairly obviously a bogus deadline. Lloyd George concluded, as Winston said, 'with tears in his voice': 'there will be war in three days.'[52] This is not quite the tone of a sternly delivered ultimatum. Churchill had himself rather undermined the force of this drama by telling a senior Irish figure (J. W. Dulanty) that 'England would not embark on further military operations in Ireland'.[53]

Gavan Duffy and Robert Barton—the most reluctant Irish signatories—laid great stress on Lloyd George's threat that immediate war would follow upon a rupture. Gavan Duffy signed to avoid 'fresh hordes of savages' being unleashed. Eamonn Duggan, on the other hand, inserted: 'I was not threatened by Lloyd George and he didn't shake any papers in my face.'[54] After all, as Duggan was well aware, the British negotiating position had collapsed on key points such as the existence of an independent Irish army and navy or the payment of an imperial contribution.

Michael Collins also dismissed the 'threat of war'. At a Cork meeting the following March, Collins explained the logic of his final decision to support the Treaty in two powerful passages:

Actually, the British were prepared to go if terms could be agreed. They had given over their claim to dominate us and hold us in subservience to their wishes. We had made this country too uncomfortable for them. There were too many ambush positions, and too many gloomy street corners in Cork and Dublin [hear, hear]. But even so, they were not militarily defeated, and we were not in the position of dictating terms of peace. Therefore, they needed not to agree to what to them would have been humiliating terms any more than we would agree to what would be to us humiliating terms [hear, hear]. And we did agree to a settlement. They agreed to withdraw their forces in exchange for political, military and economic association with them and their nations they call their 'Commonwealth'. I made it plain to all the plenipotentiaries I did not regard seriously the threat of immediate and terrible war.[55]

Collins predicted—surely accurately—that any return to conflict in Ireland would not be initiated after a formal declaration, '"immediate and terrible" or otherwise, but would develop as a result of a policeman shot here, an Irish soldier or an Irish citizen there'. He admitted: 'Duress there was, and let me tell us what it was, it was the duress the weaker nation suffers under the stronger.' But he added: 'On the British side there was duress in that world opinion pressed upon them to confirm their practice to their principles—to make an honourable peace with us, if possible.'[56]

In a celebrated mid-December speech of 1922, Churchill urged the acceptance of the Treaty. The time would come, he said, when Ulster would join southern Ireland, but such a union would have to be of Ulster's 'free will' and in 'her own time'. He praised Ulster's role in bringing about the accommodation and urged prominent ultra-unionists in Westminster and prominent republicans in Ireland to resist laying Ireland 'waste to the scourge of war' or dragging the 'name of Great Britain through the dirt in every part of the world'.[57]

Both Churchill and Collins were addressing the most profound and significant political realities of the moment. Collins's private notes reveal a scepticism about Churchill's 'ex-officer' jingoistic character. It remains the case that, if we look at the speeches of Collins—as Churchill urged—there is evidence that both men shared a similar outlook on the resolution of the crisis in Anglo-Irish relations.[58]

Churchill's essay on the Treaty, published ten years later, pays a profound tribute to the courage of Michael Collins. This article also contains a significant passage on the work of building peace after conflict.

> It is extraordinary how rarely in history have victors been capable of turning in a flash to all those absolutely different processes of action to that utterly different mood, which alone can secure them forever by generosity what they have gained by force. In the hour of success, policy is blinded by the passion of the struggle. Yet the struggle with the enemy is over. There is only then the struggle with oneself. That is the hardest of all.[59]

How did Churchill perform in this struggle with 'oneself'—'the hardest of all'?

7

The Making and Breaking of the Treaty Settlement

Then came the Great War . . . Every institution almost in the world was strained. Great empires had been overturned. The whole map of Europe has changed. The position of countries has been violently altered. The mode and thought of men, the whole conflict of affairs, the grouping of parties, all have encountered violent and tremendous changes in the deluge of the world, but as the deluge subsides and the waters fall, we see the dreary steeples of Fermanagh and Tyrone emerging once again. The integrity of their quarrel is one of the few institutions that have been unaltered in the catechism that has swept the world.[1]

Lloyd George appointed Churchill as chairman of a provisional government of Ireland committee on 21 December 1921. It was an interesting appointment. Churchill was now an ardent and effective defender of the Treaty settlement. Lloyd George appears to have felt his value in parliament outweighed any possibly over-dramatic steps in Ireland. Not every member of Lloyds George's circle was so sanguine. As part of his new duties, Churchill now had the responsibility for making sure the Treaty settlement bedded down. Churchill was, in fact, admirably equipped for the task. This involved, in essence, defending both the newly established governments in Dublin and Belfast against those who accepted no compromise on their ideal of a united Irish Republic. He felt he had bonded on a personal basis with Michael Collins during the Treaty negotiations. He was unambiguous in support of that settlement and had no desire to alter it in any way.

Indeed, he went so far in February 1922 as to request an amnesty for all IRA activists in custody for committing offences in England and Wales.[2] He was strongly opposed to British ultras like Sir Henry Wilson who sought to challenge the Treaty; equally he was totally opposed to any Irish efforts to gain more favourable terms. His attitude towards the Ulster Unionist leadership of Sir James Craig requires some comment.

In Belfast, there was a high level of sectarian violence, as the IRA continued a war against the fledgling northern state and loyalists retaliated. Inevitably this conflict hit the Catholic minority hardest. But also in the south there was continued violence. Here loyalists and Protestants were in the minority. They were on the receiving end of most of the violence: Protestants in Cork were even more vulnerable than Catholics in Belfast. Churchill's great difficulty lay in the fact that the Collins government in the south insisted that he act against Sir James Craig, while Sir Henry Wilson and many Conservative MPs in London insisted that he acted to protect southern Protestants. In both cases, Churchill was being asked to undermine men who, he believed, were essential to any prospect of stability in Ireland and, indeed, ultimate reconciliation—men whose followers might well be engaging in violence but who, in themselves, had at bottom a statesmanlike grasp of reality.

A comment, however, is necessary about Churchill's attitude towards the Boundary Commission. It is perfectly clear that, at both the beginning and the end of November 1921, Churchill was a party to offering the Irish leadership a scenario in which a boundary commission might well be a device that would, in effect, reduce Northern Ireland to an unsustainable size. There is no hint of the idea in his later private or public utterances. Why? In part, the Treaty in December conceded Ireland's right to its own navy—something Churchill opposed to the end. At some level, Churchill might have felt he had gone further towards complete independence than he had intended already. This, in turn, made any idea of placing northern unionist territory under the aegis of Dublin more problematical. More

Fig. 7. James Craig, 1st Viscount Craigavon. Orangeman and Statesman.

profoundly, the British offer on the Boundary Commission was designed to kill off the demand for a republic in Irish politics. Once it was clear that de Valera remained strong and there was a substantial intelligent republican section of opinion against the Treaty, as Churchill's assistant Lionel Curtis carefully explained to him, then the British calculation altered. The issue changed: the question of politics now was what was the best method of defeating de Valera? This was actually well understood by Tim Healy—to whom Churchill had talked about compelling Craig to accept a mere three counties. Pressure on Craig may have been possible in the context of an immediate

Irish closure on the basis of unchallenged acceptance of the Treaty, but it was not possible on the basis of an Irish polity conceivably slipping into the hands of doctrinaire republicans. Winston Churchill would have found it impossible to defend such a position both in parliament and in the country.

Churchill's initial strategy was to bring Collins and Craig to London and to ask them to hammer out a deal. On 21 January 1922 the first Craig–Collins pact was agreed.[3] The two Irish governments pledged to work together: they spoke warmly of enhanced north–south cooperation. Collins was to call off the southern boycott of Belfast business, while Craig was pledged to aid the return of the Catholic workers who had been expelled from the shipyards in 1920.[4] On the evening of 21 January, Winston Churchill and Michael Collins had dinner together at Sir John Lavery's London house, full of 'delight with themselves at having come to an agreement with Craig'.[5] But the 'moderation' of both Craig and Collins was creating discontent among their supporters; anyway, 'each was engaging in some wishful thinking about the other's position'.[6]

At this point, Churchill appeared to be in control. But not everyone in London was reassured. There was the issue of Churchill's famously impetuous character. How to act, after all, in circumstances that were incredibly difficult to read? How to balance Collins's needs as against Craig's? How far was London's expensive support for the military apparatus of the northern government justified when it threatened to bear down so hard on northern Catholics, in such a way as to bedevil the whole Irish settlement? The IRA in the north refused to accept the legitimacy of the Craig government and employed substantial violence against it. Some aides close to Lloyd George, like Tom Jones, feared that the unionist counter-response was too brutal. How to respond, on the other hand, to the increasing evidence that Collins was supporting IRA violence in the north? How, later, to respond to the apparent evidence, at the time of the Collins–de Valera pact of May 1922, that Irish republican unity was being reconstituted in a way that threatened British interests? It was a confusing world, but Churchill himself was not confused. On 10 February he told his wife:

> The full brunt of the Irish business has now come to me, and yesterday in the House for the first time. I had to deal with all the Irish questions. It is going to be very difficult to keep the goodwill of the Ulstermen while carrying out the government policy. At present, oddly enough, they seem much more friendly to me than any of the regular Conservative leaders. I have got a perfectly clear and definite view of what should be done now and how to hold the balance between the two furious factions.[7]

It soon became clear what Churchill meant by this proposition. He was determined to back Craig and his security forces in Belfast with serious financial support. But he did insist, he told Clementine on 11 February, that Ulster had to respect 'the law'. 'I will defend or conceal no illegality or irregularity of any kind.' But he was prepared to pay up. Senior people in Lloyd George's circle were annoyed; senior Treasury officials, if possible, were even more angry.[8] Churchill drew the limit at the use of air power, but he was determined to display to Craig that he would be helped. He moved away from any idea of significant territorial gains for the south. In February he told parliament that the Boundary Commission could 'conceivably'[9] affect the borders of the north 'prejudicially', but in early March Churchill assured Craig that there was nothing to fear from the Boundary Commission. The Lloyd George government, he said, believed only in minor rectifications.[10] In short, republicans were to learn that Ulster could not be coerced, whatever the price—in terms of Treasury resources or bad publicity arising out of sectarian slaughter in Belfast. On the other hand, Collins had to be supported against de Valera. In the short term, this meant a certain acceptance of the level of anti-Protestant violence in the south, no matter how angry London 'diehards' became. Churchill was sympathetic to southern loyalist complaints, but he refused to use them as an excuse for undermining the Treaty deal. The formerly Redmondite MP Stephen Gwynn declared in the *Observer*: 'Generous recognition for differing interests without regard to their numerical strength is the saving formula for Ireland.'[11] Churchill's policy was based on a more brutal *realpolitik*: 'Minorities must be left to stew in their own juice.'[12]

On 5 March 1922 Michael Collins defended the Treaty arrangement on partition. Regarding the arrangement dealing with north-east Ulster under the Treaty, he frankly confessed that it was not ideal. If the Free State was established, however, union, Collins said, was certain, as forces of persuasion and pressure were embodied in the Treaty that would bring the north-east into a united Ireland. 'With the British gone,' he said hopefully, 'the incentive to partition is gone'.[13] He was, of course, being encouraged by Churchill's message that he supported unity by consent. Collins, however, continued to believe that the problem in the north was not republican violence but unionist repression. He sent a telegram to the British government on 6 March 1922:

> Belfast parliament apparently powerless or unwilling to prevent bloodshed or to bring criminals to justice. Invariably your troops are called against our people and feeling running very high against this course of action. Suggest you send an independent investigator and my statement can be shown to be correct. Cannot over-emphasise the seriousness of the situation. Absolutely imperative that some action be taken.[14]

On 11 March 1922 Churchill was sent a further memorandum from the Irish Provisional Government, dealing with the policing situation in Belfast in 1921: it accused the Head Constable and other policemen of murdering a number of Catholics.[15] On the same day, Craig presented a rather different picture of Belfast disorder and rebutted (to his own satisfaction) specific nationalist allegations.[16] In Craig's version, the fundamental problem lay in the level of IRA provocation.

On St Patrick's Day 1922 Sir Henry Wilson prepared a report for Sir James Craig's government, 'How to Cope with the Terror'. He stressed the importance of keeping fair-minded British public opinion on side. In this context, he insisted there was need for major reform of the Special Constabulary.[17] This worried senior figures in London. It was not that they wanted to deliver a united Ireland. Rather, they feared that unionist heavy-handedness encouraged republican extremism in the island of Ireland and weakened Collins and the Treaty. It was felt that Sir James Craig was out of control. On 18 March 1922 Lionel Curtis and Tom Jones had written critically of the Unionist security build-up:

> it is impossible to assume that the formidable forces now being organised under the guise of police are solely against the danger from the South. The British government has armed and is paying for forces which it is told by the one who controls them [i.e. Craig] will in certain eventualities be turned against itself.[18]

In fact this was a rather exaggerated claim. There was, indeed, plenty of aggressive pressure from the south, as the next day was to demonstrate. On 19 March the IRA seized Pomeroy police barracks and stole all its rifles: on 20 March the operation was repeated in Maghera. Collins sanctioned an offensive that killed six policemen and Specials in the north, and the anarchy of north-east Ulster now took a turn for the worse. On 22 March Churchill sent a strong letter to Collins and Griffith concerning IRA intrusions over the border and seizure of weapons.[19] On 24 March Churchill told Sir James Craig that London had been shocked by the 'savage butchery' of the Catholic McMahon family in Belfast. He asked Craig to meet Collins in London. On 25 March Collins replied by denouncing Craig's intention to introduce further repressive legislation.

Field Marshal Sir Henry Wilson, now the MP for North Down, now erupted and publicly denounced the whole pattern of the unfolding Anglo-Irish settlement. Churchill formally replied to Wilson in a speech at Northampton on 25 March; Wilson's description of southern Ireland as a 'welter of chaos and murder' was 'by no means a truthful representation of the facts'. In fact, in most cases there was complete normality. Churchill declared himself 'encouraged' by de Valera's avowed determination at Limerick to 'wade' through Irish blood to achieve the republic. 'This is the true spirit of the Bolshevik mania, that the world is so bad and hopeless that there is nothing for it but to wade through blood towards a distant doctrinaire ideal.'[20]

Churchill had now reached the point where de Valera and Henry Wilson enjoyed a moral equivalence. This moral equivalence is even more clear in private—Churchill was to tell an Irish delegation that they had two 'torturers', Wilson and de Valera. Churchill and Wilson had first worked together in 1911; in the period since they had many areas of agreement and many areas of disagreement. They had been in a certain sense friends.[21] Placing Wilson on the same level as de Valera is, therefore, all the more shocking. This statement shows the massive extent of Churchill's investment in Collins and Craig, but events in Ireland appeared to raise doubts about the wisdom of Churchill's strategy. At the end of March it was clear that 35 Catholics and 18 Protestants had been killed in that month in Northern Ireland.

Churchill made another effort to establish a renewed Craig–Collins understanding. At the end of March, the British government sponsored an attempt to renew the Craig–Collins pact. On the eve of this meeting Sir James Craig claimed that his government did not blame the provisional government for IRA outrages in the north—though he noted language explicitly supporting northern IRA violence had been used by senior figures closely associated with the regime, such as Sean MacEoin and Eoin O'Duffy. This rather tactful (if ambiguous) message clearly indicated that he was prepared to make a second serious effort to reach a settlement.[22] After a rather difficult discussion, in which Collins apparently 'boasted'[23] of responsibility for outrages in the north, the terms of a new pact were dramatically announced by Churchill:

1. Peace is hereby declared.
2. From today, the two governments to cooperate in every way with a view to the restoration of peaceful conditions in the unsettled areas.
3. The police in mixed districts to be composed of one half Catholics and one half Protestants . . . All Specials not required for this force to be withdrawn to their homes and their arms handed in.

4. An advisory committee, composed of Catholics, to be set up to assist in the selection of Catholic recruits for the Special Police.[24]

In addition, the British government was to make available at least £500,000 for relief works—at least one-third of which was to go to Catholic workers. The essence of the new pact is clear: a reformed, non-sectarian Northern Ireland so far as security and employment policy were concerned, in exchange for an end to IRA violence (Clause 6) and Dublin recognition. Many senior unionists felt that Craig had conceded too much ground—but the prime minister himself seems to have been determined to work within the new arrangement. Craig's good faith was not put to the test.

The proposal to add Catholic recruits to the security forces failed because northern republicans refused to take the required declarations of allegiance to the northern state.[25] The *Weekly Northern Whig*, a staunch unionist supporter of the regime, explained in an important editorial on the pact that 'friendly co-operation' between north and south should be the order of the day.[26] But the leader added: 'Ulster' would never accept 'forceful incorporation in the Free State'—indeed, 'every effort to bring it about is bound to result in further alienation of the people'.

In the House of Commons, Churchill paid 'tribute . . . to the states-manlike courage and earnest good will, which had been displayed at this most critical juncture in the fortunes of Ireland by Sir James Craig [cheers]—and his colleagues in the Ulster cabinet'. Churchill expanded further on the potential significance of the new pact: 'But in addition, there is a hope in this agreement of co-operation between north and south [hear, hear]—a co-operation only forthcoming on the basis of the Treaty, a co-operation obviously fully and fatally destroyed were a republic to be set up [hear, hear].' Churchill added:

> The hope of the unity and co-operation undoubtedly opens out to Irishmen in all parts of Ireland, a prospect for the peaceful and progressive future of their country, which had never before been laid before them. In these two ways Ulster and the Ulster government have rendered supreme service not only to Ireland but to the whole empire.

Privately, however, Churchill feared that the second Craig–Collins pact had been reached three months too late, and, in consequence, Irish affairs were getting out of control.[27] But for Churchill such a 'supreme service' imposed a strong reciprocal obligation on the British government to defend the 'soil' of Ulster.[28] Simultaneously, the repressive Special Powers Act was passed by the Northern Ireland parliament.

But, if Craig received plaudits in London for striking a deal with Collins, Collins received no such reward in Dublin. Republicans were decidedly unimpressed by the new pact. On 2 April Eamon de Valera addressed a republican meeting in Dundalk. He noted bitterly of Collins: 'Certain people who were running to London day after day reminded him of little boys going to be spanked.'[29] De Valera's analysis of the second Craig–Collins pact was particularly scathing. He claimed that Sir Henry Wilson was massing an army in the north to carry out more murders, then asked of the new pact: 'What was it? It simply tells them in the north:—So murder our people and be rewarded.' Having completed the final stages of the Irish Treaty Act in parliament on 7 April, when he spoke of hope 'in this agreement' of cooperation between the north and the south, Churchill then returned to his constituency.

On 8 April 1922 Churchill spoke very pessimistically about Ireland in Dundee. Churchill signalled that he expected things in Ireland to get worse before they got better. It was 'Irish blood that would be spilled, Irish money lost, and the Irish character that would be stained by any conflict that might occur in Ireland'. The Northern Whig of Belfast described this tone as an irresponsible 'little Englanderism'; but it did reflect Churchill's relief that Britain was no longer being disgraced by violence in the island of Ireland. He had been dismayed by the international criticism of Britain's role in Ireland. Now, at least, this had stopped. 'Hatred, envy, spite are no foundations on which any form of human success or prosperity can be built.'[30] Churchill circulated a Cabinet memorandum focused on the danger of a republican *coup d'état* that would create a 'state of war' with the British Empire—a war with massive uncontrollable consequences.

On 12 April, the last day before the Easter recess, Ireland—which had taken up most of the time of this session in parliament—again dominated the Commons. Colonel Henry Page Croft, the Conservative MP for Christ Church, spoke for the Tory 'diehards'. He laid great emphasis on the exposed position of the members of the Royal Irish Constabulary and also that of the southern Protestant community. On 15 March 1922 two sergeants of the RIC had been murdered in their beds at a Galway hospital.[31] Churchill faced pleas—which he appeared to accept—that camps should be provided in England for RIC men escaping the attacks. On 27, 28, and 29 April 1922 thirteen Protestant men were killed in Cork after an IRA officer had been killed in a raid on a Protestant household.[32]

The independent Conservative Lord Robert Cecil, taking an entirely different tack, argued that the government, 'including Churchill', had intimated to the British armed forces in Ireland that they might take the law into their own hands. Cecil referred explicitly and accurately to the meeting of the Cabinet committee in June 1920. At that meeting the decision had been taken to increase the level of repression. Such men were now responsible, in Cecil's view, for the unleashed anarchy. But, for Churchill, the most important question was posed by Henry Wilson—would Michael Collins act to stop Eamon de Valera declaring a republic? Wilson assumed that it was inevitable that de Valera would declare a republic and that at that moment it would be revealed that the government had no policy.[33] Certainly Churchill refused to say what he would do in such an eventuality. Collins was absolutely sincere in his willingness to accept a status that fell short of a formalized republic. He accepted that to demand the republican idea was to attempt a dangerous humiliation of Britain. De Valera cared little for London's dignity—what if he got the upper hand in Dublin?

John Steele, the American journalist, who, along with Carl Ackerman, had played a significant role as a go-between between Sinn Fein and the government, now regarded Churchill with great favour. The main significance of the debate for Steele was that it gave Winston Churchill 'an opportunity of adding to his reputation for statesmanship which he has gained by his masterly handling of the Irish peace negotiations'.[34] His speech in reply to his critics was simply 'brilliant'.

In fact, there could be no real reply to Page Croft or Cecil, both of whom were speaking the unvarnished truth—as Churchill well knew. To say that Cecil's speech would please de Valera, as Churchill did, was a mere *ad hominem* debating point. But Churchill was genuinely infuriated by the Tory moralism—without any real strategy to deal with the Irish question. As for Page Croft, Churchill wrote to Collins on 29 April that, 'when you feel moved by some horrible event in Belfast', bear in mind the effect on English opinion of the 'massacre' of Cork Protestants and murder of RIC men, all supposedly under the protection of the Irish nation.[35] But the most significant issue for the future lay elsewhere—was Sir Henry Wilson right in his assumption that de Valera controlled the agenda in Dublin?

In mid-April the republican forces, hostile to Collins, seized the Four Courts in Dublin. In view of an intelligence report from Dublin that the Provisional government had been engaged in providing weapons for the use of the IRA in the north, Churchill baulked at supplying Collins on 16 May with the 10,000 rifles he asked for: six weeks earlier he had provided 6,000 rifles and 4,000 pistols. But, as the scholar Ryle Dwyer correctly observed, Churchill refused to see such 'matters in stark simplistic terms'. He was 'apparently not convinced' of the duplicity of Collins.[36] Even so, he was shocked by the Collins–de Valera pact of 20 May, which seemed to presage a reunified Sinn Fein.

At this sensitive moment, Carson placed an article in the *Sunday Express* on 28 May 1922, which gave the story of the 'Irish loyalists'. It was a direct rebuke to Churchill, though it did not, in fact, end the friendship they had enjoyed since 1914. It noted Churchill's concern for Jewish security on his visit to Jerusalem following the Cairo conference of March 1921.

> You can afford to spend millions upon the Jews in Palestine. Your pity overflows in rivers of blood for the alien Jews of Europe. You subsidise the Jewish state. You send it a Jewish governor. You foster and protect

these Jews at vast expense. You send your soldiers to protect their rule
over the Arabs. You guarantee them safety and security.

But nothing was to be done for the Irish loyalist population.[37]

But still Churchill kept to his course. On 31 May 1922 Churchill—in
another well-regarded speech—declared in the Commons: was Ireland
going to follow the path of anarchy already followed by Russia? 'This
great act of faith on the part of the stronger power will not, I believe, be
brought to mockery by the Irish people.' H. A. L. Fisher noted: 'The
Speaker [Whitely] says Winston's speech is the best he has ever heard.'[38]

This speech deserves some comment. When the Craig–Collins pact
was announced on 20 May 1922, Churchill's entire strategy appeared
to be in ruins. There were rumours that Churchill's nerve would
crack—his most senior official Sir James Masterton Smith thought
him in need of a holiday. Churchill had been reassured by the pro-
Treaty leadership view stated in the Dail on 19 May that republican
violence had the support of only 2 per cent of Irish people. The next
day the new pact between Collins and de Valera was announced. It was
quite a shock for the British government. It allowed for a rigged
election in which the anti-Treaty faction was to have fifty-seven
seats in the new Irish parliament as against sixty-four for supporters
of the Treaty. The compact also prescribed that a coalition government consisting of five pro-Treaty and four anti-Treaty ministers
would be formed.

Churchill insisted that the presence of the four anti-Treaty ministers, if they did not sign a declaration of support for the Treaty as
prescribed by article 17 of the Treaty, meant the Treaty was *ipso facto*
broken. This helps to explain why Republican leaders waited in vain
for their appointment to Cabinet positions. Nevertheless, he felt it his
duty to explain the position of Collins and his friends. He delayed for a
week and a half his considered response to the Collins–de Valera pact.
His words, when they came, were carefully calibrated. Michael Collins,
chaperoned by Freddie Guest, Churchill's cousin, watched on from the
distinguished visitors' gallery.

Despite the talk of 2 per cent support for violence, Ireland was threatened by anarchy, making it impossible to hold an election. Mere 'sordid ruffians and brigands' were active as well as republican 'visionaries'. They were able to take advantage of the split in the mainstream movement to operate freely. The pact would allow the government more freedom to act against this group. Further, they said, it was in the power of the 'extreme minority' in Ireland by murdering British soldiers, ex-soldiers, isolated Protestants in the south, and RIC men—as well as activity in Ulster—to bring about a government collapse in Anglo-Irish relations that would endanger the Treaty. Churchill, therefore, conceded that an improvement in social order might be a price worth paying for a delay in the expression of the free will of the Irish people on the Treaty.

Churchill then turned to the role of the northern government in the crisis. He recalled the second Craig–Collins pact of 31 March: it was almost immediately destroyed by an upsurge in violence. Craig had tried to control matters, but his efforts had failed. Catholics throughout Ireland were enraged by the loss of Catholic life in the north.

These uncertain developments justified the government's decision—opposed as it was by the opposition—to withhold final ratification of this Treaty. Churchill spoke of the significant violence directed against Protestants in the north. But there was far more violence in the south and there was widespread condemnation of the murder of six Protestants in Cork three weeks previously. Churchill concluded, with great force: 'I do not believe the members of the Provisional government are acting in bad faith':

> If we are wrong, if we are deceived, the essential strength of the Imperial position will be in no wise diminished, while the honour and reputation of Ireland will be fatally aspersed. I say to the House, whether you trust or whether you mistrust at this moment, equally you can afford to wait.

The *Spectator* reported of his late May speech that 'the tenor of Mr Churchill's speech was summed up in the words "We can afford to wait; we have done our best"'. In answer to a speech by Colonel Gretton, Mr Churchill declared that in no circumstances would the British government recognize a republic. Nonetheless, the *Spectator* opined: 'We must note our deep disappointment, indeed, our indignation, that the government said nothing about protecting the loyalists in Ireland whose cruel sufferings have been a scandal and dishonour to England.'[39] Luckily for Churchill, the Collins–de Valera 'understandings' of 20 May soon dissolved.

At the beginning of June things seemed to get worse. The seizure of two Ulster townships, Belleek and Pettigo, by republican guerrillas was described as a very grave incident by Churchill. The representatives of the provisional government at Downing Street condemned it.[40] The matter, said Churchill, then passed into another sphere. British troops moved against the IRA in Pettigo and the IRA's soldiers were 'driven pell mell over the border'.[41]

Churchill's decisive action against the 'invasion of Ulster' is sometimes seen as a function purely of his impulsive activist temperament, which can be contrasted unfavourably with the caution of other senior politicians. In fact, his action had its roots in a properly refined set of calculations. He regarded Sir James Craig as a pragmatic moderate leader of a 'furious faction' who had done his best to fulfil his various undertakings. Above all, he felt that Collins, also leader of a 'furious faction', should not be allowed to shirk the issue of breaking with de Valera by utilizing the north as an issue.

It was notable that Churchill was able to carry sometimes sceptical colleagues. Austen Chamberlain had criticized Churchill at the moment of the 'plot against Ulster'; now he was much more sympathetic, even seeing Churchill as helpful to southern unionists. On 10 June 1922 he wrote: 'Meanwhile, Belleek and Pettigo will be a good lesson to Collins and a still better lesson to the rebels.'[42] Collins continued to be moderate. 'We must conciliate elements capable of conciliation and not force everybody to fight us.'[43] De Valera made the most of Pettigo. His supporters in the press evoked the 'first movement in a campaign for the re-conquest of Ireland'.[44] Then came the decisive moment.[45] Sir Henry Wilson was murdered by IRA gunmen as he entered his London home on 22 June 1922.[46] There were many who believed, not without reason, that the gunmen acted on the orders of Collins—perhaps orders that were somewhat out of date. If so, it was all the more necessary for Collins to act in good faith with Churchill. But what if Collins did not see it that way? Churchill's positon looked decidedly weak. The *Spectator* commented:

> Mr Churchill talks vaguely if strongly about our powers of restoring order. Though we say so with shame; we do not believe the government have the power to act even if they have got the will—which we also doubt. Remember what the Churchill threat means. It means flooding the south of Ireland with troops and at the same time carrying on the very difficult business of preventing raids across the northern area. It may mean a massacre of the protestants and loyalists of the south. Anyway, it means the mobilisation of the whole British army and so the sterilising of British arms and British influences in Europe. It means a vast expenditure of money. It means a paralysis of trade.[47]

For Churchill it was an explosive moment. Would Wilson in death achieve what Wilson in life had failed to do: destroy his Irish policy? 'You are being tortured by Wilson and de Valera,' he had told a Belfast delegation on 2 June;[48] now he (Churchill) was being tortured by the ghost of Wilson. Ironically, Wilson was murdered because he was believed to be the key figure in the formation of the hated 'B' Specials in the north: at the level of the policy elite, Winston Churchill was a much more significant figure in this respect. There is a second, even deeper irony: Churchill used Collins's own crime (as it probably was) to make Collins move against de Valera, who was innocent of any involvement in the murder of Wilson.[49] The *Spectator* added: 'If we were to coerce the south, we shall be fighting against men whom we have deliberately armed, to whom we have given motor cars and lorries, to whom we have presented military and police barracks and strong places throughout the country.'

These were, indeed, appalling considerations. They did not stop Churchill indicating to Collins that decisive action against the republican threat was essential in the wake of Wilson's murder. As Collins hesitated, Churchill almost boiled over. But the *Spectator*'s fears were, in the end, groundless fears. The internal contradictions in the Irish leadership exploded when the Free State attacked anti-Treaty forces in the Four Courts on 30 June.

Churchill's policy effectively triumphed. He had shown Collins that there was a line that could not be crossed and forced him to turn away from the northern question as a means of reconstituting the unity of Sinn Fein and to contemplate instead republican challenges to his own authority in Dublin. On the other hand, as the pressures for action mounted in late June in London, Sir Neville Macready correctly claimed the credit for preventing Churchill from launching a premature British attack on the republican forces in the Four Courts.[50] Within a few days, Collins himself took the decisive action. This begs the question as to why Churchill, who did have a last minute rush of blood to the head, stood back at the very last minute; the answer has to be a certain residual trust in Collins, even though he knew Collins had supported destabilizing violence in the north.

For Churchill, the attack on the Four Courts erased all doubts about the integrity of the provisional government.

> Now [he wrote to Collins on 7 July] all is changed. Once the National Army establishes order in the south, as I do not doubt you will in a short time, a new phase will begin far more hopeful than anything we have hitherto experienced. In this phase, our objective must be the unity of Ireland. How and when this can be achieved I cannot tell, but it is surely the goal to which we must look steadfastly.[51]

Sir James Craig sent out helpful signals: he talked explicitly of his hopes for the 'whole of his beloved country'.[52] Craig's consistent willingness to hold out the possibility of Irish unity by consent was an important element in the success of Churchill's strategy.[53]

On 3 August 1922 Churchill reported to the Cabinet with some satisfaction. 'Had the cabinet been told three months ago that the Free

State government would be waging war against the rebels, as they were now doing, they would have been surprised.'[54] He told his colleagues he intended to support the Free State army with 'up to 30,000 rifles'. As for the southern loyalists, he acknowledged they were suffering in the conflict: 'Rich and poor turned out of their homes at two hours' notice.'[55] But Northern Ireland was now much more peaceful. Although Churchill acknowledged that the Treasury support for the Northern Irish security forces had been heavy, he resisted pressure within the Cabinet for any reduction in that support.

At last, Churchill had successfully dealt with a massive issue. It was widely felt that he had indeed done the state some service. But the electorate was hardly grateful, not for the last time. Michael Collins was, however, grateful. He and his colleagues in government openly stated their debt to Churchill. When Collins was shot dead in August, Churchill feared a weakening of resolve on the part of the Irish government. In fact, the opposite happened.

8

The Disintegration of Churchill's Irish Legacy

In November 1922 Churchill lost his seat at Dundee by 10,000 votes. Although the Free State government sent its people to support him, it seems that the Irish electorate largely deserted him.[1] It was an early example of a point noted by one of Churchill's biographers, Henry Pelling, that, once self-government had been delivered to Ireland, the Irish working class no longer had any strong reason to vote Liberal.[2] Churchill was ill at the start of the campaign.[3] Speaking from an invalid's chair in Dundee on 11 November 1922, he declared: 'He had no doubt the Irishman would become master in his house, and would build up according to his ideas, a decent orderly state worthy of taking a part in the affairs of the empire and the world.'[4] He expressed his delight at the Free State capture of leading republican, Erskine Childers. Churchill had hailed the bravery of Childers in the British forces during the First World War; now he was simply an enemy. Two days later it was reported: 'Turning to Ireland, Mr Churchill remarked that the treaty with that country was a great sublime act of faith, forgiveness and hope for the future which he did not believe was going to fail. The British Empire was a house of many mansions, where there was room for all.'[5] His last words as he left Dundee appear to have been about Ireland. He defended the Treaty settlement with his usual vigour. When reminded of the murders carried out by Michael Collins, he invoked the 'sponge' of oblivion. These words are an uncomfortable echo of Acton's phrase that history should not be written by a strong man with a knife followed by a clever one with a sponge. His final words in Dundee were to express his pleasure that, in the last year, 'I have been able to do something for old Ireland'.[6] As he recuperated in a nursing home, he was visited within a few hours of each other by W. T. Cosgrove and James Craig.[7]

But, even without a seat, Churchill attracted attention in Ireland. He was criticized in 1923 for his role in the Boundary Commission. In its review of William O'Brien's latest work, the *Irish Independent* referred to the alleged promise made by Churchill and the prime minister that the Boundary Commission would result in the inevitable merger of the Free State and the six counties.[8] Churchill always denied such a promise. At the Canada Club dinner at the Savoy on 28 February 1924, he warned that the Free State should be cautious: it should avoid a new 'line of barbed wire entanglement on the border'. It should look to a wider solution.[9] The truth is that both Churchill and Lloyd George encouraged the Irish pro-Treaty faction to be optimistic about Irish unity. Lloyd George did so on the basis of the role of economic factors. Churchill did so on the basis that stable leaderships in the north and the south would eventually converge. Neither appears to have laid great emphasis on the Boundary Commission as a certain lever of change, but they both allowed illusions about its possible role to grow in Dublin.

On St Patrick's Day 1924 Churchill spoke at the Irish Club in London—introduced by the Gladstonian grandee, R. B. Haldane, who recalled Parnell, 'too little remembered'. His reception was cordial. Churchill believed that the Irish had shown they were perfectly capable of managing their own affairs—'no community in the world' was more capable. Collins had vindicated the word of the Irish people by his sacrifice. It had become 'a nation once again'. All this was better than a union sustained by 'questionable means'.[10] He looked forward to the Irish Free State working closely with the British Commonwealth of nations to defend the 'utmost freedom of the individual' within a stable model of government. Irish unity was inevitable: nothing could stop it except the effort to force it. Irishmen should espouse the 'higher unity of Ireland'—cooperation between north and south and all matters of common interest. It was clear that Churchill did not believe in the desirability or capacity of the Report of the Boundary Commission to destabilize the Craig regime. On 5 September 1924 he wrote to William Coole in Fermanagh:

> A very important letter from Lord Birkenhead to Lord Balfour, written at the time the Treaty was passed, will be published in the papers of Monday next. This letter shows most clearly that the British signatories of the Treaty intended and believed that Article 12 should only deal with a readjustment of boundaries and not with a redistribution of territory. We then received the highest legal advice to the effect that no impartial commissioner could take any other view.

At this moment, Lady Lavery, wife of Sir John Lavery, wrote to Winston Churchill regretting that he was backing Ulster against the Irish Free State on the boundary question[11]—or, more accurately, regretting the militancy of Churchill's backing. Churchill was endangering his great personal triumph—the deal with Dublin. 'I felt more sorry and disappointed because I had hoped you would not, if the choice came, back Ulster against the Free State...Please do not misunderstand me to mean that I expected you to back the Free State against Ulster.'[12] On 25 September 1924 he said, 'we always thought' the Irish leaders were unwise in 'their own interest' in pressing for a Boundary Commission. 'All those who signed the Treaty had in view—an Ireland free, united, the friend of Britain—a proud contributor to the worldwide Commonwealth'.[13]

The Boundary Commission, established under Article 12 of the Anglo-Irish Treaty, had not started its proceedings until 1924. An authoritative press leak concerning its work—proposing only minor rectifications—was published on 7 November 1925. There was considerable nationalist dismay. The Tories had now returned to power. Was nationalist Ireland to be cheated? W. T. Cosgrave, the Irish premier, rushed to London to consult Stanley Baldwin—notably less sympathetic than, say, the now departed Lloyd George.

There was a possible escape route for all concerned. Winston Churchill, now returned not just to parliament but to government as Tory Chancellor of the Exchequer, was to play the decisive role, but it could not have been achieved without the firm support of both the Irish premiers, Craig and Cosgrave. Article 5 of the Treaty had committed the Free State to a share of the United Kingdom public debt, subject to agreement between the two governments. A possibility existed, therefore, of a 'trade off'—to use Enda Staunton's phrase[14]—between the abandonment of Article 12 and the gaining of concessions under this article. There was an important facilitating historical context. The new Irish state faced significant financial difficulties. Throughout the second half of the nineteenth century it was widely felt in Ireland that the country was overtaxed—a view supported by English and Irish liberals.[15] However, after 1906 the new liberal welfare reforms changed the financial relationships. Indeed, a significant point of the impulse behind the 1916 Rising lay in the idea that nationalists had to act before the Irish people were seduced by old age pensions and the other comforts of the nascent welfare state. Inevitably, for an independent Ireland it became impossible in the 1920s to maintain the inherited level of social provision. On 1 December Churchill walked into the Treasury Board Room, announced that he understood that the Irish government was disappointed by the Boundary Commission, but the results, 'he could truly say', were 'very much what he had expected'.[16] But what to do next? The new tripartite agreement on 3 December between the governments of the United Kingdom, the Irish Free State, and Northern Ireland revoked the powers of the Boundary Commission and maintained the existing boundary of Northern Ireland.

Churchill then repaid the Irish by giving them a good financial settlement. As he explained to Parliament:

> As the price of autonomy the Free State had already accepted a lower standard of public expenditure than rules in this country ... they have lowered the salaries of their teachers, they have reduced their old age

pensions, they have not followed our later developments of unemploy-ment insurance, or of pensions for widows or of pensions at 65 years of age.[17]

The tripartite agreement of 1925 formalized Dublin's acceptance of the legitimacy of the Belfast regime. In principle, it also allowed the space for friendly cooperation between the north and the south. At first it appeared as if this was on the cards.

James Craig declared in February 1926:

> I have always taken the view that the illustrations I have used with regard to the two friendly neighbours holds equally strong when one considers that for future times the north and south have got to live together as neighbours and the prosperity of Northern Ireland does undoubtedly affect the prosperity of southern Ireland and a peaceful and prosperous southern Ireland reflects on the north . . .
>
> Therefore a man is short sighted indeed and no patriot to his country who would see one portion standing out prosperous, rich, happy and content if, on the other side, he was to see despondency, poverty and going down the hill instead of going up. So it is for the government of the south and the government of the north to turn their hands rather from the matters which may have divided them in the past to concen-trate on the matters which really affect the people in their own area with the view that the whole of Ireland, and not one part of it alone, may be prosperous.[18]

In March 1926 Churchill returned to Belfast and spoke at the Ulster Hall. He explained his position with great care: 'At the moment when Ulster accepted the 1920 Act and withdrew her opposition to a measure of autonomy for the rest of Ireland, he became one of the defenders of the rights of Ulster.' He insisted that Irish unity would come about only through the 'free and unfettered' choice of the north. He was totally opposed to 'unfair economic pressure'. His long-term preference remained for Irish unity within the Empire—but he accepted that many in Ireland thought that unrealistic. At any rate, the Irish question had entered a 'stable phase'. There would be no constitutional change for many years ahead. He then added a final flourish, acknowledging 'old friends, good comrades, my father's work'.[19]

In November 1926, also, Kevin O'Higgins, a leading figure in the Free State government, attempted to revive an old Sinn Fein policy of the 1905–17 era: the proposal to create a Kingdom of Ireland with its own unified parliament. In such a settlement Kevin O'Higgins believed that unionist, British, and Irish interests would be met. Churchill, he told Hazel Lavery, was 'breast-high' for it, and even Carson was a little intrigued. For one modern scholar, John M. Regan: 'This was the apogee of the counter revolution,' for, as O'Higgins acknowledged at the end of his letter, 'the Dublin coronation was still a long way off'.[20]

In Belfast, Sir James Craig was keen to maintain the doctrine of 'parity', that is 'step by step'—an equivalent level of social services within the rest of the kingdom. The main financial question of devolution was whether Britain could be persuaded to replace the imperial contribution (whereby Northern Ireland was expected to pay its share

Fig. 8. Ronald McNeill, 1st Baron Cushendun. Churchill's enemy turned friend.

of defence expenditure) by a payment making 'parity' of social welfare possible, regardless of Belfast's capacity to pay for it. This was achieved in 1926 on Churchill's watch, by a separate agreement supplementing Ulster's employment fund. In March 1926 it was hardly surprising that he had to defend himself in parliament from the charge that he was treating Northern Ireland too generously. Certainly, he was consciously allowing the Belfast government to escape the financial constraints of the Government of Ireland Act of 1920. He did not, therefore, need to be quite so coy when he wrote to Carson in 1927: 'It is strange how kind Ulstermen have been to me . . . you, in particular, have always been a good friend to me, both in the war and afterwards as much as you possibly could.'[21] It was not that strange. In 1930, one Treasury officer noted: 'Any honest statement of the position can not help pointing out that we now subsidise Northern Ireland to the tune of £1 million a year or more.'[22] Of course, it is worth adding that Ronald McNeill, now Churchill's chief secretary in the Treasury, was the same Ronald McNeill, the Unionist MP, who had struck him with a flying object in parliament in 1912.

In 1926, however, Irish republicanism reconstructed itself yet again as a political force as the more realistic 'politicos' split from the purists. In 1927 Kevin O'Higgins, a natural ally for Churchill, was murdered. De Valera's growing political influence from 1926 onwards offset Churchill's calculations for Ireland. He had not really considered this possibility. In response to de Valera taking power in Dublin in 1932, Churchill declared in a newspaper article: 'We would no more allow hostile hands to be laid on the liberties of the protestant north than we would allow the Isle of Wight or the castles of Carnarvon or Edinburgh to fall into the hands of the Germans or the French.'[23]

But it was de Valera who was now in power in Dublin and Churchill who was on the political margin. Everything seemed to assist de Valera in his progress towards dismantling the Treaty settlement. Even before he came to office in March 1932, on 11 December 1931, the Statute of Westminster empowered dominion parliaments to repeal or amend any act of the UK parliament. In 1936 Edward VIII abdicated: in Dublin, on 11 December, the Constitution (Amendment No. 27) Act removed the king from the Irish Constitution.

But more important was the decision in the 1937 Irish Constitution to revoke the explicit recognition given to Northern Ireland in the 1925 agreement. In international law this was a meaningless move—treaties must be observed. Governments cannot in this sphere act unilaterally. But, in terms of Irish politics, the effect of a Dublin territorial claim on Northern Ireland as embodied in Articles 2 and 3 of the 1937 Constitution was highly significant. It could be said to have opened up an era of cold war between north and south that did not end until the Good Friday Agreement of 1998 remodelled these articles. The Treaty implied, and the 1925 agreement formalized, Dublin's recognition of the legitimacy of Northern Ireland. Winston Churchill was central to both developments. The 1937 Constitution destroyed that building block—essential for any model of north–south cooperation leading to Irish unity by consent. Churchill was not to live to see its reinstatement in the agreement of 1998.

For Churchill, even worse was to follow when Neville Chamberlain became prime minister. In 1939 the 'Treaty' ports in Ireland were given up by London—partly in a vain attempt to persuade Hitler that peaceful negotiation and conciliation was the best path. For Chamberlain the idea was to convince Europe that old historical animosities could be alleviated by negotiation and concession; for Churchill the retention of these naval facilities in Ireland had been a theme of his career since he had first visited them in 1912. Churchill responded with disbelief:

> Now we are to give them [the ports] up unconditionally to an Irish government composed of men—I do not wish to use hard words—whose rise to power has been proportionate to the animosity with which they have acted against this country, no doubt in pursuance of their own patriotic impulses, and whose present position is based on the violation of solemn Treaty arrangements.[24]

He recalled his own experience in the admiralty:

> The admiralty of those days (1921) assured me that without the use of those ports it would be very difficult, perhaps almost impossible, to feed this island in time of war. Queenstown and Berehaven shelter the flotillas which kept clear the approaches to Bristol and the English Channel, and Lough Swilly is the base from which access to the Mersey and the Clyde is covered. In a war against an enemy possessing a numerous and powerful fleet of submarines, those are the essential bases from which the whole operation of hunting submarines and protecting incoming convoys is conducted. If we are denied the use of Lough Swilly and have to work from Lamlash, we should strike 100 miles from the effective radius of our flotillas. These ports are, in fact, the sentinel towers of the western approaches by which the 45 million people on this island so enormously depend on foreign food for their daily bread and by which they carry on their trade, which is equally important to their existence.[25]

Resonant as the words were, they had little impact. Churchill was now an isolated, eccentric figure. His fears were in the end absolutely justified. At the moment of their articulation, they were disregarded completely. Churchill's career had many frustrating moments, but few were to rival this one, which presaged Munich itself. Churchill was entirely isolated on the issue. 'Blessed are the peacemakers,' cried the Daily Express. The Times welcomed the 'refreshing spectacle' of a 'settlement' of a 'long standing dispute', especially in 'a period in the world's history in which reason and legality have repeatedly been overlooked by emotional violence'.[26] The prime minister stated this approach would bring stability to the Middle East—though, of course, he hoped even more it would bring stability to Europe.

There is one final footnote to these, the grimmest days of Churchill's political career. Churchill was grateful for the Unionist support and sympathy that he continued to receive in the wilderness year of 1938. Of the silver cup—engraved with quotations from speeches on Ulster by his father, himself, and his son Randolph—sent by Lord Craigavon (James Craig, as was) as a Christmas present in December 1938, Churchill wrote to his wife: 'I wish some of the dirty Tory hacks who would drive me out of the party could see this trophy.'[27] The fact remains, however, that although the Unionist government did protest against the deal on the Irish ports, their protest was a qualified one. Lord Craigavon, in the end, professed a willingness to be 'bribed' by government contracts for Belfast firms.[28] Some observers believed that Craigavon in essence supported the policy of appeasement. The low-key betrayal by a friend brings home the full extent of Churchill's powerlessness in 1938.

But it was not just Churchill who was marginalized—in his view it was Ireland itself. In his essay on Parnell—assisted by his cousin Shane Leslie—published in 1938, Churchill lamented the new-found insignificance of Ireland:

> Modern youth now sees home-rule Ireland, a sullen impoverished group of agricultural counties leading a life of their own, detached from the march of Britain and the British Empire, incapable of separate appearance in any way, except in small and discordant roles, upon the world stage. But in the days of which we write, Ireland and the Irish affairs dominated the centre of British affairs, while Britain herself was universally envied and accepted as the leader in an advancing and hopeful civilisation.[29]

In the same year Churchill acknowledged in a newspaper article that Irish America was unreconciled to Britain and that his 1912 Belfast speech vision of the Irish as a contented section of the 'English speaking peoples' was dead. Ireland regarded Churchill as completely irrelevant. Churchill's excellent essay on Parnell is a double lament: a lament for the loss of his vision of Ireland working alongside Britain on the world stage and a lament for himself. His own remarkable work in stabilizing the Irish settlement was now forgotten, just as the 'youth of today' had forgotten that Ireland had ever been an important issue in British politics. Few in independent Ireland cared about this loss of historic status. For them Churchill's and Redmond's vision of a Dublin parliament linked in legal harmony with the British Empire was redundant. Ireland may not have been the largest Catholic country in the world, but it was the largest English-speaking Catholic country. Here was a role worth playing.

9

Churchill and Irish Neutrality

The choice is between the old, faulty democracies of today and the slave-compounds. Or worse, the carrying of the lash in the slave compounds. Faced with that choice, the Irish will choose the faults of today, that there may be a tomorrow with which to mend them. The British too.[1]

Winston Churchill's years of frustration in the political wilderness were coming to an end. Chamberlain, of course, still hoped to avert war with Hitler. But in August 1939 Germany signed a treaty with Russia, protecting her eastern flank. On 1 September Germany invaded Poland. Churchill was invited once again to become First Lord of the Admiralty two days later. One of his first acts was to ask his most loyal friend, the Irishman Brendan Bracken, to become his parliamentary private secretary.

Irish neutrality infuriated Churchill. By October 1939 he had advised the Cabinet 'to take stock of the weapons of coercion'.[2] He tried unsuccessfully to persuade the Cabinet to take back the Treaty port of Berehaven. He described the Irish refusal to cooperate as 'odious' and said he was 'sick' of Ireland.[3] The IRA decided to add its own contribution to the tension by launching a bombing campaign in England. Churchill asked: 'What does Intelligence say about possible succouring of U-boats by Irish malcontents in the west of Ireland? If they throw bombs in London, why should they not supply fuel to the U-boats? Extreme vigilance should be practised.'[4] It was perhaps fortunate that the British naval attaché in Dublin was not an alarmist on this score.[5] It should, however, be noted that, after the war, Admiral Eberhard Gott told his British interrogators that German U-boats were able to surface, rest, and repair in Irish territorial waters throughout the war and up to the end of the war were receiving very considerable information about anti-U-boat minefields from the German intelligence service.[6]

On 10 May Neville Chamberlain—much liked by de Valera—resigned, and Churchill became prime minister. 'I hope it is not too late,'[7] Churchill muttered. News of German triumphs dominated the headlines almost daily in May and June. The Allied armies retreated towards Dunkirk and began their evacuation on 26 May. Hitler stopped his panzers 18 miles short of Dunkirk, predicting that the 'British won't come back in this war'.[8]

In May 1940 Victor Gollancz published in his patriotic Victory Books series a book by the Irish socialist republican and admirer of Jack London, Jim Phelan, entitled *Churchill can Unite Ireland*. The book is an intellectual oddity, which is not to say it is incoherent. It places itself firmly in the John Mitchel tradition of outright and full-blooded denunciation of British oppression in Ireland. But it, nonetheless, accepts—while acknowledging explicitly that many Irish people did not—that Hitlerism is a greater evil than British capitalism. Phelan wrote:

> If the British people do not stand off Nazism, if they tolerate the lies and swindling and cheap histrionics of Hitler's admirers past danger point, they and we will be stamped out of existence. There will be no more of pseudo-democratic British capitalism, which some Irish might think a good thing. But there will also be an end to the incipient Irish republic. The fighting republican politically-alert people of Ireland can not allow the British to lose.[9]

Rather wildly, Phelan called for a conference involving Churchill and Irish politicians. Eamon de Valera and Lord Craigavon should meet within a week with Churchill. The conversation should be attended also by Irish socialist anti-fascists such as republican Paedar

O'Connell and playwright Sean O'Casey, plus—rather quaintly—'one man taken at random from an Irish peasant holding'.[10] This was a delightful reductionist Marxist fantasy but hardly a practical proposal. But the idea of an offer of Irish unity for an end to Irish neutrality was part of the real world of politics. This time Churchill 'can call upon Lord Craigavon to prove his loyalty'. For Phelan, in the context of 'a war totally unlike any preceding, there is no time to maintain polite fictions'. He was confident that this time there would be no Curragh mutiny: in other words, no Unionist resistance to the will of the British state. He felt that de Valera would offer in return for unity an Irish common defence against Hitler—though it might be better to place French rather than British soldiers in Ireland as part of this arrangement. Phelan, for all his Irish republican leftism, writes as one convinced that Churchill was a great British leader who understood the need for Irish support. He concluded in an emotional passage:

> With all its myriad faults we, the Irish, will fight for this western end of Europe. For little things that will be bigger and shall mean likeable things that will be better. For the taste of sweet milk hot from the cow and the lazy lying to smoke by a river; for apples in Covent Garden and trout in Killarney; for the bustle of London's West End and the lonely lorries on the Great North Road; for the smoke of turf in Tipperary and the talk of the miners in Rhondda and a tap room in an English village where I can hear the Gaelic spoken, every night, by 20-odd hard-eyed young fellows in air-force blue, some but an hour back from tearing at the iron heel. For these things, foolish or otherwise, a man can fight and be easy.[11]

The idea that the early spring and early summer of 1940 provided the ideal context for a move towards Irish unity, which would, in turn, lead to a united Irish participation in the war against Hitler, was not confined to left-wing romantics. As one nationalist later wrote in an open letter to Churchill: 'If the Orange card was the card to play for Britain in dividing Ireland, then there was, at the time of Dunkirk, a sense in which it might have been the ace of trumps in the hands of

Fig. 9. David Low Cartoon, 'Irish Argument', June 1940 (reproduced in 'Years of Wrath'). Illustration showing British resentment to Irish neutrality.

Hitler.'[12] In other words, Northern Ireland, because it prevented de Valera's entry into the war on the British side, was a strategic weakness. In the end, of course, Northern Ireland was a strategic asset.

The international conflict placed enormous strain on a small neutral state like Ireland. In a Senate speech in 1939, some months before the outbreak of war, de Valera had outlined a clearly defined policy of neutrality. Nevertheless, it is important, however, to note that Irish foreign policy was not only defensive and fearful—as was entirely understandable—but also watchful and hopeful. In particular, there was an effort from the autumn of 1939 to trade Irish influence in America—in favour of continued American neutrality—for German support for Irish unity at the end of the war.

Of course, it remained the case that it would have been exceedingly difficult for de Valera to bring Ireland in on the British side, even if he had such an inclination. Opinion in the country was simply too divided and de Valera faced a significant threat from the IRA on his left. Eamon de Valera was never likely to forget that it was John Redmond's decision to support the British in the First World War, which in the end destroyed his leadership of Irish nationalism. Even Churchill did not ignore the fact that de Valera acted under serious political constraint.

> Three-quarters of the people of southern Ireland are with us but the implacable malignant minority can make so much trouble that de Valera dare not do anything to offend them. All this talk about partition and bitterness that would be healed by a union of Northern Ireland will amount to nothing. They will not unite at the present time and we can not, in any circumstances, see the loyalists of Northern Ireland down.[13]

'Three-quarters' was, to say the least, a generous figure, but this analysis was not without a certain grip on reality.

On 3 April 1940 Churchill met David Gray—who was on his way through London to take up the post of US Representative in Dublin. At this point, and for some weeks thereafter, Gray—like Jim Phelan—was convinced that the way forward was for the British government to order the Ulster Unionist leadership to accept Irish unity in exchange for an end to Irish neutrality. Over plovers' eggs, Churchill was extremely civil to a man who was, after all, Roosevelt's cousin and certainly not an isolationist. Nevertheless, in response to Gray's proposal, he roared in his 'quarterdeck' manner: 'If you have come here to offer me a bribe to sell out Ulster for any kind of American support, you had better go back.'[14] Gray reported: 'He [Mr Churchill] said he was sick of the Irish, that the English had given them a generous settlement and that immediately they began to break their engagements and were now stabbing England in the back.'[15] Five weeks later, on 10 May, Chamberlain resigned and Churchill became prime minister; but Churchill's tone on the Irish question altered. Now the British sought to offer a deal on partition to Dublin, but just as quickly the Irish state gravitated towards an ever-more triumphant Germany. Professor Reynolds has written that 'the proposal foundered on the refusal of the Irish leader, Eamon de Valera, to enter the war, and of the Ulster Unionists to end partition'. It should be added that, of these two factors, the first was rather more decisive than the second.[16]

On 11 May 1940 de Valera did criticize the German invasion of Belgium and the Netherlands. The Irish envoy in Berlin, William Warnock, was exasperated. The Germans had not been pleased. The German archives record Warnock as having used some rather striking 'personal' language to reassure them—implying that Ireland was merely waiting for the right moment to strike against Britain, having struck too early in 1916.[17] Churchill remained uneasy about any attempt to coerce the Ulster Loyalists, but on 27 May the War Cabinet agreed:

1. To make an immediate approach to de Valera in order to bring home the danger facing Eire, and the need in order to combat it, for early and full cooperation with this country. In particular, we should ask for the use of Berehaven for the Navy.
2. To invite Lord Craigavon to agree that the Government of Northern Ireland should take part in an All-Ireland Council *during the period of the present Emergency*.[18]

Some in the War Cabinet favoured an even more explicit offer of Irish unity. Professor Paul Canning has written: 'By watering down "2" in an attempt to make it palatable to Craigavon, the War Cabinet virtually assured that it would be unacceptable to de Valera and therefore "1" would be lost.' However, the truth is that once such a discussion had begun in earnest between London and Dublin, it would have been very difficult to place limitations upon it. The momentum towards Irish unity would have been a strong one. At the beginning of June 1940 Sir John Maffey, the British ambassador in Dublin, told David Gray, his US counterpart, that Lord Craigavon, the Ulster premier, had recently been called to London, where he had been given 'merry hell' and all but ordered to 'end partition on the best terms he could'.[19]

On 17 June the Irish Department of External Affairs, worried by some recent public talk from Hitler about compromise with the British Empire, asked for reassurance that this did not mean 'the abandonment of Ireland' and the withdrawal of German support for the 'final realisation of Irish demands'.[20]

On 21 June 1940 Joe Walshe, the secretary general of the Department of Foreign Affairs, informed de Valera: 'British defeat has been placed beyond all doubt.'[21] It is hardly surprising that the intense and sometimes public debate within the unionist elite in Belfast in June 1940—a debate in which senior figures known to Churchill such as Basil Brooke and the Marquess of Dufferin and Ava[22] favoured an offer of Irish unity to bring the full weight of Ireland into the war against Hitler—received practically no attention in Dublin.[23] The French high command, as if to support Walshe's point, surrendered on 22 June; Jim Phelan's genial idea that French soldiers, rather than British, guard Ireland was now dead.

At this precise juncture de Valera had discussions in Dublin with the British government's representative, Malcolm MacDonald, Chamberlain's ally. The fact that Churchill allowed MacDonald, whom he despised for his role in the concession of the Treaty ports, to take up this mission, speaks volumes. Quite explicitly, de Valera acknowledged that, even if the British agreed the extension of his 1937 Constitution over the whole country, Dublin would not guarantee to join the war effort. It 'might', but only with a 'very big question mark after might'. MacDonald was later to defend de Valera's decision, but it is worth noting that, at the time, he also pointed out correctly that de Valera's decision would enormously strengthen support for partition in England. Churchill had supported the dialogue with de Valera: 'the key to this is de Valera showing some loyalty to crown and empire,'[24] he had said. He was certainly prepared to offer a British declaration accepting the principle of a united Ireland. There is no clearer sign of the desperation of Britain's position. But there was growing awareness in London that there was no real possibility of a deal, especially as the Germans intensified the pressure on Ireland. 'Get this clear,' Frank Aiken, a senior Cabinet member, declared in response to a visitor telling him of interesting divisions within the northern Cabinet; 'we are never going to abandon our neutrality'.[25]

The *Irish Independent*, on 5 July, carried a rather worrying report: 'At the Wilhelmstrasse it was stated that the position of Ireland is similar to that existing in Belgium before the German invasion.' The next day the *Belfast Northern Whig* published a number of German press threats against Ireland. In a draft telegram dated 5 July, Churchill wrote that 'de Valera and his party are reconciling themselves to throwing in their lot with the Germans, whom they think are bound to win'.[26] On 9 July de Valera ended all doubt on the subject by telling the *New York Times* that he was committed to a policy of 'strict neutrality' even in the context of Irish unity. Matters now moved on. Craigavon felt confident enough to urge a British invasion of the south—tactfully employing only Scottish and Welsh troops.

The British then had decided on their response. Churchill, for all his anger, acted with considerable forbearance. In Churchill's notes for his 'secret speech' to the House of Commons on 20 June 1940, on the 'Fall of France', the following reference is made: 'Question of Ireland. Greatly influenced by a great army developing here. Germans would fight in Ireland under great disadvantages. Much rather they break Irish neutrality than me.'[27] This was the new British policy.[28] British–Irish military staff talks in May 1940 reached agreement that, in the event of a German invasion, the defence forces would fight for twenty-four hours before requesting British assistance. The Chief of Staff of the Irish army would have to assure de Valera that it was a real invasion, 'not just a matter of a few odd parachutists'. Advance columns of British forces could be in Dublin within two and a half hours of receiving the call to move south.[29]

Churchill continued to grumble ferociously about Irish neutrality, but he accepted the fact of its existence. On 7 December 1940 Churchill told the US President that he would not coerce Northern Ireland. In fact, the government was more concerned about Belfast's contribution to the war effort.[30] A young civil servant in the Cabinet secretariat, later to be prime minister, Harold Wilson, drew up a report criticizing the contribution of the Northern Ireland workforce to the war economy—a criticism it is clear Churchill accepted.[31]

In February 1941 the veteran Irish–American columnist Mark Sullivan wrote in the *Washington Post* that Churchill avoided public mention of Ireland in his speeches—but everyone was aware of its possible strategic importance. Mark Sullivan feared that Hitler would attempt a simultaneous descent upon the two islands, Britain and Ireland. He concluded:

> Ireland is today in the position occupied by Norway, Denmark, Holland and Belgium before Germany fell upon them. She is in danger as the others were in danger. Like the others her only possible help is Britain. Again, like the others, she is unwilling to invite Britain in to give her that help—until it is too late.[32]

A secret memorandum of the Irish Department of External Affairs, dated May 1941, detailed thirteen areas of cooperation with Britain. They included information on transport and military facilities in Ireland, free air space for British planes, broadcasting facilities, collection of and passing-on of information, a coast watch service, routing of official German and Italian communications through Britain, internment of spies, and blacking-out of areas at British request. Ireland also provided much food for Britain.[33] Belfast was, however, now facing the savage impact of Nazi onslaught: between 8 April and 7 May 1941, 950 citizens were killed in German air raids. The Luftwaffe planes that made the April attack had 'massed' over neutral Eire, in the opinion of British intelligence.

On 20 May 1941 the British government informed the Belfast government that it was reconsidering the introduction of conscription in Northern Ireland. Publicly, at least, the Ulster Unionists supported the idea, but the Irish government and many in British public life remained sceptical. Churchill himself was on record in pointing out that the threat of conscription in Ireland in 1918 had been highly counterproductive. General Sir Hubert Gough of the 'Curragh mutiny' fame, no less, joined forces with two survivors of the Redmondite tradition, Henry Harrison and Maurice Healy, to argue against the idea. Before the end of May it was clear that Churchill had dropped the notion.[34] It was rightly observed that 'it is unfortunate that the impression has been allowed to grow up that Churchill was in favour of conscription'.[35] Churchill remained consistently irritable about Ireland; though others in the Cabinet took comfort in the Irish contribution to the workforce in wartime England, Churchill warned that the German embassy in Dublin would include spies in their number.[36] Churchill's cousin Shane Leslie was serving in the Home Guards under Sir Hubert Gough, the commander-in-chief. Leslie and Gough supported the idea that existing fighting units of Irishmen in the British army should be regrouped as a brigade or division, to lend the Irish serving in the British army a more distinctive identity. There is a distinct irony here. Gough, one of the Curragh mutineers, and Leslie, a former Redmondite parliamentary candidate, were now united behind the old Redmondite view that it was best to give the Irish serving in the British army as distinct an identity as possible. During the First World War—for reasons that applied equally to the Welsh—the high command did not see it as a practical idea. In September 1941 Churchill told Leslie he was very sympathetic to the idea, but again the War Office vetoed it on the grounds of practicality.[37]

A second British offer of unity was to be made in far more propitious circumstances—for the British. On the early morning of 8 December 1941 Sir John Maffey, the British representative in Dublin, delivered a special message to de Valera from Churchill. The context was clear: in the immediate aftermath of the Japanese attack on Pearl Harbor, American involvement in the war against the Axis was certain. The note passed over included the celebrated phrase: 'Now is your chance, now or never, a nation once again.'[38] The following day Churchill made it clear that a 'nation once again' did not imply any imposed deal on partition. It meant above all that Ireland would regain its national honour by involvement in the struggle against fascism. But it is worth recalling that Churchill was aware that important and younger elements in the Ulster Unionist Cabinet would accept Irish unity as a price for Irish support in the war against Hitler. This, therefore, gives the message rather more potential meaning. Did de

Valera miss an opportunity to solve the partition issue? His son denies the point. 'Such a theory is without foundation, grossly misleading and patently false, for to take one important point, the unionists had not been consulted.'[39]

In defence of his father's policy, Terry de Valera has recently written that Britain rather than Germany was the most likely invader of Ireland, and that Britain's intentions towards Ireland were less benign than those of the Nazis. In particular, Terry de Valera stresses the significance of a British War Cabinet memorandum of 8 October 1940, in which it was decided that, in the event of a German invasion of Ireland, the RAF should be prepared to use poison mustard gas, a gas that could hardly have discriminated between Irish and German.[40] Terry de Valera's observation also adds that his father's inclination was not to explore the offer: 'As he told me, his primary worry and concern at this point in time was not the solution to partition, but rather the grave danger of an imminent invasion by the British on some pretext for such.'[41]

De Valera was hardly out of tune with nationalist sentiment. But, although de Valera turned down Churchill's offer, the American entry into the war did lead to a different type of Irish neutrality; now, a neutrality that already favoured the Allies did so much more. The recently declassified British official history of MI5's Irish section gives, in effect, the founding text of what, in Ireland, is known as the 'pragmatic pro-neutrality argument'.[42] As Professor Christopher Andrew makes clear in his introduction, the document is an anti-Churchill critique. It argues that Irish neutrality on balance helped Britain; Dr Garret FitzGerald has suggested that it was hardly neutrality, properly understood, at all.[43] The thesis essentially is that de Valera could not have brought a partitioned Ireland into the war on the British side without creating massive internal Irish conflict. In that event, Ireland's contribution of over 40,000 men and women to the British armed forces, and many more to its industrial labour force, could not have been made. Meanwhile, potential intelligence problems were sorted out by an unusually high degree of cooperation—a remarkable level, indeed, given traditional Anglo-Irish tensions. It was not always relaxed cooperation. Hugh Trevor-Roper, a British intelligence officer, relaxing on a Dublin break, was arrested by Irish police. But, on the whole, British and Irish cooperation was good.

But such an account avoids two key issues. In a context in which a move to end neutrality was linked to a firm British statement of support for Irish unity, it might not have been beyond de Valera's political capacity to persuade a majority of the electorate.[44] More particularly, de Valera, after America's entry into the war, would have had the advantage of being on the probable winning side and the advantage that the USA would probably support Irish unity. Secondly, this MI5 document does not face up to the full strategic thrust of Churchill's argument that the Irish Treaty ports were vital to British security. Berehaven, after all, was beyond the range of German dive-bombers and long-range fighter air cover; it would have offered secure anchorage for British ships waiting to counter German raiders trying to attack the Atlantic convoys. With facilities in Ireland, the effective air reconnaissance essential to anti-submarine warfare would have been much easier. Denial of the Irish ports to the Royal Navy was reckoned by the Admiralty to have cost 368 ships and 5,070 lives during the war.[45] The leading Irish opposition politician James Dillon wrote: 'I could never forget that the west coast of Ireland was littered with the bodies of English seamen who had been bringing supplies to us.'[46] As the MI5 document concludes:

> There can be very little doubt that when de Valera decided to adopt the policy of neutrality, entailing as it did, the refusal to grant the British navy the use of the Eire ports, he provided the British people with an overwhelming case for the maintenance of partition, which he himself would so much have liked to see ended.

It is this same point that Malcolm MacDonald made directly to de Valera on 21 June 1940.

It might be useful to place this MI5 document against another later report. In May 1947 Lord Rugby (previously Sir John Maffey, the wartime British representative in Dublin) completed, with the help of a distinguished intelligence official, Dick White, a further British survey of the working of Irish neutrality. Rugby noted that Ireland was quite separate from the case of other neutral countries such as Portugal and Switzerland, whose neutrality gave advantages to both sides. In his view, 'Irish neutrality had been useful only to our enemies'. The survey covered naval, air, and security aspects. The Irish, said Rugby, had been given 'full liberty of choice': but would Ireland side with its neighbours against Hitler? The strategic weakness created when Ireland had not done so was quite startling.

Rugby here inserted a rather grim passage:

> It is obvious that when Britain is waging a war in Europe she can, as in the past, gain great strength and security from bases in the Irish coastline. Indeed, our island containing 50 million fed and maintained by supplies coming across the Atlantic Ocean would seem doomed to perish without these facilities. It was no doubt fortunate that the enemy did not fully develop plans for Atlantic warfare on a calculation of the advantages afforded to them by the neutrality of Eire.

The German aeroplanes that attacked Belfast—creating in one night the greatest loss of life of any British city outside London except Coventry—massed over Eire: at least thirty-four British airmen were interned in Ireland, but others had died trying to avoid internment in the effort to get home. Much was owed to German incompetence and failure to grasp the scale of their opportunity: German intelligence (if not the German foreign office) invested in the IRA, absurdly, 'as if Dublin Castle still existed'. Maffey's most fascinating comment is of some subtlety: 'If the Germans had left politics alone and been content to operate an underground network of agents for espionage in Eire, there is no doubt Eire neutrality would have afforded immense possibilities.' Here, Maffey is suggesting that the Germans should have worked with the Anglophobia of large sections of the ruling party and the Irish elites; by pitching their tent with the underground subversives of the IRA, the Germans missed their main opportunity. The loss of sailors had been heavy and, but for Northern Ireland, the situation would have been much worse. But it was accepted that Ireland refused to allow Germany any base to operate against Britain and that by the end of 1943 the level of cooperation was high.[47]

10

'Saving them from themselves'

Their [Irish] conduct will never be forgiven in this war by the British people...we must save these people from themselves.

(Churchill to Attlee, 5 May 1943)[1]

But, of course, the strategic significance of Northern Ireland was also enhanced by the American intervention in the war. The province was to be a crucial base for US soldiers—some of whom appeared to have been secretly stationed there even before the US formal entry into the war. In the summer of 1942, Churchill, Lloyd George, and John Andrews, the Northern Ireland premier, dined in London. The broad context was London's desire to improve the efficiency of Belfast's industrial contribution to the war, but the chat ranged over historical matters. Andrews was told that both Lloyd George and Churchill wanted to see a united Ireland more closely linked to Britain and they felt that the north could play a key role in that—but he was also told that neither Churchill nor Lloyd George regretted his support for the principle of consent. One irony was passed over at this lunch: Andrews's minister in charge of public security was William Grant, one of the shipyard workers who had almost turned over Churchill's car in Belfast in 1912. Churchill was also well aware that loyalist recruitment in Northern Ireland was not impressive. There was, of course, now no competitive recruitment with nationalists, as had happened in the First World War: on the contrary, as nationalists stayed at home, unionists feared that they would step into jobs vacated by loyalists who took the path of voluntary recruitment.

Churchill, however, remained more hostile to Irish neutrality. At a Cabinet meeting on 22 February 1943, Churchill surprised his colleagues by announcing that he proposed to settle the Irish question 'now during the war'. When a number of ministers resisted this idea, Churchill retreated. L. S. Amery noted in his diary: 'Ulster will bitterly resent any idea of trying to persuade her to come in under de Valera if the latter should at the last moment lend a base or two to America.'[2] Of course, any serious practitioner of *realpolitik* or, indeed, any serious strategist for a united Ireland would have been looking for such an opportunity. But de Valera was not. Churchill, as always, underestimated the strength of anti-British sentiment in nationalist Ireland. When Andrews resigned as prime minister of Northern Ireland in the same month, Churchill wrote that, but for the north, Britain would 'have been confronted with slavery and death, and the light which shone so strongly throughout the world would have been extinguished'.[3] In May 1943 he talked of saving the Irish from themselves.

It was a striking way of putting it, but not one that would have been appreciated in Ireland itself. On 14 March 1944 Churchill told the House of Commons that the restrictions of travel between Britain and all of Ireland were merely part of the first step designed to isolate southern Ireland from the outside world in the critical period of the war that was approaching. Another part of that step, the prime minister said, was designed to isolate Britain from southern Ireland, where the Axis agents had been receiving important information about the allied war effort. Churchill said the initiative in the latest Irish developments had been taken by the United States because of the danger to American armed forces from Axis missions in Dublin, but the British government fully supported the request for the removal of these missions. Churchill acknowledged that the step was a painful one. He was well aware of the 'large numbers of Irishmen who are fighting so bravely in our armed forces...they have kept alive the martial honour of the Irish race'. But he added: 'There is also the future to consider. If a catastrophe were to occur to the allied armies which could be traced to the retention of the German and Japanese representatives in Dublin, a gulf would be opened between Great Britain on the one hand and southern Ireland on the other, which even generations would not budge.'[4]

The *New York Times* editorial strongly supported Churchill's announcement. 'Specifically it must be intended to keep the Germans from knowing where, when, in what force and by what force and by what means, we shall attempt to land on the French coast. There would be bitter resentment if the answers came from Dublin.'[5] Americans would not support a British invasion of Ireland. They had kind thoughts about the Irish as St Patrick's Day approached. The British had shown great patience, and there was now no danger that their policy on this point would change.

On 19 March 1944 Churchill told Roosevelt he would propose stopping ships going from Ireland to Portugal and Spain, as it might compromise the D-Day landings.[6] American (OSS) intelligence confirmed that the Germans were gaining a good deal of useful intelligence in Ireland. Roosevelt unsuccessfully requested that Ireland break diplomatic relations with Germany and Italy.[7] In March 1944 Churchill publicly described retention of Axis facilities in Dublin as 'substantial disservice to the Allied cause'. It is worth noting, however, that Irish weather stations in the west of Ireland freely supplied the Allies with helpful data in the lead-up to the invasion. In February 1945 the Irish government allowed the British to establish a radar station on their territory, but even so the UK government decided to make no effort to help the Irish 'to get on the bandwagon'—as others were doing—with a late declaration of war on Hitler.[8] As victory in the world war neared, the Northern Irish government naturally moved to consolidate its position. This was, after all, the perfect moment. The prime minister of Northern Ireland, Sir Basil Brooke, asked for help in keeping southern Irish labour out of his part of Ireland. The problem of 'migrant labour'—that is, emigrants from the south and Donegal—had much concerned the Unionists since 1942, and in February 1945 Sir Basil Brooke told his Cabinet that he would raise the matter with Winston Churchill in March.[9]

Brooke said that the social services which were being instituted in Ulster on the same lines as those in England, with the higher wages, were going to attract a lot of labour from the Free State and there was a real danger that Ulster in a short time would lose its political colour. The prime minister agreed and said it ought to be done now, during the war. The prime minister dilated on Ulster's services to the empire – she had left her foot in the door so it could not be closed. If all Ireland had belonged to the Free State, the entrance to the Mersey and the Clyde would have been impossible. We had run it pretty fine as it was.[10]

As if the Ulster Unionist position was not strong enough, de Valera offered condolences to the German legation on the death of Hitler on 3 May 1945. The Labour journal, *New Statesman*, in disbelief, commented on de Valera's policy:

And on Thursday, 3 May 1945 (not 225 AD, but 1945 AD) the *Times* reported that Mr de Valera called on the German Minister in Dublin to express his condolences on Mr Hitler's death. Mr de Valera in the previous week must have seen the photographs of Dachau and Buchenwald. He is a Roman Catholic and the head of a state which purports to back his whole policy and actions upon the Christian religion and the Catholic Church. In Mr de Valera's condolences we can see the degradation of civilised beliefs which made Hitler and the Nazi regime possible.[11]

Actually, the Irish government had banned the British parliamentary delegation report on Buchenwald produced in March 1945, though, of course, de Valera was well aware of its contents. A few days later Churchill turned, in his victory speech, to the role of Dublin—the pain left by his remarks has not been entirely extinguished to this day. Churchill declared:

Owing to the actions of Mr de Valera, so much at variance with the temper and instincts of southern Irishmen, who hastened to the battle-field to prove that ancient valour, the approaches which the southern ports and airfields could so easily have guarded, were closed by the hostile aircraft and U-boats.

This was, indeed, a deadly moment in our life and had it not been for the loyalty and friendship of Northern Ireland, we should have been forced to come to close quarters with Mr de Valera, or perish forever from the earth.

However, with a restraint and poise to which I venture to say history will find few parallels, His Majesty's government never laid a hand upon them, though at times it would have been quite easy and natural. We left the de Valera government to frolic with the Germans and later with the Japanese representatives to their hearts' content.[12]

Churchill attempted to soften the tone of his speech by making warm reference to three members of the 'Irish race' who had won VCs. Unfortunately for the premier, the examples chosen were not likely to have an effect on Irish public opinion. John Patrick Kennealy, apparently a Tipperary-born agricultural labourer, had, in fact, been born Leslie Robinson in the north of England and was a pupil of King Edward Grammar School. After joining the Royal Artillery at the start of the war, Robinson got bored and became involved in various scrapes. After one of these, he was held at the Irish Guards detention centre. After his release, Robinson absconded and fell in with a group of Irish migrant labourers, one of whom, John Patrick Kennealy, had returned to Ireland while leaving his papers behind. British intelligence was very alarmed by these cases. They knew that there was a trade in these papers, but the Germans never seem to have taken advantage of it,[13] while a great British war hero did. Robinson took these papers, reinvented himself, and joined the Irish Guards, who had impressed him during his period of detention. He won his VC for twice—over a two-day period—charging 200 Germans firing a Bren gun from the hip, inflicting heavy casualties in the closing stages of the Tunisian campaign. A wartime hero to be sure, but quite without any relatives in Tipperary to hail his bravery.

Captain E. S. Fogarty Fegan had been born in South Sea, Hampshire, of Irish parentage in 1891—a naval officer who had served in the First World War and with the Australian Royal Navy in the inter-war period. In November 1940 Fogarty Fegan ordered his ship, the *Jervis Bay*, formerly a liner, to make for the German warship that threatened his Atlantic convoy. Despite being outgunned, crippled, and in flames, the *Jervis Bay* held the enemy's fire for nearly an hour before she went down. Fogarty Fegan's brave self-sacrifice was declared to have saved the lives of many merchant seamen. At least thirty-three of the thirty-eight merchant men with the convoy were saved. But Fogarty Fegan's family had been too long out of Ireland for Churchill's words to have any resonance in that country.

Finally, Churchill mentioned the case of Lieutenant Commander Eugene Kingsmith Esmonde. Unlike Churchill's other two heroes, the Esmondes were, indeed, a well-known Irish political family: Sir Thomas Grattan Esmonde had even briefly joined Sinn Fein from 1907 to 1908. Eugene Esmonde was a scion of the junior branch of this Wexford landed family. Esmonde was the leader of a squadron of six Fairey Swordfish torpedo-carrying planes that, in 1942, attacked three big German warships—the *Scharnhorst*, the *Gniesenau*, and the *Prince Eugen*. Embarking on this mission, Esmonde and his men must have known that they would be likely to die. The German ships were attempting to slip through the Straits of Dover to a German port, with strong fighter cover and with formidable naval protection. Not one of the six planes returned. Eugene Esmonde, while being born near Barnsley, was educated at the elite Jesuit boarding school Clongowes in Ireland. However, the political associations of Eugene Esmonde were hardly attractive in de Valera's Ireland. His father, Dr John Esmonde, had been Redmondite MP for Tipperary in 1910–15. He died of an illness contracted at a recruiting meeting.[14] One son, John Lymbrick Esmonde, was elected after his father's death for the same seat while serving in the British army.[15] He served in the forces that put down the Easter Rising and subsequently became a Fine Gael TD. His half-brother was Eugene Esmonde, who won the VC in 1942. Here was Churchill's final piece of bad luck; the Esmondes were precisely the type of established Catholic family who disliked de Valera's government, and de Valera was well aware of their dislike.

The press reaction was rather complex. Churchill created so much anger in Ireland that he was even attacked for not mentioning his Irish generals, who were of course, of Protestant and unionist background and, in the case of Alanbrooke, actually an Orangeman. Churchill believed he had acted tactfully in this respect, but there was so much anger in Dublin he was not given the benefit of the doubt. In the Dublin press G. A. Quinn replied angrily, reminding Churchill that de Valera had been determined that this country should not be used as a base for attack upon England:

> It is a strange fact that among the Irish heroes supplied to him by his advisers on this occasion, none thought to remind Mr Churchill of the Irish nationality of Montgomery and Alexander, who played no small part in a glorious victory but then perhaps the English people themselves do not, nor would they want to know it, now that the war is over.[16]

A provincial nationalist paper, the *People's Press*, admitted:

> As Mr Churchill sees it and probably, as most Englishmen see it, at a deadly moment in the life of England, Northern Ireland showed 'loyalty and friendship', while Eire refused her the ports and airfields which could have kept her sea approaches from being closed by hostile aircraft and u-boats. But for the help given by Northern Ireland, England would have had to choose between seizing the ports and perishing forever from the earth. It is a distressing thought that but for partition, Ireland would have had to choose between invasion and participation in the war. The 26 counties were let stay out because the six counties were let in. There is still a more chastening question: is perpetual partition the price that has to be paid for six years of neutrality? Are Eire and Northern Ireland to remain at close quarters and never to become one?[17]

On 18 May the *Irish Times* editorial responded:

> It was only to be expected that, in his broadcast to the British nation commemorating the Allies' crushing victory in the war, Mr Winston Churchill would make some remarks concerning Ireland's neutrality. There is no doubt that Mr de Valera's decision to keep this country outside the world conflict came as a grievous disappointment not only to the British, but also to the people of the whole Commonwealth. Few outside this island remembered, or bothered to remember, that this decision had been reached some time before the war broke out. It also is true that, particularly in the early days of the war, Ireland's existence as a neutral country hampered the defence of Great Britain. The loss of the Irish ports, which had been handed back to Mr de Valera not very long

before the outbreak of the struggle, was felt keenly by the admiralty; and Mr Churchill was fully entitled, speaking to his people in the first glowing flush of victory, to criticise the attitude of the Irish government. Nevertheless, we have an uneasy feeling that possibly he went just a little too far. Admittedly, he tempered his biting references to the Taoiseach by a warm tribute to those citizens of the Irish State who gave such noble service to the Allied cause in the ranks of His Majesty's forces; but his suggestion that Mr de Valera's government spent its time during the war in 'frolics' with the Germans and Japanese was, to say the least of it, a slight overstatement.

Within a few days de Valera replied:

> Mr Churchill makes it clear that in certain circumstances, he would have violated our neutrality and that he would justify his action by Britain's necessity...if accepted [this] would mean that Britain's necessity would become a moral code and when this necessity became sufficiently great, other people's rights were not to count...That is precisely why we have the disastrous succession of wars...
>
> Mr Churchill is fiercely proud of his nation's perseverance against heavy odds. But we in this island are still prouder of our people's perseverance for freedom through all the centuries...I regret that it is not to this nobler purpose that Mr Churchill is lending his hand, rather than, by the abuse of a people who have done him no wrong, trying to find in a crisis like the present, excuse for continuing the mutilation of our country...Meanwhile, even as a small partitioned nation, we shall go on and strive to play our part in the world, continue unswervingly to work for the cause of true freedom and for peace and understanding between all nations.[18]

Sir John Maffey, the British representative in Dublin, was exasperated.[19] He felt that Churchill had given de Valera a chance to behave like a serious leader. After de Valera's reply, Churchill told his son that he had spoken in the 'heat of the moment'. He added: 'The idea of Eire sitting at our feet without giving us a hand annoyed me.'[20] In his war memoirs he glossed over the episode.

The conventional wisdom is that Churchill's attack on de Valera backfired: that it was an example of the hangover of an imperialist colonialist mentality. Sir John Maffey's irritation is perhaps the most suggestive—the British representative in Dublin was annoyed because it allowed de Valera to project his narrow nationalist story before his own people. This is a fair analysis. De Valera's reply was very popular in Ireland. However, it is worth pointing out that the Irish ambassador in Washington, Robert Brennan, sought to have this speech of de Valera's on the record in Congress, but could not find 'one of our old friends' to do so.

In fact, de Valera's reply had little wider impact. The argument that a British invasion of Ireland or, more particularly, a seizure of the Treaty ports—if necessary *in extremis* to defeat Hitler—would have been an act of a similar sort to those aggressive actions of Hitler which had led to the world war had little resonance in 1945. Dr Paul Murray has, however, with some force, recently written:

> Churchill's entire argument rested in the postulate…that self-defined British interests enforced an absolute right of enforcement, no matter what the consequences might be for other nations. De Valera exposed the weakness of Churchill's position with deadly effect, striking where he was most vulnerable, and assuming the role of political moralist more convincingly than his adversary had been able to do.[21]

The difficulty with this argument is that it reduces the issues at stake in 1940 to one issue—British self-determination or Irish self-determination—when, in fact, they were considerably broader, involving the survival of large swathes of humanity. To those who knew how little interest Ireland had in May–June 1940 in the ending of partition, de Valera's references to partition were equally unimpressive. Then there is the case of the US representative in Dublin, David Gray: Gray believed the captured German documents showed that Ireland had a tacit relationship of support of Germany in exchange for an end to partition. Gray found nothing to fault in Churchill's speech. Churchill, though, appears to have felt his tone was bitter, even spiteful, and a matter for regret. His own essay on the Treaty had talked about 'perils inherent in the moment' of victory; the 'harder battle' was the battle with 'oneself'; did he feel he had failed by his own standard?

It is clear that Churchill continued to be troubled by the reflection that he had not lived up to his own standards of magnanimity and statesmanship. He was particularly disturbed by the idea that he had failed to learn the lesson taught by the 'great Castlereagh'—the second Marquess of Londonderry—and thus a very distant kinsman and Britain's greatest Foreign Secretary. 'We have the great Castlereagh—so ignorantly traduced—after a generation of struggle with France, threatening in the day of triumph to go to war with his Prussian and Russian allies rather than have France dismembered or oppressed.'[22] For Churchill, the greatest error was to indulge in the emotions of revenge and spite. Post-conflict he was soon to go out of his way to send warm messages to Dublin.

Four decades later, Churchill's assessment of Irish neutrality resurfaced again as an issue in practical politics. When Margaret Thatcher was being ushered by her officials towards the signing of the Anglo-Irish Agreement of 1985, she experienced several moments of doubt. She did not really know how she could trust *any* Irish government. This led her to ask on 14 February for an assessment of Irish neutrality in the Second World War—how many British lives had been lost? The task was delegated to E. C. 'Ted' Hallett, a Foreign Office official. Hallett allowed that the Chiefs of Staff had told the Cabinet in the late summer of 1940 that 'by the use of Berehaven we should be able to operate a further 180 miles west than is possible for any bases in the UK'.[23] But it also drew attention to the view of the US Chief of Staff, General Marshall, that the decisive factor here was German control of the French coast, which, in effect, reduced the significance of Berehaven as the Germans were so well placed to threaten shipping around the south coast of Ireland. Hallett argued—not unreasonably—that it was impossible to give a figure for the number of British lives lost as a specific result of Irish neutrality, as so many factors were involved. The report does not mention, however, that the Admiralty files do contain a precise figure: 5,070 dead sailors. Hallett's report stresses areas of mutual cooperation, as does the Maffey–White document of 1947–8; but it does not include the darker themes of that document—the darkest of all, of course, being Maffey's mature assessment that the Germans would have done better to work with the grain of Anglophobia of Ireland's ruling elites rather than flirt with the IRA. Suitably reassured, Margaret Thatcher felt able to move ahead towards the Anglo-Irish Agreement, though she was soon to be greatly disappointed by the security cooperation obtained and later condemned it as her one major error of policy.

Pushed out of office by the Labour landslide of 1945, a reflective Churchill returned to the theme of Ireland in his 1947 essay 'The Dream'. It opens with a moment of recollection.

> One foggy afternoon in November 1947 I was painting in my studio at the cottage down the hill at Chartwell. Someone had sent me a portrait of my father, which had been painted for one of the Belfast conservative clubs about the time of his visit to Ulster in the home rule crisis of 1886. The canvas had been badly torn, and though I am very shy of painting human faces, I thought I would try to make a copy of it.[24]

The story then fades into a dreamlike sequence, in which Churchill's father questions him about developments in world history since his death. Naturally, Randolph asked about Ireland:

> What happened to Ireland? Did they get home rule?
> The South got it but Ulster stayed with us.
> Are the South a republic?
> No one knows what they are. They are neither in nor out of the empire. But they are much more friendly to us than they used to be. They have built up a cultured Roman Catholic system in the South. There has been no anarchy or confusion. They are getting more happy and prosperous. The bitter past is fading.
> 'Ah,' he said, 'how vexed the Tories were with me when I observed there was no English statesman who had not had his hour of home rule'. Then, after a pause, 'What about the home rule meaning 'Rome rule'?
> It certainly does, but they like it. And the Catholic Church has now become a great champion of individual liberty.[25]

The point here is that Churchill rapidly found a new dividing line after the defeat of Nazism. Either a system preserved the essentials of individual freedom or it did not. By this standard, Ireland passed the test. Irish Catholics and Irish Americans were enthusiastic anti-communists. In 1948 the new inter-party government in Ireland declared itself to be a republic. It was a surprise move, somewhat chaotically executed. Churchill, at this moment, clearly made every effort to restrain himself and his use of language. He was not going to repeat the error of the victory speech. Churchill responded in parliament:

Some of the important elements, which, a few years ago, formed the British Empire, are falling away like autumn leaves, over wide areas in many parts of the globe. It is a fashionable mood in these areas to sever connections with the Crown and to retain only such association with this island as carries with it material advantage. Take first the case of Southern Ireland or Eire. I must confess that I was astonished to learn some weeks ago of Mr Costello's decision to sever the last link with the Crown which even Mr de Valera had deemed it necessary to preserve. I have for many years held a consistent view about Ireland. I expressed it nearly a quarter of a century ago, in 1925 or 1926, when I was invited, as Conservative Chancellor of the Exchequer, to address the Ulster Unionists in Belfast. Perhaps I may read for a moment what I then said:

'I have declared again and again that neither by threats, or violence, or by intrigue nor yet by unfair economic pressure shall the people of Ulster be compelled against their wish to sever the ties which bind them to the United Kingdom or be forced, unless by their own free and unfettered choice, to join another system of government.'

I was therefore glad to hear the answer which the prime minister has just given to my Right Hon. friend and to show that in this matter at any rate there is no difference between us. On that occasion, a quarter of a century ago, in the Ulster Hall, I added the following:

'I may cherish the hope that some day all Ireland will be loyal, will be loyal because it is free, will be united because it is loyal, and will be united within itself and united to the British Empire.'

Strange as it may seem, I still cherish that dream.

I shall always hope that some day there will be a united Ireland, but at the same time, that Ulster or the northern counties will never be com-pelled against their wishes to enter a Dublin parliament. They should be courted. They should not be raped. As the minister responsible for carrying out the cabinet decisions embodied in the Irish Treaty of 1921, I have watched with contentment and pleasure the orderly Christian society, with a grace and culture of its own and a flash of sport thrown in, which this quarter of a century has seen built up in Southern Ireland, in spite of many gloomy predictions. I well know the grievous injury which Southern Irish neutrality and the denial of the Southern Irish ports inflicted upon us in the recent war, but I always adhered to the policy that nothing, save British existence and survival, should lead us to regain those ports by force of arms, because we had already given them up.

Churchill then moved on to discuss the Irishmen who had fought in the British forces. He mentioned, in particular, Brendan Finucane, the exceptional young RAF pilot who died in 1942 after his plane crash-landed in the sea off the French coast after being hit by anti-aircraft fire—one of Jim Phelan's 'hard eyed young fellows' in Air Force blue. Finucane's father had taken part in the 1916 Rising and he, unlike the other VCs mentioned in 1945, might have been considered to be more authentically Irish. It is worth noting that Finucane's father had joined the RAF as a radio operator in 1939.[26]

In the end we got through without this step. I rejoice that no new blood was shed between the British and Irish peoples. I shall never forget—none of us can ever forget—the superb gallantry of the scores of thousands of southern Irishmen who fought as volunteers in the British army, and of the famous Victoria Crosses which eight of them gained by their outstanding valour. If ever I feel a bitter feeling rising in me in my heart about the Irish the hand of heroes like Finucane seems to stretch out to soothe it away. Moreover, since the war, great antagonisms have grown up in this world against communist tyranny and Soviet aggression. These have made new ties of unity of thought and of sympathy between the Irish and the British peoples, and indeed throughout the British islands, and they deeply stir Irish feelings. The Catholic Church has ranged itself among the defenders and champions of the liberty and the dignity of the individual. It seemed to me that the passage of time might lead to the unity of Ireland itself in the only way in which that unity can be achieved, namely, by a unison of Irish hearts.

There can, of course, be no question of coercing Ulster, but if she were wooed and won of her own free will and consent, I, personally, would regard such an event as a blessing for the whole of the British empire and also for the civilised world. It was indeed strange and, if I may say so, characteristically Irish that this moment above all others should be

selected by the Dublin government for breaking that last tenuous connection with the Crown and proclaiming themselves a foreign republic.
This decision may well prevent for ever that united Ireland, the dream
of which is cherished by so many ardent Irish patriots. In this way
Mr Costello and his colleagues have constituted themselves the authors
of permanent partition. It is they who have dug a gulf between Southern
and Northern Ireland deeper than ever before. They have made a gulf
which is unbridgeable except by physical force, the use of which I regret
to see Mr de Valera in his latest speeches does not exclude.

We cannot tell at what point our present decline will stop, but I cannot
conceive it within the bounds of possibility that any British parliament
would drive the people of Ulster out of the United Kingdom and force
them to become the citizens of a foreign state against their will. So far as
we can tell from the newspapers, from the prime minister's reply on
Tuesday and his answer just given to my Right Hon. friend across the
Floor of the House, the socialist government seem to have acted rightly in
bringing home to the Dublin government the many serious injuries they
would inflict upon themselves and upon Irishmen in this country and in
many parts of the world by forcing us to regard them legally as foreigners
and aliens.[27]

Of course, in Dublin only the references to Irish unity had resonance.
On 29 October 1948 Harold Nicolson, along with the British ambas-
sador, Lord Rugby, dined in the Kildare Street Club in Dublin with the
Irish premier John A. Costello and his foreign minister, Sean Mac-
Bride. Costello and MacBride were delighted by 'Winston having said
he longed for a united Ireland'. Walter Elliott, a Conservative MP who
was present, replied: 'Make no mistake, what Winston meant was an
Ireland united under the Crown.'[28]

There is an interesting footnote to this intervention in parliament.
Shortly afterwards, Churchill spoke to J. W. Dulanty after the annual
Remembrance Day ceremony at the Cenotaph in London. After the
Irish diplomat had laid a wreath in memory of those killed in the two
world wars, Churchill approached Dulanty and said he was glad to see
him at the ceremony. Churchill added: 'I said a few words in Parliament the other day about your country because I still hope for a
united Ireland. You must get these fellows in the North in, though you
can't do it by force.' Before Churchill said goodbye, he told Mr

Dulanty: 'There is not, and never was, any bitterness in my heart towards your country.'[29] On May 10 1949 he repeated his criticisms of Irish neutrality to Dulanty, but praised Ireland for keeping the secret of D-Day, which 'they knew all about'.[30]

The declaration of the republic had, in Churchill's words, dug a 'ditch', opened a 'gulf', between the two parts of Ireland.[31] This was the real significance of the events. Ireland's status was in a sense substantively unchanged.

> I do not wish to exaggerate the significance of the step which the Dublin government are resolved to take. From the point of view of their relations with this country, it is not of a very novel character. Mr de Valera's External Relations Act did not prevent Irish neutrality in war, in mortal war, or the denial to us of the use of the ports on which our life sometimes depended. The External Relations Act did not prevent Mr de Valera's government from having an Irish minister in Berlin and in Rome, and German and Italian ministers in Dublin. I have no doubt whatever that he only retained the use of the symbol of the Crown for matters of domestic and local convenience. Therefore, it seems that the severing of this link implies no real or material change—whatever may be the sentimental issues involved—in the position which has been accepted and endured for the last ten years or more.[32]

There was, perhaps, one further moment of discomfort. He was surprised at Attlee's announcement that Eire was neither to be a member of the Commonwealth nor 'in the category of foreign countries'. Churchill said he was not bound by it—but on return to office left it as it was.[33] In January 1951 Churchill irritated Basil Brooke over lunch in London: 'He was obviously thinking of a united Ireland, I tried to disabuse him.'[34]

In May 1951, over a few drinks, Churchill told Frederick Boland, who succeeded Dulanty as ambassador to Britain, that he had wanted Ireland to see one of his horses, *Canyon Kid*, run in the Irish Derby, but that the horse had died of heart failure. 'You know I have had many invitations to visit Ulster but I have refused them all. I don't want to go there at all. I would much rather go to southern Ireland.

Maybe I'll buy another horse with an entry in the Irish derby.'[35] The dead horse, alas, became a metaphor for Anglo-Irish relations. A symbol: in 1954 Churchill's nag, *Red Winter*, won the Ulster derby.[36] The boozy Boland chat was all very amicable but empty of any real political content. Basil Brooke, the prime minister in Northern Ireland—the same Basil Brooke who had supported Irish unity if it was the price of defeating Hitler—declared (erroneously) in October 1951 that no parliament, even the one in London, could take away Stormont's powers.[37] Churchill, in the Conservative election manifesto, declared that the 'destiny' of Northern Ireland was 'forever bound up with Britain and the British Empire'.[38] On 22 November 1951, now back in power, Churchill warmly received Basil Brooke at Downing Street and the talk was all of military contracts for Belfast. On 3 May 1951, Brooke saw Churchill in Downing Street, and this time the conversation was more satisfactory to the Ulster PM; indeed, on 11 May 1951, Churchill issued a strong statement of support for the Unionist candidate in the Derry by-election.[39]

In 1951 also, Churchill's cousin Shane Leslie lectured in Chicago. There was little hope of Irish unity, even though he supported it. He called instead for 'non-political committees' to be appointed by the two Irish governments to discuss practical issues in the Bank of Ireland building in Dublin. Even this minimalistic suggestion was not taken up either in Dublin or in Belfast.

In September 1953 Churchill stood at the doorstep of 10 Downing Street and shook hands with Eamon de Valera. The *London Letter* of the *Irish Times* drew attention to the remarkable fact that the two men had never met before. Both men were now nearing the end of the long spans of leadership—in de Valera's case rather longer than Churchill. He had, after all, been prime minister from 1932 to 1948, while Churchill's longest spell had been from 1939 to 1945. It might be said that both men became, in effect, political adults in the nineteenth century. But this nineteenth-century heritage did little to unite them.

The truth is that de Valera was in certain respects a typical twentieth-century revolutionary, a survivor of a period of turmoil,

Fig. 10. De Valera and Churchill meeting, 10 Downing Street, 1953. Patrician embodiments of competing nationalisms?

who sedulously exploited the aspirations of the revolution in order to cling tenaciously to power for decades. Churchill's life reflected rather more the chance defeats and victories of a politician in a liberal democracy, albeit a liberal democracy threatened, in his heroic moment, by a fascist dictatorship. But Mary C. Bromage is correct to detect in the two men a 'patrician love' of country and national history. This is what they truly had in common: ally this to a common anti-communism and we have the basis for the genial luncheon party at 10 Downing Street.[40] De Valera talked about mathematics—to Churchill's incomprehension—but pleased his host by saying he would not have left the Commonwealth in 1948. De Valera's own note of the occasion said: 'I spoke first of a possible unification of the country. To this he replied that they could never put out the people of the Six Counties, so long as they wished to remain with them. There were also political factors which no Conservative could ignore.'[41]

Eamon de Valera certainly failed to alert him to issues of anti-Catholic discrimination in Northern Ireland. A few months later the fate of northern Catholics was raised by the nationalist MP and wartime pro-German internee Cahir Healy in parliament. [42] Churchill was slow to see the problems of anti-Catholic discrimination in the north: 'Mr Churchill replied to Mr Healy saying that he thought these issues were all settled happily a long time ago . . .'.[43] Churchill's reply was genial—his cousin Shane Leslie was in friendly contact with Healy and attempting to act as a link between Healy and Churchill[44]—but quite without substance.

On 16 December 1955 Churchill blithely spoke of a growing 'measure of goodwill' between the Republic of Ireland and Northern Ireland that would not be within the power of a small minority to alter. Accepting the freedom of the cities of Belfast and Londonderry, he told a Mansion House dinner he welcomed the Irish Republic as a member of the United Nations: 'The passage of years and a general broadening of thought will show many points on which we shall be in agreement.'[45] In particular, the Irish Republic and Britain would find themselves in the closest accord in fighting communism. The old battle cries were fading at last. Even so, Dublin managed one last insult. De Valera described Churchill as having been for a long time an enemy of Ireland and dangerous, and sent the 'hopelessly inappropriate' Frank Aiken—anti-Protestant, sectarian Anglophobe—as official representative to Churchill's state funeral.[46] Churchill himself would have hated rather more the *Irish Times* obituary, which dated his long 'unhappy' relationship 'with Ireland to his arrival in Dublin Castle at the age of two'.[47]

However, John E. Sayers, one of his wartime personal staff, was editor of the *Belfast Telegraph*, and his language was rather warmer. He noted that 'the Anglo-Saxon race which sired Winston Churchill still has its ancient power, not to overcome with missiles, but the power to shape and temper the human spirit, to hold aloft the flame of liberty'.[48] Sayers went on to say that he was sure that Churchill would have welcomed the end of the 'cold war'[49] on the island of Ireland signalled by the recent O'Neill–Lemass meetings between the premiers in Belfast and Dublin. Indeed, Charles J. Haughey, the Republic's Minister of Agriculture and son-in-law of Sean Lemass, visited Belfast in February and denounced those who lived still in the mindset of 'fifty years ago', and predicted 'fifty wonderful years' ahead for Ireland, north and south. It was not to be. Within three years, the era of the 'Troubles' opened. It was a typical Churchillian illusion, but this time he could not be blamed for its failure.

Conclusion

It is no accident that Mary C. Bromage in her *Churchill and Ireland* noted Churchill's citation of Emerson's castigation of a 'foolish consistency' as 'the hobgoblin of little minds'.[1] Bromage found it a comfort as she grappled with the many twists and turns of Churchill's Irish rhetoric and policy. It has to be confessed that Churchill is not always the best guide to his own positions on the Irish question.

In 1928 he told a young friend James Scrymegeour-Wedderburn (later the eleventh Earl of Dundee) that he had resisted the paramilitary mobilization of the Ulster Unionists longer than anyone in the Cabinet. Similarly, he claimed that he had been the last Cabinet member to acknowledge the need for negotiation with the IRA in 1921.

In fact, as early as 1913, Churchill had insisted that the threats and illegality of the Ulster Unionists did not rule out negotiation and compromise with them. As for the IRA, he urged talks in May 1921, some weeks before a majority of the relevant Cabinet committee.

In many instances, Churchill's Irish stances fitted rather suspiciously all too neatly with his contemporary political ambitions. His embrace of home rule after 1906 made him, as a recent Tory convert, much more acceptable to his new party and his colleagues in the Liberal government. His Bradford assault on the Ulster Unionists in March 1914 was certainly again determined, in part, by a renewed desire to win popularity in the Liberal Party following the controversy over naval estimates. The subsequent more unionist tone of his pronouncements—though it includes, of course, the effective alliance with Michael Collins—was also compatible with his British political ambitions, including his return to high office under the Tories in 1925.

Who is the real Churchill? The Churchill who insisted on the importance of the Bolshevik–Sinn Fein link in 1920 or the Churchill who later told his cousin (Clare Sheridan) not to confuse the Russian with the Irish revolutionaries, who were essentially Catholic, patriotic, and pure in their intention?[2] Some of his contradictions are purely conjunctural—a desperate attempt to make the Treaty negotiation succeed. He told Henry Wilson that a return to war was likely if negotiations failed (Wilson did not believe him), while he told J. W. Dulanty, a key Irish figure, that it was unlikely. At the end of November 1921 he may have hinted to Tim Healy that the Boundary Commission might reduce Northern Ireland to three counties; by 1924 he insisted that his view had always been that the Boundary Commission could make only small changes. In the modern era, all this recalls nothing so much as the ambiguous language over IRA decommissioning employed by Tony Blair to secure the Good Friday Agreement. Churchill himself forgot about IRA decommissioning, which was a key British demand in late 1920. Contrary to popular belief, there was no actual clear-cut mendacity here—just a certain ambiguity on important cognate details of the settlement though not the predominant terms of the settlement itself.

The view of Churchill's Irish policy as being primarily motivated by a self-serving opportunism has, in recent years, been linked to another source of criticism. If Churchill's ardent imperialism was a subject once avoided in Churchillian literature, it is no more. His Victorian and even eighteenth-century mindset receives much comment. For many, especially British liberals and Irish nationalists, there is a simple connection between this mindset and his Irish policy.

On 26 May 1941 Churchill had a difficult conversation with J. W. Dulanty, de Valera's representative in London. Churchill bluntly told Dulanty that the Irish 'had lost their soul'. Dulanty, then the Dean of the Faculty of Technology at the Manchester School of Technology, had supported Churchill's unsuccessful campaign for the Manchester seat in 1908.

Churchill recalled in this conversation others who had backed him for the seat: John Redmond and Tom Kettle, 'one of your finest modern minds'. It is easy to understand Churchill's regard for Redmond and Kettle. Both had believed passionately that the German violation of Belgian neutrality justified the British position in the First World War. Kettle, a former nationalist MP for Tyrone and a gifted academic, was respected by Balfour as well as by Churchill. He died at the front on 9 September 1916, when he led his Division 'B' company out of its trench during the attack on Ginchy. Dulanty was well aware that the new political class in Dublin regarded such men with disdain. Churchill's sympathetic reference to them did not soften his insult but rather deepened it. Dulanty concluded:

> He [Churchill] is regarded by some, not in any fault-finding way, as having an eighteenth century mind. As I left Downing Street I thought of a speech I heard him make over thirty years ago exhorting the English to look on Irish problems with a modern and unprejudiced mind. He himself looks today on Ireland with a mind which is neither.[3]

However, as a corrective, it is worth looking at the views of Churchill's Cabinet colleague Ernest Bevin, later to be the Foreign Secretary who extracted Britain from India. Nothing is more striking here than Ernest Bevin's remarks to J. W. Dulanty:

> [Bevin] said he thought Mr Churchill's attitude to us was far more liberal than I had given him credit for. 'Remember,' he said, 'how fiercely he opposed the Indian Reforms of 1935. Remember, how when he lost that battle he stood up in the House of Commons and said that although he did not agree with the Government of the day his fight with them was over and he would do his best to help forward the new plans for India. He says frequently to me that he is willing to come out of India any day but that he is not prepared to leave British troops or other facilities to enable the Hindus to oppress the Moslems. His one desire today after winning the war is to realise his dream of a Parliament of Man and he is continually quoting Tennyson's lines.' (He refers presumably to 'Locksley Hall')

'When the war drums throb no longer, when
the battle flags were furled,
In the Parliament of Man, the federation of the World.'[4]

Bevin linked this flexibility to a flexibility on Ireland:

He has said to me repeatedly—'I would do anything to get a United Ireland but I would not coerce the Six County Government'. What do you mean by 'coerce' [Bevin] enquired. 'By coercion I mean having troops there and using physical force to compel these people to take a course against their will. But I am willing to use pressure and have indeed done so. I have also used persuasion and am ready to do these things again, but I must have something from Mr de Valera on which I can build.' I asked X what he thought Mr Churchill meant by 'something on which he could build'. 'He meant some gesture of friendship towards both the Six County Government and Great Britain,' said [Bevin].[5]

The tone of this discussion is important. The liberal–Irish nationalist critique of Churchill is at one level perfectly correct: his mind was saturated with (liberal) imperialist assumptions. But there is also a process of evolution and the requirements of a political agenda, in which—to give the most obvious example—the need to defeat Nazi Germany sweeps all before it. Churchill's determination to negotiate and preserve the Treaty is an early example of the same phenomenon. The related problem with the liberal–nationalist critique of Churchill on Ireland is that it does not fully engage with Churchill's carefully calibrated response to that critique. What is at issue here is the tenacious legacy of Gladstonian liberalism within British politics, particularly the legacy of that tradition's view of the Irish question.

Churchill insisted that he was a Gladstonian in the sense that from about 1907 onwards he accepted the case for Irish self-governance. He believed that a democratic case had been established; he believed also that the Westminster parliament ought to respond to it sympathetically. He was convinced by 1912 that a Dublin parliament would be a friend to Britain, and that, indeed, Britain would be strengthened rather than weakened by the concession of Irish autonomy. He also believed that it was a huge mistake to attempt to coerce Ulster Unionists into a united Ireland, but it is clear that he would have been delighted if they had been successfully persuaded. Such a 'united' Ireland would inevitably be a friend to Britain. Churchill was aware that not everyone in British politics accepted his version.

In early 1922 the former prime minister, H. H. Asquith, criticized the Irish Treaty so recently signed. Where was the spirit of Gladstonian 'reconciliation'? What was the theme of justice to Ireland? Where was the sense of a need for historic redress? Churchill's reply as the minister in effective charge of government policy is fascinating. It drew on a knowledge of history that has now disappeared from British political life and a sharp wit:

> Mr Asquith had denied that they had any right to claim in their Irish settlement they were following in the footsteps of Mr Gladstone. In what happened before, as well as in the settlement as it had appeared, if they studied the facts, they would see that they were following, to a very large extent, and in many respects with painful accuracy, in the footsteps of Mr Gladstone. For the best part of five years, Mr Gladstone pursued a regime of coercion in Ireland, and it was only at the end of that period that he turned round and offered a home rule solution to the men he had previously described as marching through rapine to the dismemberment of the empire.[6]

This is a devastating riposte. The account of Gladstone's journey from 1881 to 1886 is correct. The power of the reply lies in the ability to combine this level of knowledge—derived from his biography of his father—with a self-critical, cynical version of this recent political past while sharing it with the wider public. It is the very opposite of sterile 'sound-bite' politics. Of course, Winston Churchill was well aware of the great weakness at the heart of Gladstone's Irish record. In his essay on Chamberlain in his volume *Great Contemporaries* he made the point with great force:

> Gladstone was blind to the claims and cause of protestant Ulster resistance. He displayed an indifference to the rights of the people

of Northern Ireland which dominated the liberal mind for a whole generation. He elevated this myopia to the level of a doctrinal principle. In the end we all reached together a broken Ireland and a broken United Kingdom.[7]

But, in the spirit of his reply to Asquith in 1922, Churchill might have gone further: he might have said that, having attempted to deny the reality of the Ulster question in 1886, Gladstone finally conceded in explicit terms in parliament in May 1893 the logic of the partitionist case. It could be argued that Asquith's course during the home rule bill crisis of 1912–14 merely echoed that of Gladstone's in the second home rule bill controversy of 1893. But this would have been pedantic: while Gladstone belatedly, in May 1893, came to terms with the problematic nature of his Ulster policy, the liberal tradition in Britain ignored the Grand Old Man's intervention. As a result, Churchill's critique is unanswerable—with the consequence that the consent principle had, in a sense, to be forcibly rediscovered by Tony Blair in the late 1990s before a renewed settlement could be reached in Ulster.

Is there, or ought there to be, a Churchillian legacy for Ireland? When Churchill met de Valera in 1953, de Valera told him that Ireland's decision to leave the Commonwealth in 1948 had been a mistake. Churchill was delighted, for the obvious reason that he believed in Ireland maintaining close institutional connections with Britain. Yet, more than sixty years later, little of a substantive nature has been heard about Ireland rejoining the Commonwealth.

Part of the explanation lies in Ireland's decision to join the European Union. Since 1972 Ireland has been part of an international club of substance as well, of course, as a member of the United Nations. Perhaps as important as the economic and institutional aspects of Ireland's European membership is the emotional focus: an intense love, if not always a requited one. Ireland has attempted to escape British predominance by embracing the European project. In Dublin, European social liberalism has replaced Catholic nationalism as the dominant ideology. When the Irish economy decisively crashed in 2011, it required a

European bail-out financed by France and Germany. But the first impulse of the French and German leaderships had been to pass the Irish burden back on Britain. After all, did not Britain have the closest ties and, therefore, the most to lose from the Irish collapse? The British had to explain that a complex history between the two islands forbade that option—though they did lend £7 billion to aid the Irish recovery.

But, despite this sobering moment, Ireland has still not contemplated a return to the Commonwealth. Ironically, the 'modernizing' Irish elites of today are less sympathetic than de Valera to the idea. To the argument that it is a useful institution in the modern world wooed by countries such as Mozambique and Algeria, Ireland replies that these countries had not defined themselves by opposition to Britain. Perhaps surprisingly, neither the Queen's enormously successful visit to Ireland in 2011 nor the Irish state visit to London in 2014 has made any difference to this sentiment. The immense effort of official commemoration of the Irish dead of the First World War signalled an awareness on the part of official Ireland that Irish unity by consent—if it ever came about—could not be achieved on a stable basis was linked overwhelmingly to a narrowly republican version of Irish history. Indeed, if Irish unity never came about, such a respect for these broader traditions could help to bring about more harmony in a divided island. But this is as far as the process went.

Winston Churchill would, no doubt, have welcomed this as much as he would have welcomed the triumph of principle of 'consent' for the north-east, of which he might be considered to have been an early champion. But he would have been disappointed by the failure to achieve a reconciliation based on the profound intimacy that is, in fact, the dominant reality of the relationship between the two people. The Churchill who was delighted by the success of the royal visit to Dublin in 1911 would have been delighted by the royal visit a century later. He would have noted that mainstream Irish nationalism now accepted the consent principle in the north, pretty much in line with his own views since 1909 and more particularly since 1920. But he would have

Fig. 11. Churchill visits Queen's University Belfast, 1926. Belfast acknowledges Churchill's generosity.

detected also—despite all the high-flown orations—that the reality of the relationship between Ireland and Britain was not the one he had fought for. In particular, he was disappointed by the fact that the Irish both in Ireland and America did not see their history as part of his history of the 'English-speaking peoples', as he had so passionately hoped in 1912.

It has become increasingly fashionable since 2001 (as the inquest on the Iraq War continues) to criticize the myth of strong leadership, in general, and the Churchill myth in particular.[8] In this assessment, Churchill is like a stopped clock, right twice a day, right on Hitler and Nazism, right on Stalin and Communism, and nothing much else. His Irish policies have frequently been employed as part of the case for the prosecution. This book has attempted to reassess the ambitious, complex, and, at times, deeply flawed nature of Churchill's engagement with Ireland. At the simplest level, it is worth asking the question where is the twentieth-century Irish political leader who could write such a powerful essay on a British political leader as Churchill wrote on Parnell? Churchill had a favourite Irish story, one he loved to repeat: 'British bomber over Berlin, caught in the searchlights, flak coming up, one engine on fire, rear-gunner wounded, Irish pilot mutters, "Thank God DeV kept us out of this bloody war."' The joke expresses a pleasure in the joys of contradiction and paradox that was never far from Churchill's attitude towards the Irish. If we allow ourselves to think of that pilot as Churchill's heroic Brendan Finucane and recall the same Finucane family's engagement in the Ulster Troubles on the republican side, the ambiguity becomes even greater.[9]

Churchill's legacy in Ireland is characterized by this kind of intense paradox. In the home rule crisis of 1912–14, he spoke of the need to 'comfort the soul of Ireland'; if this was not done, 'there could be no peace'.[10] He criticized the 'insulting condition of inferiority', to which, as he said, Unionists relegated the Irish members at Westminster. His strong denunciation of Unionist arrogance in 1914 was recalled in 1941 by the Socialist Party in Belfast, which felt it justified their description of Northern Ireland as a 'near fascist state'.[11] But in 1941 Churchill was in an entirely different, rather more pro-Unionist place. During the home rule debate he insisted that 'an Irish parliament could harm England but little, even if it had the will to do so'.[12] Yet, in mid-June 1940, the Irish government had approached a triumphant Germany worried that some of Hitler's talk about compromise with the British Empire might mean the withdrawal of German support for 'the final realisation of Irish demands'.[13]

Churchill had arrived at this point in significant measure because of his embrace of the consent principle for Northern Ireland. He was a sponsor of partition but he never *really* desired that it should last so long. Yet his own actions as Chancellor of the Exchequer were in large measure responsible. He broke the Treasury consensus of 1921–2 that Northern Ireland should pay for its own upkeep and indeed make a contribution to the imperial army, navy, and civil service. In the early twenty-first century Treasury expenditure per head in Northern Ireland is 23 per cent higher than the rest of the United Kingdom. No one individual contributed more to this outcome than Winston Churchill—a partition of Ireland that the economic facts of life tend to sustain.

NOTES

Introduction

1. Sonja Tiernan, 'In Defence of Barmaids: The Gore-Booth Sisters take on Winston Churchill', *History Ireland* (May/June 2012), 20/3: 34–8; Gerard Noonan, *The IRA in Britain, 1919–23: In the Heart of Enemy Lines* (Liverpool, 2014), 245. Richard Purcell and J. P. Connolly, pro-Treaty IRA officers, canvassed for Churchill, as they wished to protect pro-Treaty politicians (also Austen Chamberlain) against anti-Treaty diehards (correspondence between Alfred Cope, Desmond Fitzgerald, and Richard Purcell, November 1922, UCD, p8–1391/107).
2. John J. Horgan, *Irish Media: A Critical History since 1922* (London, 2012), 124.
3. Hugh Leonard, *DA/A Life/Time Was* (London, 1981), 28.
4. PRONI, D2846/2/15/33, 15 October 1904.
5. PRONI, D2846/1/2/8, 'The Ulster Crisis and the Plot that Failed'.
6. PRONI, D3084/C/P/2/19, comment dated 26 May 1915.
7. PRONI, D3084/C/B/29/61, 1 February 1919.
8. PRONI, D3099/2/5.
9. *Irish Independent*, 30 January 1965; see Clare Sheridan's memoir *Nuda Veritas* (London, 1927).
10. The best account of Churchill's humane approach is Alan S. Baxendale, *Winston Leonard Spencer Churchill: Penal Reformer* (Bern, 2007), 173–4; for a judicious treatment of this point, see Ashley Jackson, *Churchill* (London, 2011), 118–20.
11. Mary Soames (ed.), *Speaking for Themselves: The Personal Letters of Winston and Clementine Churchill* (London, 1998), 261, 14 August 1922.
12. Paul Kent Alkon, *Winston Churchill's Literary Imagination* (Lewisburg, PA, 2006), 72.
13. Warren Kimball, 'That Neutral Ireland', prepared for the Churchill Centre in 2011, is a good overview.
14. '"Worse than a Protestant or even an atheist": J. K. Bracken, "The Radical Stonemason from Templemore"', *History Ireland*, 12/3 (2004) <http://www.historyireland.com/20th-century-contemporary-history/worse-than-a-protestant-or-even-an-atheist-j-k-bracken-the-radical-stonemason-from-templemore/> (accessed 4 September 2015).

15. H. Montgomery Hyde, *The Londonderrys* (London, 1979), 109–10.
16. Neil C. Fleming, *The Marquess of Londonderry* (London, 2008), 166–7.
17. 'How Winston Became an Artist', *Weekly Northern Whig and Belfast Post*, 7 January 1922.
18. Roy Jenkins, *Churchill: A Biography* (London, 2001), 358.
19. *Irish News*, 24 January 2015.
20. Peter Gray and Olwen Purdue (eds), *The Irish Lord Lieutenancy c.1549–1922* (Dublin, 2012), 237; J. R. B. McMinn (ed.), *Against the Tide: J. B. Armour, Irish Presbyterian Minister and Home Ruler* (Belfast, 1985), 156.
21. *Irish Independent*, 16 October 1923; Turtle Bunbury, *The Glorious Madness: Tales of the Irish and the Great War* (Dublin, 2014), 145–57.
22. Patrick Marrinan, *Churchill and the Irish Field Marshalls* (Belfast, 1986), is the full treatment of this topic.
23. Alex Danchev and Dan Todman (eds), *War Diaries 1939–1945: Field Marshall Lord Alanbrooke* (London, 2002), p. xix, reveals that the young Churchill rode into Ladysmith alongside two of the 'fighting Brookes'.
24. Arthur Lynch, *The Rosy Fingers: The Building Forms of Thought and Action in the New Era* (London, 1929), 203.
25. Adam Begley, *Updike* (New York, 2014), 442; John Updike, *Memories of the Ford Administration* (London, 1992), 357.
26. Isaiah Berlin, *Mr Churchill in 1940* (London, 1949), 15.
27. The award-winning 1988 RTE documentary, directed by Eoghan Harris, *Darkness Visible: The Art of Manic Depression*, has an important discussion by the psychiatrists Anthony Clare and Anthony Storr on the subject of Churchill, Collins, and the 'Black Dog' depression they both experienced.
28. Laurence James, *Churchill and Empire: Portrait of an Imperialist* (London, 2013).
29. Jonathan Rose, *The Literary Churchill: Author, Reader, Actor* (New Haven and London, 2014).
30. See, e.g., Philip Hensher's review of James, *Churchill and Empire*, in the *Spectator*, 22 July 2013.
31. Winston Churchill, *The Aftermath (The World Crisis: 1918–1928)* (New York, 1929), 291.
32. For confirmation, see Alan O'Day, *The English Face of Irish Nationalism* (Dublin, 1997); Eugene Biagini, *British Democracy and Irish Nationalism* (Cambridge, 2007).
33. Michael MacDonagh, *Parliament* (London, 1902), 333.
34. This is a paraphrase from the third verse of Rudyard Kipling's 'The Young British Soldier' in the first series of his *Barrack-Room Ballads* (London, 1892): 'First mind you steer clear o' the grog-sellers' huts | For they sell you Fixed Bay'nets that rots out your guts | Ay, drink that 'ud eat the live steel from your butts— | An' it's bad for the young British soldier.'
35. Eugene Biagini, 'The Third Home Rule Bill', in Gabriel Doherty (ed.), *The Home Rule Crisis* (Cork, 2014), 277.
36. *Belfast Telegraph*, 26 January 1965.

Chapter 1

1. Winston Churchill, 'The Dream', in John Gross (ed.), *The Oxford Book of Essays* (Oxford, 2008), 366.

2. See the important article by Catherine B. Shannon, 'Lord Randolph Churchill's Irish Apprenticeship and its Aftermath, 1877–85', in Robert McNamara (ed.), *The Churchills in Ireland 1660–1965: Connections and Controversies* (Dublin, 2012), 68.

3. Shannon, 'Lord Randolph's Irish Apprenticeship', 69.

4. *Punch*, 10 April 1880.

5. James Redpath, 'The Famine in Ireland—How a Great Fund is Spending—A Talk with Lord Randolph Churchill about the Duchess of Marlborough Fund', *New York Daily Tribune*, 5 March 1880.

6. *New York Daily Tribune*, 1 March 1880.

7. *New York Daily Tribune*, 1 March 1880.

8. N. D. Palmer, *The Irish Land League Crisis* (New Haven, CT, 1940), 89.

9. *Connaught Telegraph*, 3 July 1880.

10. Winston Churchill, *My Early Life* (London, 1930), 2.

11. Winston Churchill, *My Early Life* (London, 1930), 2.

12. Winston Churchill, 'Charles Stewart Parnell', in *Great Contemporaries*, 2nd edn (London, 1938), 271.

13. Paul Bew, *Enigma: A New Life of Charles Stewart Parnell* (Dublin, 2012), 94–105. For the most recent treatment of the Phoenix Park Murders, see Felix M. Larkin, 'Lord Frederick Cavendish and the Phoenix Park Murders of 1882', *History Ireland*, 22/3: 28–31.

14. F. E. Hamer (ed.), *The Personal Papers of Lord Rendel* (London, 1931), 7.

15. Churchill, 'Charles Stewart Parnell', 268.

16. Churchill, 'Charles Stewart Parnell', 270.

17. *Spectator*, 3 March 1883.

18. R. F. Foster, 'To the Northern Counties Station: Lord Randolph Churchill and the Prelude to the Orange Card', in F. S. L. Lyons and R. J. Hawkins (eds), *Ireland under the Union: Varieties of Tension* (Oxford, 1980), 241.

19. Shannon, 'Lord Randolph's Irish Apprenticeship', 81.

20. Shannon, 'Lord Randolph's Irish Apprenticeship', 81.

21. Roy Foster, *Lord Randolph Churchill: A Political Life* (Oxford, 1981), 141.

22. Churchill, 'Charles Stewart Parnell', 272.

23. W. S. Churchill, *Lord Randolph Churchill*, 2 vols (London, 1906), i. 395.

24. Lord George Hamilton, *Parliamentary Reminiscences and Reflections 1868–1885* (London, 1916), 279–80.

25. S. Ball (ed.), *Dublin Castle and the First Home Rule Crisis: The Political Journal of Sir George Fottrell* (Cambridge, 2008), 113.

26. 'Parnellite Toryism', *Spectator*, 25 July 1885.

27. Thomas MacKnight, *Ulster As It Is* (London 1896), ii. 94.

28. Michael J. F. McCarthy, *The Nonconformist Treason or the Sale of the Emerald Isle* (Edinburgh and London, 1912), 151.
29. Bew, *Enigma*, 122.
30. Churchill, 'Charles Stewart Parnell', 272.
31. William O'Brien, *Evening Memories* (Dublin and London, 1920), 93.
32. Anthony J. Jordan, *Churchill: A Founder of Modern Ireland* (Westport, 1995), 29. For a sensitive discussion of this issue, see Foster, *Lord Randolph Churchill*, 226, 395.
33. Peter Gordon (ed.), *The Political Diaries of the Fourth Earl of Carnarvon, 1857–1890: Colonial Secretary and Lord-Lieutenant of Ireland* (Cambridge: Cambridge University Press, 2009), 413, 15 January 1886.
34. Peter Clarke, *Mr Churchill's Profession: Statesman, Orator, Writer* (London, 2012), 63.
35. MacKnight, *Ulster As It Is*, ii. 90–4.
36. Foster, 'To the Northern Countries Station', 279–80.
37. 'Churchill in Ireland: An Incendiary Tour by the Conservative Leader', *Atlanta Constitution*, 23 February 1886.
38. 'Churchill in Ireland: An Incendiary Tour'.
39. A. B. Cooke and J. R. Vincent, *The Governing Passion: Cabinet, Government and Party Politics in Britain 1885–6* (Hassocks, 1974), 74–5. See also Arthur A. Baumann, *The Last Victorians* (London, 1927), 272.
40. *Evening Standard*, 15 April 1886, speech at Beaconsfield Club.
41. Richard Temple, *Letters and Character Sketches from the House of Commons* (London, 1912), 19.
42. *Spectator*, 3 April 1889.
43. *Spectator*, 12 April 1890.
44. *Spectator*, 27 May 1893.
45. R. E. Quinault, 'Lord Randolph Churchill and Home Rule', *Irish Historical Studies*, 22/84 (1979), 377–403.
46. Baumann, *The Last Victorians*, 160.

Chapter 2

1. Con Coughlin, *Churchill's First War* (London, 2012), 70.
2. Robert McNamara, 'Winston Churchill: The Untold Story of Young Winston and his American Mentor', in Robert McNamara (ed.), *The Churchills in Ireland 1660–1965: Connections and Controversies* (Dublin, 2012), 210–11. On Cuba, see Patrick Maume, '"Cuba, the Ireland of the West": Irish Daily Independent and Irish Nationalist Responses to the Spanish American War', *History Ireland*, 16/4 (July–August 2008).
3. Paul Addison, *Churchill: The Unexpected Hero* (Oxford, 2006), 15.
4. Turtle Bunbury, *The Glorious Madness: Tales of the Irish and the Great War* (Dublin, 2014), 178.

5. *Weekly Irish Times*, 3 February 1980.
6. Winston Churchill, *My Early Life* (London, 1930), 294.
7. Anthony J. Jordan, *Churchill: A Founder of Modern Ireland* (Westport, 1995), 20.
8. TNA:PRO CO903/9, 1 January 1902, Corofin speech, *Kilkenny People*, 27 September 1900.
9. Jordan, *Churchill*, 25.
10. Jordan, *Churchill*, 22.
11. Lynch's Francophilia was to make him a strong supporter of the First World War.
12. *Irish Times*, 4 September 1918.
13. *Winston Churchill: His Complete Speeches, 1897–1963*, ed. Robert Rhodes James, 8 vols (New York and London, 1974), i. 277, 29 April 1954.
14. *Churchill: His Complete Speeches*, ed. Rhodes James, i. 317.
15. Paul Bew, *Conflict and Conciliation in Ireland 1890–1920* (Oxford, 1987), 18–19.
16. 'The New Irish Scheme', *Irish Independent*, 30 September 1904.
17. Winston S. Churchill Papers, Churchill College, Cambridge, Cambridge Chartwell Collection (hereafter CHAR), 2/18/5, October 1904.
18. Sir Joseph West Ridgeway had been appointed Irish under-secretary in 1887: a highly competent unionist official, identified with the strategy of the Balfour period, he had, nonetheless, strongly supported the principle if not the details of devolution to be found in the Dunraven proposal (see L. P. Curtis, *Coercion and Conciliations in Ireland 1880–1892: A Study in Conservative Unionism* (Princeton, 1963), 421). Sir Robert Hamilton, who attracted remarkably little public attention then or since, had been a key figure in Gladstone's conversion to home rule. Thomas Drummond had famously asserted in the 1830s that property had its duties as well as its rights. (Cf. R. Barry O'Brien, *Irish Wrongs and English Remedies* (London, 1887).)
19. W. S. Churchill, *Lord Randolph Churchill*, 2 vols (London, 1906), i. 446.
20. Paul Bew, *Enigma: A New Life of Charles Stewart Parnell* (Dublin, 2012), 120.
21. *Irish Independent*, 13 May 1905.
22. J. B. Lyons, *The Enigma of Tom Kettle* (Dublin, 1989), 68.
23. *Irish Independent*, 22 February 1905.
24. *Irish Independent*, 10 October 1906.
25. Churchill, *Lord Randolph Churchill*, i. 305. For the best review of the historiography on the subject, see Robert McNamara, 'Winston Churchill, the Historian of Ireland', in McNamara (ed.), *The Churchills in Ireland*, 184–7.
26. Peter Clarke, *Mr Churchill's Profession: Statesman, Orator, Writer* (London, 2012), 206.
27. Churchill, *Lord Randolph Churchill*, i. 436.
28. Ashley Jackson, *Churchill* (London, 2011), 98.
29. *Ulster Herald*, 4 August 1906.
30. *Ulster Herald*, 4 August 1906.

31. *Daily News*, 31 December 1906; see also *Irish Independent*, 12 October 1906, 29 October 1906, 9 November 1906.
32. *Irish Independent*, 11 January 1907.
33. Dermot Meleady, *John Redmond: The National Leader* (Dublin, 2013), 106–7.
34. *National Leader* (Dublin, 2014), 106–7.
35. *Churchill: His Complete Speeches*, ed. Rhodes James, i. 881.
36. Ronan Fanning, *Fatal Path: British Government and Irish Revolution 1910–1922* (London, 2013), 26.
37. W. F. Monypenny, *The Two Irish Nations: An Essay on Home Rule* (London, 1913), 54.
38. T. M. Healy, *Letters and Leaders of My Day* (London, 1928), ii. 483, April 1908.
39. *Spectator*, 25 April 1908.
40. *Spectator*, 25 April 1908.
41. *Irish Times*, 22 April 1908.
42. *Irish Times*, 23 April 1908.
43. Martin John Broadley, *Louis Charles Cesartelli: A Bishop in Peace and War* (Manchester, 2007), 185. Churchill, however, was not just opposed by those who followed the Catholic bishops; a small group of Irish radical feminists also opposed him.
44. *Irish Independent*, 22 April 1908.
45. *Irish Independent*, 11 August 1908.
46. *Churchill: His Complete Speeches*, ed. Rhodes James, i. 1087.

Chapter 3

1. W. F. Monypenny, *The Two Irish Nations: An Essay on Home Rule* (London, 1913), 3.
2. Alvin Jackson, *Home Rule: An Irish History* (London, 2003), 108; M. Wheatley, 'John Redmond and Federalism in 1910', *Irish Historical Studies*, 32/127 (May 2001), 345.
3. Patrick Maume, *The Long Gestation: Irish Nationalist Life 1891–1918* (Dublin, 1999), 228; John Kendle, *Ireland and the Federal Solution* (Oxford, 1989), 260; Alan J. Ward, 'Frewen's Anglo-American Campaign for Federalism 1910–21', *Irish Historical Studies*, 15/59 (March 1967), 256–75.
4. *Irish Independent*, 5 August 1911.
5. *Belfast Evening Telegraph*, 25 January 1912.
6. CHAR 2/259/4/5.
7. *Weekly Irish Times*, 17 February 1912.
8. Tom Kettle's book *Open Secret of Ireland* has recently been republished (2007) in the Classics of Irish History series, published by the University College Dublin Press, with a fine introduction by Senia Paseta.
9. Winston Churchill, 'Introduction', in Jeremiah MacVeigh, *Home Rule in a Nutshell* (London, 1912), p. iv.

10. Churchill, 'Introduction', in MacVeigh, *Home Rule*, p. vi. Churchill was always obsessed with this theme, as his *A History of the English Speaking Peoples* (New York, 1956–8) demonstrates: but by 1938 he openly admitted that Irish Americans felt no affinity with Britain. Jonathan Rose, *The Literary Churchill: Author, Reader, Actor* (New Haven and London, 2014), 211.

11. CHAR 2/60/1.

12. *Weekly Irish Times*, 17 February 1912. 'Knighthood for a Hall', *Northern Whig*, 28 February 1912, echo of Churchill meeting.

13. *Weekly Irish Times*, 10 February 1912.

14. *Weekly Irish Times*, 10 February 1912.

15. *Weekly Irish Times*, 10 February 1912.

16. *Weekly Irish Times*, 3 February 1912.

17. Patricia Jalland, *Liberals and Ireland: Ulster Question in British Politics to 1914* (Hassocks, 1980), 56–65.

18. *Belfast Evening Telegraph*, 7 February 1912.

19. *Irish Independent*, 2 August 1912.

20. Violet Bonham Carter, *Winston Churchill as I Knew Him* (London, 1965), 297.

21. Terence O'Neill, *Autobiography* (London, 1972), 31–2.

22. *Weekly Irish Times*, 17 February 1912.

23. *The Times*, 9 February 1912.

24. *The Times*, 9 February 1912.

25. *Irish Independent*, 9 February 1912.

26. For an excellent discussion, see James Loughlin, *The British Monarchy and Ireland: 1800 to the Present* (Cambridge, 2007), 279–85.

27. Michael J. F. McCarthy, *The Nonconformist Treason or the Sale of the Emerald Isle* (Edinburgh and London, 1912), 328–9.

28. Patricia Jalland, 'Irish Home Rule—Finance: A Neglected Dimension of the Irish Question, 1910–1914', in Alan O'Day (ed.), *Reactions to Irish Nationalism* (Dublin, 1987), 302–7.

29. *Weekly Irish Times*, 17 February 1912.

30. *Belfast Telegraph*, 29 January 1965.

31. *Weekly Irish Times*, 17 February 1912.

32. 'Mr Churchill Hooted in Belfast', *Weekly Irish Times*, 17 February 1912.

33. *Belfast Newsletter*, 19 February 1912.

34. *Belfast Telegraph*, 9 February 1912.

35. *Weekly Irish Times*, 17 February 1912.

36. McCarthy, *The Nonconformist Treason or the Sale of the Emerald Isle*, 336.

37. Monypenny, *The Two Irish Nations*, 77.

38. Monypenny, *The Two Irish Nations*, 65.

39. *Witness*, 1 February 1912.

40. *Weekly Irish Times*, 17 February 1912.

41. *Roscommon Herald*, 2 February 1912.

42. *Weekly Irish Times*, 17 February 1912.

43. *Weekly Irish Times*, 17 February 1912.
44. *Weekly Irish Times*, 17 February 1912.

Chapter 4

1. Ronan Fanning, *Fatal Path: British Government and Irish Revolution 1910–1922* (London, 2013), 68.
2. *Weekly Irish Times*, 12 July 1912; *Irish Independent*, 4 July 1912.
3. *New York Times*, 12 August 1922.
4. 'Sir Edward Carson's Reply to Mr Churchill', *Weekly Irish Times*, 18 August 1912.
5. *Weekly Irish Times*, 7 September 1912.
6. *Irish Independent*, 14 September 1912.
7. *Irish Independent*, 10 October 1912.
8. Michael Sheldon, *Young Titan: The Making of Winston Churchill* (London, 2013), 283; see also Gordon Lucey, 'When Churchill was Wrong on Ulster', *Belfast Newsletter*, 22 February 2012.
9. *Northern Whig*, 9 October 1913.
10. Andrew R. Muldoon, 'Making Ireland's Opportunity England's: Winston Churchill and the Third Irish Home Rule Bill', *Parliamentary History*, 15 (1996), 329.
11. *Northern Whig*, 9 October 1913.
12. Timothy Bowman, *Carson's Army, the Ulster Volunteer Force* (Manchester, 2007), 65.
13. B. Clifford and J. Marsland, *Lovat Fraser's Tour of Ireland* (Belfast, 1992), 14.
14. Dermot Meleady, *John Redmond: The National Leader* (Dublin, 2013), 250.
15. *Spectator*, 25 October 1913.
16. T. M. Healy, *Letters and Leaders of my Day* (London, 1928), ii. 508–9, 16 August 1912.
17. Healy, *Letters and Leaders of my Day*, ii. 532, 15 December 1913.
18. Healy to Maurice, in Healy, *Letters and Leaders of my Day*, ii. 535, 26 January 1914.
19. 'Sir Arthur Paget on Ulster', *Weekly Irish Times*, 28 February 1914.
20. *Weekly Irish Times*, 28 February 1914.
21. Patrick Maume, 'The *Irish Independent* and the Ulster', in D. G. Boyce and Alan O'Day (eds), *The Ulster Crisis* (London, 2005), 213; see full *Irish Times* report of Paget, 28 February 1914.
22. *Witness*, 13 February 1914.
23. Paul Bew, *Ideology and the Irish Question* (Oxford, 1994), 105.
24. *Weekly Irish Times*, 21 March 1914.
25. Trevor Wilson (ed.), *The Political Diaries of C. P. Scott* (London, 1970), 78.
26. Laurence James, *Churchill and Empire: Portrait of an Imperialist* (London, 2013), 75–6.

27. PRONI 2486/1/2/18, 'The Ulster Crisis and the Plot against Ulster', note dated 10 April 1914.
28. Richard Toye, *Lloyd George and Churchill: Rivals for Greatness* (London, 2007), 115.
29. Alan F. Parkinson, *Friends in High Places: Ulster's Resistance to Home Rule* (Belfast, 2012), 209.
30. *Observer*, 29 March 1914.
31. *Witness*, 20 March 1914.
32. *Observer*, 29 March 1914.
33. *Weekly Irish Times*, 28 March 1914.
34. Jonathan Rose, *The Literary Churchill: Author, Reader, Actor* (New Haven and London, 2014), 173.
35. *Weekly Irish Times*, 28 March 1914.
36. Ian Chambers, *The Chamberlains, Churchill and Ireland 1874–1922* (Youngstown, NY, 2006), 215.
37. Chambers, *The Chamberlains, Churchill and Ireland*, 208.
38. Ian F. W. Beckett (ed.), *The Army and the Curragh Incident* (London, 1986), Sir Francis Hopwood to Lord Stamfordham, 21 March 1914.
39. Beckett (ed.), *The Army and the Curragh Incident*, 169, account of the events 19–23 March 1914, Lt Col. McEwen.
40. Paul O'Brien, *A Question of Duty: The Curragh Incident* (Dublin, 1914), 42.
41. Fanning, *Fatal Path*, 113.
42. Fanning, *Fatal Path*, 108.
43. Douglas Russell, *Winston Churchill: Soldier: The Military Life of a Gentleman at War* (London, 2006), 372–3.
44. Hansard, 21 April 1914, col. 766, speech of F. Hall.
45. Churchill's statement on 22 April in parliament, in *Winston Churchill: His Complete Speeches, 1897–1963*, ed. Robert Rhodes James, 8 vols (New York and London, 1974), iii. 2291–2.
46. *Weekly Irish Times*, 25 April 1914.
47. Chambers, *The Chamberlains, the Churchills and Ireland*, 209.
48. Keith Jeffrey, *Field Marshall Sir Henry Wilson* (Oxford, 2006), 124.
49. *New York Times*, 23 March 1914.
50. Beckett (ed.), *The Army and the Curragh Incident*, 117, notes by Lt. Col I. G. Hogg on the events of 20–23 March 1914. Hogg and Churchill had joined the army together.
51. Beckett (ed.), *The Army and the Curragh Incident*, 358, 3 April 1914.
52. Beckett (ed.), *The Army and the Curragh Incident*, 357, Brigadier General H. P. Gough to Brigadier General J. E. Gough, 3 April 1914.
53. Michael Brock and Eleanor Brock (eds), *Margot Asquith's Great War Diary 1914–1916* (London, 2014), 108, 8 May 1915.
54. Memorandum by Winston S Churchill (Asquith Papers), n.d., in Randolph Churchill, *Winston S. Churchill: Companion, Volume II, Part 3, Documents 1911–14* (London, 1969), 1411–13.

55. Edward David (ed.), *Inside Asquith's Cabinet: From the Diaries of Charles Hobhouse* (London, 1977), 165, note of 24 March of Cabinet on 23 March.
56. Mark Pottle (ed.), *Champion Redoubtable: Diaries and Letters of Violet Bonham Carter* (London, 1998), 56.
57. Hansard, 30 March 1914, col. 1078.
58. *Irish Independent*, 31 March 1914.
59. Hansard, 30 March 1914, col. 1081.
60. *Weekly Irish Times*, 4 April 1914.
61. *Weekly Irish Times*, 28 March 1914.
62. 'London Letter', *Belfast Telegraph*, 21 April 1914.
63. *Northern Whig*, 25 April 1914.
64. 'Mr Churchill and Sir Edward Carson', *Manchester Guardian*, 28 April 1914.
65. Geoffrey Lewis, *Carson: The Man who Divided Ireland* (London, 2005), 159.
66. *Westmister Gazetter*, 28 April 1914.
67. *Daily Express*, 28 April 1914.
68. *Pall Mall Gazette*, 28 April 1914.
69. Meleady, *John Redmond*, 271.
70. Meleady, *John Redmond*, 284.
71. Winston Churchill, *The Aftermath (The World Crisis: 1918–1928)* (New York, 1929), i. 187.
72. Douglas Newton, *The Darkest Days: The Truth behind Britain's Rush to War, 1914* (London, 2014), 61–7.
73. Lionel Curtis, *Civitas Dei* (London, 1937), ii. 356.
74. Lewis, *Carson*, 167.
75. Churchill, *The Aftermath*, i. 148.
76. Fanning, *Fatal Path*, 107.
77. Michael Brock (ed.), *H. H. Asquith: Letters to Venetia Stanley* (Oxford, 1985), 227.

Chapter 5

1. Ian Colvin, *The Life of Lord Carson* (London, 1936), 21.
2. Clare Sheridan, *Nuda Veritas* (London, 1927), 100.
3. John Redmond, 'Introduction', in Michael MacDonagh, *The Irish at the Front* (London, 1916), 13.
4. Colvin, *The Life of Lord Carson*, 13, 81.
5. Turtle Bunbury, *The Glorious Madness: Tales of the Irish and the Great War* (Dublin, 2014), 154.
6. Stephen Sandford, *Neither Unionist nor Nationalist: The 10th Irish Division in the Great War* (Dublin, 2015), 43.
7. MacDonagh, *The Irish at the Front*, 74.
8. Myles Dungan, *Voices from the Great War* (Dublin, 2014), 79; John Bligh, 'John Fitzgibbon of Castlerea: A Most Mischievous and Dangerous Agitator', in Brian Casey (ed.), *Defying the Law of the Land* (Dublin, 2013), 201–19.

9. Stuart Ward, 'Parallel Lives, Poles Apart: Commemorating Gallipoli in Ireland and Australia', in J. Horne and Edward Madigan (eds), *Towards Commemoration: Ireland in War and Revolution 1912–1923* (Dublin, 2013).

10. Bunbury, *The Glorious Madness*, 178.

11. MacDonagh, *The Irish at the Front*, ch. 1, 'The Immortal Story', 74.

12. Kevin Myers, *Ireland's Great War* (Dublin, 2014), 99. Colonel Patterson has described Fr Finn, chaplain to the Dublin Fusiliers, rushing, seriously wounded himself, to give the last rites to 500 dead or dying Irish soldiers, before he was cut down. *With the Zionists in Gallipoli* (London, 1916), 88.

13. Patrick Maume, *The Long Gestation: Irish Nationalist Life 1891–1918* (Dublin, 1999), 234.

14. Mary Soames (ed.), *Speaking for Themselves: The Personal Letters of Winston and Clementine Churchill* (London, 1998), 188.

15. *Spectator*, 13 May 1916.

16. *Manchester Guardian*, 16 May 1916.

17. Geoffrey Best, *Churchill: A Study in Greatness* (Hambledon and London, 2002), 81.

18. Alvin Jackson, *Home Rule: An Irish History* (London, 2003), 163–77.

19. PRONI 0/1633/1/2/203, Lillian Spender to Wilfrid Spender, 25 May 1916.

20. Lilian Spender to Wilfrid, 5 November 1917, in Margaret Baguley (ed.), *World War I and the Question of Ulster: The Correspondence of Lilian and Wilfrid Spender* (Dublin, 2009), 295.

21. Anthony J. Jordan, *Churchill: A Founder of Modern Ireland* (Westport, 1996), 64.

22. Philip Ollerenshaw, *Northern Ireland in the Second World War: Politics, Economic Mobilisation and Society, 1939–45* (Manchester, 2013), 164.

23. 'Urges Harmony in Ireland: "Churchill says only Irish Disputes Prevent Self-Government"', *New York Times*, 12 December 1918.

24. Churchill may have been misled by the quality of the intelligence he received from Dublin which emphasized 'elements of weakness' despite the 'apparent strength of Sinn Fein' and 'liberal' and 'modern ideas' in the North. CHAR 2/59/5, Document dated 17 Oct 1917.

Chapter 6

1. Winston Churchill, *The Aftermath (The World Crisis: 1918–1928)* (New York, 1929), 305.

2. Hansard, 4 December 1919, col. 2883. *Winston Churchill: His Complete Speeches, 1897–1963*, ed. Robert Rhodes James, 8 vols (New York and London, 1974), iii. 2883.

3. T. Ryle Dwyer, *Michael Collins and the Civil War* (Cork, 2012), 138.

4. Richard Toye, *Lloyd George and Churchill: Rivals for Greatness* (London, 2007), 220–1.

5. Maurice Walsh, *Bitter Freedom: Ireland in a Revolutionary World 1918–23* (London, 2015), 193.

6. D. M. Leeson, *The Black and Tans: British Police and Auxiliaries in the Irish War of Independence 1920–21* (Oxford, 2011), 31–2.

7. Sir Ormonde Winter, *Winter's Tale: An Autobiography* (London, 1955), 335.

8. Churchill, *The Aftermath*, 302.

9. Wilson Papers, 26 July 1920, quoted in Paul Bew, Peter Gibbon, and Henry Patterson, *Northern Ireland, 1921–96: Political Forces and Social Classes* (Manchester, 1995), 52; original in Martin Gilbert, *Winston S. Churchill: Companion, Volume V, Part 2, Documents The Wilderness Years, 1929–1935* (London, 1981), 1150.

10. Charles Townshend, *The Republic: The Fight for Irish Independence* (London, 2013), 154.

11. TNA:PRO, Home Office, 317/70, Sir John Anderson to Winston Churchill, 13 November 1928. Churchill had asked both H. A. L. Fisher and Sir John Anderson to look at the Irish section of *The Aftermath*.

12. Carl Ackerman, 'Janus Headed Ireland', *Atlantic Monthly* (June 1922), 812.

13. Anthony J. Jordan, *Churchill: A Founder of Modern Ireland* (Westport, 1996), 67.

14. Ross O'Mahony, 'The Sack of Balbriggan and Tit for Tat Terror', in David Fitzpatrick (ed), *Terror in Ireland* (Dublin, 2012), 164.

15. O'Mahony, 'The Sack of Balbriggan and Tit for Tat Terror', 66.

16. *The Times*, 17 October 1920.

17. Richard Abbott, *Police Casualties in Ireland* (Cork, 2000), 169.

18. 'Churchill Asserts we would Aid Irish', *New York Times*, 17 October 1920.

19. *Chicago Daily Tribune*, 17 October 1920.

20. *San Francisco Chronicle*, 17 October 1920; *Chicago Tribune*, 17 October 1920.

21. John Steele, 'Newspaper Bureau: Scene of Irish Deal, Negotiations with Government Carried on in *Chicago Tribune* London Office', *New York Times*, 12 December 1920.

22. J. M. Kenworthy, *Sailors, Statesmen and Others: An Autobiography* (London, 1933), 191–2.

23. Roy MacLaren has recently claimed that, behind the scenes, Churchill argued that MacSwiney should not be allowed to die. See R. MacLaren, *Empire and Ireland* (Montreal and Kingston, 2015), 177.

24. Arthur Mitchell, *Revolutionary Government in Ireland: Dail Eireann 1919–1922* (Dublin, 1995), 214.

25. *Churchill: His Complete Speeches*, ed. Rhodes James, iii. 3026.

26. Laurence James, *Churchill and Empire: Portrait of an Imperialist* (London, 2013), 147.

27. See the introduction to Paul Bew and Patrick Maume (eds), *Wilfrid Ewart: A Journey in Ireland* (Dublin, 2007), p. xx.

28. Wilson Diary, 22 November 1920, in Martin Gilbert, *Winston S. Churchill: Companion, Volume IV, Part 2, Documents July 1919–March 1921* (London, 1977), 1248.

29. Walsh, *Bitter Freedom*, 276.
30. R. Fanning et al. (eds), *Documents on Irish Foreign Policy*, i. 1919–1922 (1998), 219.
31. Paul Bew, *Ireland: The Politics of Enmity, 1786–2006* (Oxford, 2007), 415.
32. Kenworthy, *Sailors, Statesmen and Others*, 198.
33. Paul Addison, 'The Search for Peace in Ireland', in J. W. Muller (ed.), *Churchill as Peacemaker* (Cambridge, 1997), 201.
34. Roy Jenkins, *Churchill: A Biography* (London, 2001), 362.
35. Ian Chambers, *The Chamberlains, the Churchills and Ireland 1874–1922* (Youngstown, NY, 2006), 236.
36. Kevin Matthews, 'Churchill and Ulster', in Robert McNamara (ed.), *The Churchills in Ireland 1660–1965: Connections and Controversies* (Dublin, 2012), 131–2.
37. M. Hopkinson (ed.), *The Last Days of Dublin Castle* (Dublin, 1999) (Sturges saw Cabinet memo, 25 May).
38. Hopkinson (ed.), *The Last Days of Dublin Castle*.
39. Hopkinson (ed.), *The Last Days of Dublin Castle*.
40. See also 'Our London Letter', *Irish Independent*, 6 January 1906.
41. Martin Gilbert, *Winston S. Churchill: Companion, Volume IV, Part 3, Documents April 1921–November 1922* (London 1977), 1507–8.
42. *Spectator*, 1 July 1921.
43. John Julius Norwich, *The Duff Cooper Diaries 1915–51* (London, 2005), 153–6, 5 November 1921.
44. Churchill to Lloyd George, in Gilbert, *Winston S. Churchill: Companion, Volume IV, Part 3*, 1667.
45. Tom Jones, *Whitehall Diary 1916–25*, ed. Keith Middlemas (Oxford, 1969), 60.
46. Frances Stevenson, *Lloyd George: A Diary* (London, 1971), 236–77.
47. F. Callanan, *T. M. Healy* (Cork, 1996), 578.
48. 'C. P. Scott Diary', 2–5 December 1921, in Trevor Wilson (ed.), *The Political Diaries of C. P. Scott*, (London, 1970).
49. Mark DeWolfe (ed.), *Holmes–Laski Letters: The Correspondence of Mr Justice Holmes and Harold J. Laski 1916–1935* (Oxford, 1953), i. 386–7, Laski to Holmes, 8 December 1921.
50. Wilson papers, 5 December 1921, in Gilbert, *Winston S. Churchill: Companion, Volume IV, Part 3*, 1684. See Keith Jeffery, *Field Marshall Sir Henry Wilson: A Political Solder* (Oxford 1996), 266.
51. Mary C. Bromage, *Churchill and Ireland* (Notre Dame, IN, 1964), 76.
52. H. A. L. Fisher diary, 6 December 1921, in Gilbert, *Winston S. Churchill: Companion, Volume IV, Part 3*, 1685.
53. Mitchell, *Revolutionary Government*, 325.
54. *Weekly Northern Whig* and *Belfast Post*, 24 December 1921.
55. *Co. Cork Eagle and Munster Advertiser*, 18 March 1922.
56. *Co. Cork Eagle and Munster Advertiser*, 18 March 1922.
57. 15 December 1921 (Austen Chamberlain Papers), in Gilbert, *Winston S. Churchill: Companion, Volume IV, Part 3*, 1691.

58. Peter Hart, the most scholarly of the Collins biographers, insisted that Collins profoundly disliked Churchill. Peter Hart, *Mick: The Real Michael Collins* (London, 2006).

59. J. W. Muller (ed.),*The Irish Treaty, Thoughts and Adventures* (Wilmington, DE, 2009), 239.

Chapter 7

1. Hansard, 16 February 1922, cols 1279–82.

2. D. Ferriter, *A Nation and not a Rabble: The Irish Revolution 1913–23* (London, 2015), 255.

3. For details and presentation, see Paul Bew, *Ireland: The Politics of Enmity, 1786–2006* (Oxford, 2007), 424–5.

4. Henry Patterson, *Class Conflict and Sectarianism in Belfast* (Belfast, 1980), remains the classic analysis.

5. John Julius Norwich (ed.), *The Duff Cooper Diaries 1915–51* (London, 2005), 156, 22 January 1922.

6. T. Ryle Dwyer, *Michael Collins and the Civil War* (Cork, 2012), 50.

7. Winston S. Churchill to Clementine Churchill, 10 February 1922, in Martin Gilbert, *Winston S. Churchill: Companion, Volume IV, Part 3, Documents April 1921–November 1922* (London, 1977), 1766.

8. See TNA:PRO, T/63/61 g 256/049, Otto Niemayer's document on this subject, 26 May 1922.

9. Gilbert, *Winston S. Churchill: Companion, Volume IV, Part 3*, 652.

10. Kevin Matthews, *Fatal Influence: The Impact of Ireland on British Politics, 1920–1925* (Dublin, 2004), 78.

11. *Observer*, 1 April 1922.

12. Ronan Fanning, *Fatal Path: British Government and Irish Revolution 1910–1922* (London, 2013), 36.

13. *Leinster Leader*, 11 March 1922.

14. PRONI HA 31/1/1928, telegram from Collins to Churchill, 6 March 1922.

15. CHAR 22/12A/25–32.

16. CHAR 22/12A/30–34.

17. 'Sir Henry's Advice to Ulster', *Ballymena Observer*, 3 June 1922.

18. TNA:PRO CO 906/30, 'Memorandum in the Present Position of the Imperial Government'.

19. CHAR 22/12A/42/J.

20. *Weekly Freeman*, 1 April 1922. On the same day Collins had written to Churchill again denouncing Craig's repressive measures. CHAR 22/12/A51.

21. See, on this point, for example, Churchill's correspondence with Wilson in March 1916, in Keith Jeffrey, *Field Marshal Sir Henry Wilson* (Oxford, 2006), 174.

22. *Irish Times*, 29 March 1922.

23. Lady Spender's diary, 6 April 1922, records her husband Wilfrid Spender's view of these negotiations: 'Collins, who, he says, is like the hero of an American film drama, was very truculent... did not attempt to deny responsibility for outrages in Ulster... indeed, he boasted of them' (PRONI D1633/2/24).

24. *Irish Times*, 31 March 1922.

25. Fearghal McGarry, *Eoin O'Duffy: A Self-Made Hero* (Oxford, 2005), 102.

26. *Weekly Northern Whig*, 1 April 1922.

27. Winston S. Churchill, draft uncirculated Cabinet memorandum, 4 April 1922, in Martin Gilbert, *Winston S. Churchill: Companion, Volume IV, Part 3*, 1847.

28. Ibid.

29. *Freeman's Journal*, 4 April 1922.

30. *Weekly Northern Whig*, 5 April 1922.

31. Elizabeth Malcolm, *The Irish Policeman 1822–1922: A Life* (Dublin, 2006), 220.

32. On the suffering of southern Protestants, see Peter Hart, *The IRA at War 1916–23* (Oxford, 2005), ch. 9; for events in Cork, see Brian Walker's recent fine essay on the Dunmanway killings, 'Counting the Cost: The Price of Mass Murder', *Irish Independent*, 31 May 2014.

33. Sir Henry Wilson Diary, 12 April 1922, in Gilbert, *Winston S. Churchill: Companion, Volume IV, Part 3*, 185–9.

34. 'Irish Criticism in Commons gets Churchill's Fire: Peace Negotiator Defends British Policy', *Chicago Daily Tribune*, 13 April 1922.

35. Winston Churchill, *The Aftermath (The World Crisis: 1918–1928)* (New York, 1929), 386.

36. Dwyer, *Michael Collins and the Civil War*, 180.

37. *Weekly Northern Whig* and *Belfast Post*, 3 June 1922.

38. H. A. L. Fisher Diary, 31 May 1922, in Gilbert, *Winston S. Churchill: Companion, Volume IV, Part 3*, 1906.

39. *Spectator*, 2 June 1922.

40. *Weekly Northern Whig*, 3 June 1922.

41. *Weekly Northern Whig*, 10 June 1922.

42. Robert C. Self (ed.), *The Austen Chamberlain Diary Letters: The Correspondence of Sir Austen Chamberlain with the Sisters Hilda and Ida, 1916–37* (Cambridge, 1995), 192.

43. *Weekly Northern Whig*, 17 June 1922, Mr Collins in Ulster.

44. *Weekly Northern Whig*, 17 June 1922.

45. *Weekly Irish Times*, 25 March 1922.

46. See Hart, *The IRA at War*, ch. 6, for the conspiracy theories surrounding the murder. For a judicious review of the literature, see Paul Murray, *The Irish Boundary Commission and its Origins* (Dublin, 2011), 126.

47. *Spectator*, 30 June 1922.

48. TNA:PRO CO906/25.

49. 'Sinn Fein's Great Crime', *Ballymena Observer*, 30 June 1922.

50. Dwyer, *Michael Collins and the Civil War*, 241.
51. Matthews, *Fatal Influence*, 82; Professor Matthews does not accept that Churchill had a serious commitment to the view (p. 89), but he does accept that those who worked closely with him on the issue felt it was his genuine position.
52. *Northern Whig*, 1 May 1923.
53. Bew, *Ireland: The Politics of Enmity*, 425.
54. Gilbert, *Winston S. Churchill: Companion, Volume IV, Part 3*, 1947–8.
55. Charles Townshend, *The Republic: The Fight for Irish Independence* (London, 2013), 141.

Chapter 8

1. The Irish students, who appear in all accounts as Churchill's loyal supporters, at the end were also supporters of the Dublin government.
2. Review of Ross McKibbin, *The Evolution of the Labour Party, 1910–1924*, in *Historical Journal*, 18/3 (1975), 670–2.
3. *The Times*, 12 November 1922.
4. 'Mr Churchill in the Fight', *Observer*, 12 November 1922. See also M. Laffan, *Judging W. T. Cosgrave* (Dublin, 2014), 4.
5. *Manchester Guardian*, 15 November 1922.
6. Martin Gilbert, *Churchill: A Life* (London, 1991), 851.
7. Ephesian, *Winston Churchill* (London, 1927), 224.
8. *Irish Independent*, 5 May 1923. William O'Brien, in *The Irish Revolution* (London, 1923), 441–2, claimed that 'two reliable' sources had told him that Churchill had, as Collins claimed, promised 'vast territories' to the Free State, under the Boundary Commission.
9. *Winston Churchill: His Complete Speeches, 1897–1963*, ed. Robert Rhodes James, 8 vols (New York and London, 1974), iv. 3434, 28 February 1924.
10. *Irish Independent*, 18 March 1924.
11. John P. McCarthy, *Kevin O'Higgins: Builder of the Irish Free State* (Dublin, 2006), 245.
12. CHAR 2/136/30–34.
13. Martin Gilbert, *Winston S. Churchill: Companion, Volume V, Part 1, Documents The Exchequer Years 1922–1929* (London, 1979), 3470, 25 September 1924.
14. Enda Staunton, 'The Boundary Commission Debacle 1925: Aftermath and the Implications', *History Ireland* (Summer 1981), 42.
15. Thomas Lough, *England's Wealth, Ireland's Poverty* (London, 1896).
16. CHAR 22/56.
17. *Churchill, His Complete Speeches*, ed. Rhodes, James, iv. 3789, 9 December 1925.
18. *Derry Standard*, 19 February 1926.
19. *Irish Times*, 3 March 1926.

20. John M. Regan, *The Irish Counter-Revolution 1921–36: Treatyite Politics and Settlement in Independent Ireland* (Dublin, 1999), 266.
21. H. Montgomery Hyde, *Carson: The Life of Sir Edward Carson* (London, 1953), 489.
22. TNA:PRO, Treasury Papers, T160/430/12302, Bewley to Waley, 24 November 1930.
23. Iain S. Wood, *Britain, Ireland and the Second World War* (Edinburgh, 2010), 12.
24. *Churchill: His Complete Speeches*, ed. Rhodes James, vi. 5948–55, 5 May 1938.
25. *Churchill: His Complete Speeches*, ed. Rhodes James, vi. 5948–55, 5 May 1938.
26. Paul Bew, 'History is Never Once in Northern Ireland', *The Times*, 30 November 2001.
27. James Loughlin, *Ulster Unionism and British National Identity* (London, 1995), 92.
28. See Paul Bew, Peter Gibbon, and Henry Patterson, *The State in Northern Ireland: Political Forces and Social Classes* (Manchester, 1979), 70, n. 48, which explains Spender's outlook.
29. Winston Churchill, 'Charles Stewart Parnell', in *Great Contemporaries*, 2nd edn (London, 1938).

Chapter 9

1. Jim Phelan, *Churchill can Unite Ireland* (London, 1940), 18. For Phelan's exotic career as IRA man, bank robber, jailbird, tramper, and later darling of the BBC, see Andrew Lees, 'The Rolling English Road', *Dublin Review of Books*, Issue 72.
2. Andrew Baker, 'Anglo-Irish Relations 1939–41: A Study in Multi-Lateral Diplomacy and Military Restraint', *Twentieth Century British History*, 15/4 (2015), 363.
3. Anthony J. Jordan, *Churchill: A Founder of Modern Ireland* (Westport, 1996), 171.
4. Jordan, *Churchill*, 171.
5. Michael Kennedy, *Guarding Neutral Ireland* (Dublin, 2008).
6. Geoffrey Sloan, 'Ireland and the Geopolitics of Anglo-Irish Relations', *Irish Studies Review*, 15 (2007), 239–75; see also Robert Fisk, 'German U-Boats Refuelled in Ireland, Surely Not', *Independent*, 17 September 2011.
7. John Lukacs, *Five Days in May: London 1940* (New Haven, 1999), 13.
8. Andrew Roberts, *The Storm of War: A New History of the Second World War* (London, 2000), 64.
9. Phelan, *Churchill can Unite Ireland*, 10.
10. Phelan, *Churchill can Unite Ireland*, 113.
11. Phelan, *Churchill can Unite Ireland*, 119.
12. Denis Ireland, *Letter from Ireland* (Belfast, 1945), 'Ulster and the Peace: An Open Letter to Mr Churchill'.
13. Jordan, *Churchill*, 171.

14. Paul Bew, *A Yankee in de Valera's Ireland: The Memoir of David Gray* (Dublin, 2012), 38–9.

15. Bew, *A Yankee in de Valera's Ireland*, 39.

16. David Reynolds, *In Command of History: Churchill Fighting and Writing the Second World War* (London, 2004), 195.

17. Bew, *A Yankee in de Valera's Ireland*, 134.

18. Paul Canning, *British Policy towards Ireland 1921–41* (Oxford, 1985), 268.

19. T. Ryle Dwyer, *Irish Neutrality and the USA 1939–47* (Dublin, 1977), 54.

20. Telegram from Dublin from E. Hempel, the German legate, dated 17 June 1940, in *Documents on German Foreign Policy 1918–1948* (London: HMSO, 1954), series D 1937–1945, vol. IX, no. 473,603.

21. C. Crowe et al. (eds), *Documents on Irish Foreign Policy*, vi. *1931–1941* (Dublin, 2008), 249.

22. Jeffrey Mayer, 'The Marquess of Dufferin and Ava: The Tragic History of Basil Blackwood', *Standpoint* (April 2014).

23. Bew, *A Yankee in de Valera's Ireland*, p. xx.

24. Jordan, *Churchill*, 174.

25. John Bowman, *De Valera and the Ulster Question* (Oxford 1982), 237. Aiken's words confirm Lord Londonderry's analysis, sent to Churchill at this time. Brian Barton, *The Belfast Blitz: The City in the War Years* (Belfast, 2015), 557.

26. David Freeman, 'Winston Churchill and Eamon de Valera', in Robert McNamara (ed.), *The Churchills in Ireland 1660–1965: Connections and Controversies* (Dublin, 2012), 165.

27. *Secret Session Speeches: Delivered by the Rt Hon Winston S Churchill DM, CH, MP to the House of Commons 1940–43* (London, 1946), 16.

28. Thomas Hachey, 'Nuanced Neutrality, Irish Identity: An Ideological Legacy', in T. E. Hachey (ed.), *Turning Points in Twentieth Century Irish History* (Dublin, 2010), 84.

29. Michael Kennedy and Victor Laing (eds), *The Irish Defence Forces 1940–49: The Chief of Staff's Reports* (Dublin, 2011), p. xxv.

30. Warren F. Kimball (ed.), *Churchill and Roosevelt: The Complete Correspondence* (Princeton, 1989), i. 106–7.

31. Philip Ollerenshaw, *Northern Ireland in the Second World War: Politics, Economic Mobilisation and Society, 1939–45* (Manchester, 2013).

32. *Washington Post*, 11 February 1941.

33. Jordan, *Churchill*, 176.

34. Ollerenshaw, *Northern Ireland in the Second World War*, 162–5; Bryce Evans, *Ireland during the Second World War: Farewell to Plato's Cave* (Manchester, 2014), 22–3.

35. *Spectator*, 28 May 1941.

36. M. Gilbert, *Winston S. Churchill: Companion, Volume III, Documents 1914–1916* (London, 1972), 953.

37. Otto Rauchbauer, *Shane Leslie: Sublime Failure* (Dublin, 2009), 74.
38. Canning, *British Policy towards Ireland*, 314.
39. Terry de Valera, *A Memoir* (Dublin, 2004), 212.
40. De Valera, *A Memoir*, 176; cf. also J. P. Duggan, *Ireland and the Third Reich* (Dublin, 1985). But see Ray Raymond, 'Irish Neutrality and Anglo-Irish Relations, 1921–41', *International History Review*, 9/3 (August 1987), 459.
41. De Valera, *A Memoir*, 212.
42. Eamon O'Halpin (ed.), *MI5 and Ireland 1939–45: The Official History* (Dublin, 2003).
43. Garret FitzGerald, *Ireland and the World: Further Reflections* (Dublin, 2005), 124. See, most recently, Ronan Fanning, *Eamon de Valera: A Will to Power* (London, 2015).
44. Henry Patterson, *Ireland since 1939: The Persistence of Conflict* (Dublin, 2006), 57–61.
45. Patterson, *Ireland since 1939*, 57–61.
46. Maurice Manning, *James Dillon: A Biography* (Dublin, 1999), 169.
47. TNA:PRO KV4/4/49, Rugby's assessment introduced by a note from White, dated 7 May 1947.

Chapter 10

1. E. O'Halpin, *Spying on Ireland: British Intelligence and Irish Neutrality during the Second World War* (Oxford, 2008), 240.
2. Paul Addison, 'The Search for Peace in Ireland', in J. W. Muller (ed.) *Churchill as Peacemaker* (Cambridge, 1997), 208.
3. 'Underlying Consistency', *Belfast Telegraph*, 25 January 1965.
4. *New York Times*, 18 March 1944.
5. *New York Times*, 15 March 1944.
6. Churchill to Roosevelt, 19 March 1944, in Warren F. Kimball (ed.), *Churchill and Roosevelt: The Complete Correspondence* (Princeton, 1989), iii. 57.
7. Anthony Cave Brown, *Bodyguards of Lies* (Guildford, CT, 2007), 543–4.
8. TNA:PRO Cab.6/66/62/9, 'World Organisation: The position of Southern Ireland', Lord Cranborne's text, dated 21 February 1945.
9. The matter is first discussed in the Andrews era, in early 1942; see PRONI Cab.4/496/5; for Brooke's remarks in February 1945, see PRONI Cab.4/615/5.
10. Lord Moran, *Churchill at War 1940–5* (London, 2002), 295, 1 March 1945.
11. Leonard Woolf, 'The Little Man: An Obituary of Adolf Hitler', *New Statesman*, 13 May 1945.
12. Richard Toye, *The Roar of the Lion: The Untold Story of Churchill's World War II Speeches* (Oxford, 2013), 79.
13. TNA:PRO LV/V/1440. Assessment of the security problem of a neutral Eire? This report was started on the 7 May 1947 and completed on 18 December 1947.

14. Patrick Maume, *The Long Gestation: Irish Nationalist Life 1891–1918* (Dublin, 1999), 227.
15. Paul Bew, *Ideology and the Irish Question* (Oxford, 1994).
16. 'Mr Churchill's Remarks: Dublin Man's Letter', *Roscommon Herald*, 19 May 1945.
17. *The People's Press*, 19 May 1945.
18. Tim Pat Coogan, *De Valera: Long Fellow, Long Shadow* (London, 1993), 617.
19. Richard Toye, '"Phrases make History here": Churchill, Ireland, the Rhetoric of Empire', *Journal of Imperial and Commonwealth History*, 30 (2010), 549–70.
20. Toye, *The Roar of the Lion*, 108.
21. Paul Murray, *The Irish Boundary Commission and its Origins* (Dublin, 2011), 65.
22. J. W. Muller, *Thoughts and Adventures: Churchill Reflects on Spies, Cartoons, Flying, and the Future* (Wilmington, DE, 2009), 240.
23. TNA:PRO Cab. 164/1733.
24. Winston Churchill, 'The Dream', in John Gross (ed.), *The Oxford Book of Essays* (Oxford, 2008), 362.
25. Churchill, 'The Dream', 366.
26. Steven O'Connor, *Irish Officers in the British Forces 1922–45* (London, 2014), 172–3.
27. Hansard, 25 October 1948, col. 31.
28. Harold Nicolson, *Diaries and Letters 1945–62*, ed. Nigel Nicolson (London, 1968), 153.
29. Claire Simpson, 'Churchill Wanted a United Ireland, Archives Reveal', *Irish News*, 18 November 2014.
30. C. Crowe et al. (eds), *Documents on Irish Foreign Policy*, ix. *1948–1951* (Dublin, 2014), 383–4.
31. Hansard, 25 November 1948, col. 1417.
32. *Irish Times*, 26 November 1948.
33. *Spectator*, 3 December 1948.
34. PRONI 3004/D/42, Sir Basil Brooke Diaries, 29 January 1951.
35. *Irish News*, 18 November 2014.
36. *Washington Post*, 25 July 1954.
37. *Irish Times*, 8 October 1951.
38. *Irish Times*, 18 October 1951.
39. PRONI 3004/D/42, Sir Basil Brooke Diaries, 3 May 1951, 11 May 1951.
40. Mary C. Bromage, *Churchill and Ireland* (Notre Dame, IN, 1964).
41. Anthony J. Jordan, *Churchill: A Founder of Modern Ireland* (Westport, 1996), 197.
42. For the reason for Healy's internment alongside British fascists in London, see Christopher Norton, *The Politics of Constitutional Nationalism in Northern Ireland, 1932–70* (Manchester, 2014), 51–4, which sets the event within the context of a wider northern nationalist flirtation with Germany. In August 1940 three senior northern nationalist politicians—Senator MacLaughlin (a close associate of Cardinal Macrory) and John Southwell and Peadar Murney—'decided' at a meeting in Dublin, tempted by the German

legislation, to place the Catholic minority in the north under the protection of the Third Reich. (B. Barton, *Northern Ireland and the Second World War* (Belfast, 1995), 123.) Healy was interned for planning to act in supporting this project.

43. Kevin McCay, 'Fermanagh Unionism 1921–72', University of Ulster, Ph.D. 2013, p. 276. Walton Newbold, the ex-communist MP who became a Churchill ally, wrote to him as early as 19 March 1941: 'you have evaded the issue as to equality of opportunity of the Catholics of the six counties of Northern Ireland' (CHAR 20/20/13/14).

44. PRONI D2991/B/130/6, Leslie to Healy, 17 June 1953.

45. 'Churchill Expects Amity among Irish', *New York Times*, 17 December 1953.

46. John Ramsden, *Man of the Century: Winston Churchill and the Legend* (London, 2002), 263; Bryce Evans and S. Kelly (eds), *Frank Aiken* (Dublin, 2014), 88–90, 141–4.

47. *Irish Times*, 25 January 1965.

48. *Belfast Telegraph*, 30 January 1965.

49. *Belfast Telegraph*, 26 January 1965.

Conclusion

1. Mary C. Bromage, *Churchill and Ireland* (Notre Dame, IN, 1964), p. xii.

2. Jonathan Rose, *The Literary Churchill: Author, Reader, Actor* (New Haven and London, 2014), 176.

3. For this report, see C. Crowe et al. (eds), *Documents on Irish Foreign Policy*, vii. 1941–1945 (Dublin, 2010), 83–4.

4. Crowe, *Documents on Irish Foreign Policy*, vii. 227.

5. Crowe, *Documents on Irish Foreign Policy*, vii. 227.

6. *Co. Cork Eagle and Munster Advertiser*, 28 January 1922.

7. Winston Churchill, 'Joseph Chamberlain', in *Great Contemporaries* (London, 1937), 88.

8. e.g. Simon Heffer, 'The Churchill Myth', *New Statesman*, 9–15 January 2015.

9. Thanks to Eamon Mallie for this point.

10. *Daily Telegraph*, 1 May 1912.

11. Red Hand pamphlet published by the Socialist Party, 34 Berry Street, Belfast, 1941.

12. *Daily Telegraph*, 1 May 1912.

13. Telegram from Dublin from E. Hempel, the German legate, dated 17 June 1940, in *Documents on German Foreign Policy 1918–1948* (London: HMSO, 1954), series D 1937–1945, vol. IX, no. 473,603, quoted in Paul Bew, *A Yankee in de Valera's Ireland: The Memoir of David Gray* (Dublin, 2012), p. xvii.

PICTURE CREDITS

INDEX